FANNY
TROLLOPE

A REMARKABLE LIFE

I remember reading in some book that an autobiography written with perfect sincerity, and recording the real feelings of its author, would be an invaluable work; and such a work I am determined to attempt.

Frances Trollope, *A Clever Woman*, vol. 1, p. 97

I have assuredly great pleasure in thinking that this record of my remarkable life may be not only interesting, but useful to my fellow creatures.

Frances Trollope, *A Clever Woman*, vol. 3, p. 305

Instead of melting down my materials into one mass and constantly speaking in my own person . . . I have resolved to adopt and enlarge upon the excellent plan of Mr Mason in his Memoirs of Gray. Whatever narrative is necessary to explain, connect, and supply, I furnish it to the best of my abilities; but in the chronological series of Johnson's life, which I trace as distinctly as I can, year by year, I produce, wherever it is in my power, his own minutes, letters or conversation, being convinced that this mode is more lively, and will make my readers better acquainted with him. . . . Indeed I cannot conceive a more perfect mode of writing any man's life.

Boswell's Preface to his *Life of Dr. Johnson*

FANNY TROLLOPE

A REMARKABLE LIFE

Teresa Ransom

FOREWORD BY
VICTORIA GLENDINNING

ALAN SUTTON PUBLISHING LIMITED

First published in the United Kingdom in 1995
Alan Sutton Publishing Ltd · Phoenix Mill · Far Thrupp · Stroud
Gloucestershire

Reprinted 1995
Reprinted with corrections 1996
First paperback edition 1996

British Library Cataloguing in Publication Data

Ransom, Teresa
Fanny Trollope
I. Title
828.709

ISBN 0-7509-0950-1 (hardback)
ISBN 0-7509–1269-3 (paperback)

Typeset in 10/13 pt New Baskerville.
Typesetting and origination by
Alan Sutton Publishing Limited
Printed in Great Britain by
Butler & Tanner, Frome, Somerset.

For Mark, Sally and
Victoria

Rae

Christmas 2003

Lots of Love

Grandad &

Nan.

x

Contents

List of Illustrations

MILTON

TROLLOPE

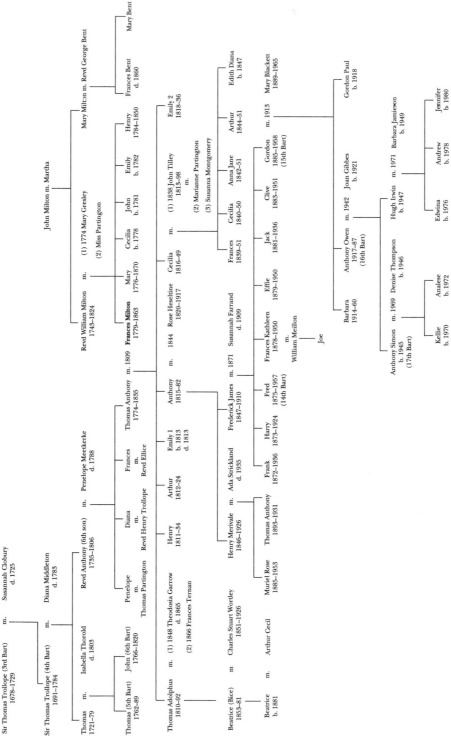

Foreword

by Victoria Glendinning

The subtitle of this book, 'A Remarkable Life', is as apt as the title of the novel by Fanny Trollope from which the phrase is taken: *A Clever Woman*. Fanny Trollope was a very clever woman. She is chiefly known to posterity as the mother of the great Victorian novelist Anthony Trollope. In this, posterity may have made a category error.

Until he was well into middle age, it was Trollope's mother who was the famous one in the family. She was not just well known: she was, as we would say, *seriously* famous. It was her name that persuaded publishers to take on Anthony's early work. Yet she did not begin to write until she was over fifty, and then only because the financial situation of the family was so desperate that she could think of no other way of generating some money.

She had instant success, and never looked back, producing between 1832 and 1856 no less than forty books, comprising 115 volumes. Those who have read or (like myself) written about Anthony Trollope's life, know very well how forceful and gifted his mother was. We have been impressed by her indomitable courage and resourcefulness, and felt sympathy for her in her difficult marriage, in her long widowhood, and in the dreadful loss from tuberculosis of four of her six children. With her scatty schemes, her optimism, her forthright manners and her unorthodox appearance she has also sometimes appeared almost as a comic figure.

She had a healthy ego, and liked to be the centre of her circle. As mother to her surviving children, Tom and Anthony, any account of her attitudes and behaviour may on occasion cause raised eyebrows. She is, in short, not unfamiliar as a 'character'. But even though many readers of her son's novels may also have read one or two of hers or, more likely, her first and best-known book *Domestic Manners of the Americans*, she has not, up until now, been studied seriously and comprehensively as a writer.

Fanny Trollope's writing is at the centre of this biography. Other books have been written about her 'remarkable life', but no one, before Teresa Ransom came along, has made a case for Fanny Trollope as a significant author. Ransom has read everything that she wrote, and her conclusions are humbling. It seems shameful and extraordinary, after reading this biography, that Fanny Trollope's work has not been properly recognized before, when that of so many other and less effective women writers from the past have been resurrected and reprinted.

Fanny Trollope is revealed as a true radical – by temperament, not by ideology, for I think she would have rejected the label with shrieks of horror. Her politics, such as they were, and they were pretty vague, were Tory. Yet she constantly, instinctively, and fearlessly challenged the conventional attitudes of her time, particularly where women were concerned. She thought women should enter the professions and that there should be equality between the sexes. Her heroines are not meek and mild, but show a feisty independence which generally pays off. Her observation of social manners is malicious and very funny. Nor is domestic life and the relationship between the sexes her only subject, as was often the case with women novelists.

From first-hand observation, she wrote in her fiction about the inhuman treatment of black people in America and of small children in textile mills in the industrial north of England, and about the degrading conditions prevailing in workhouses. And this was before Harriet Beecher Stowe, Charles Dickens or Mrs Gaskell had turned their attention to these social evils. She was always beady-eyed, caustic and salty, and she did not pull her punches, either in her novels or in her travel-books. She was not a decorous lady-traveller; she insisted on being lowered down into salt-mines, and toured cathedral vaults where uncoffined bodies lay rotting in heaps.

All this, plus her oblique but still startling candour about intimate matters, made her not only famous but notorious. She was considered by the largely male critical establishment of her time as distressingly unfeminine, and condemned as 'vulgar', as lacking in 'good taste and decorum'. It is precisely this satirical zest that makes her writing seem so lively and readable today.

Her legacies to her son Anthony were energy, endurance and application. Much has been written about his regular working hours and about how he would start to write a new book almost as soon as he had finished the last. That is exactly what his mother did – while running a household and caring for family invalids at the same time.

Nor is that all. There are many similarities between the mother's work and the son's, some of them pleasantly trivial; they both like to rush off at a tangent and make pronouncements about, for example, what makes a successful dinner-party; they both like to infiltrate the Trollope family dog, Neptune, into their stories. It is known that Anthony Trollope's anti-evangelical prejudice came to him through his mother, and the relationship between her eponymous *Vicar of Wrexhill* and her son's Mr Slope has been remarked.

But Teresa Ransom has found some interesting new plot-links between

Fanny's novels and those of Anthony Trollope. Because of the essentially limited experience of even the most enterprising woman in the nineteenth century, she did not have his grasp of the worlds of business, politics and public affairs. But any new study of Anthony Trollope's work will henceforward have to take account of his mother's, particularly *Charles Chesterfield* and *The Blue Belles of England*. She wrote (from experience) about ill-tempered and obsessional husbands, taking on marriage rather than the conventional topic of courtship, in a way echoed by Anthony in *He Knew He was Right*. Her *Uncle Walter* may have been a starting-point for the Barchester novels. It makes one wonder: behind how many novelists who have 'lasted' (through arbitrary quirks of taste, the market, the canon, sexism . . .) is there some unknown or half-forgotten literary parent – whether literally a parent or not – without whom they might never have found a voice?

Teresa Ransom was well placed to write this book. She is Australian, like the remaining direct descendants of Fanny Trollope, who have given her access to family material. She is obliquely one of the family herself, through the marriage of a great-aunt to the Revd Charles Trollope, a connection of Anthony's. She has discovered a great deal that is new about Fanny Trollope's original family, the Miltons, and their different homes in and around Bristol. One of the strengths of this book is the author's sense of place.

Fanny Trollope was a competent and indefatigable homemaker who, with varying members of her family, moved constantly between lodgings and rented houses both in England and abroad. Not content with discovering and documenting these locations, Teresa Ransom has wherever possible searched them out, visited them, and photographed them.

This adds greatly to the vividness of her account, and is the more valuable because Fanny used whatever raw material was to hand in writing her novels; her settings are nearly always based on where she was living at the time, or on a place she had just left. She also made use of the appearance and conversation of people she had recently met for her fictional characters, which makes her novels an excellent source for contemporary modes and manners. At the time, this habit made friendship with her something of a hazard. From a distance of over a century, the closer acquaintance with Fanny Trollope and her work which this book provides is nothing but a privilege.

Acknowledgements

In my research for this book I owe much to other writers who have pioneered the journey of Fanny Trollope and her family and who have laid down a firm foundation of facts from which I have been able to explore in various directions. Wherever possible I have referred to the original source for information. Where this has not been possible, usually for economic reasons, I have relied on the research of others. Any mistakes are my own.

I have used family memoirs, autobiographies, and contemporary letters to build this portrait. I have had access to copies of Fanny Trollope's letters to Julia Pertz, by permission of the Houghton Library, Harvard University, and these have been of enormous value. Access to much of the other material held in American universities and collections, has had to be via the scholarship of others. My debt to them has been documented in the notes, but I would particularly like to mention Helen Heineman's scholarly work, *Mrs Trollope: The Triumphant Feminine in the Nineteenth Century*.

My very special thanks go to Hugh Trollope, Fanny's great-great-great-grandson, for sharing his knowledge and generously lending family papers, books and photographs.

I would also like to thank Victoria Glendinning for her encouragement and support; Madame Catherine Brooks for discussing and sharing with me her research on Fanny Trollope; Mr and Mrs Glen Tollet of Heckfield House (the old Vicarage), Mr and Mrs Tony English of Harrow Weald House Farm, Mr and Mrs Phillip Hulme of Grandon at Hadley, and Dr and Mrs Barr of Carlton Hill, for welcoming me into their houses, allowing me to take photographs, and for sharing information with me; Joanna Corden for research on Grandon, at Barnet Archives and Local History Library; Bob Thomson, Local History Librarian of Harrow Library Services, who helped me to try and solve the whereabouts of the Harrow Weald Farm; John Williams, City Archivist, Bristol Record Office, for information on John Milton and his son the Reverend William Milton; Miss S.M. Shepard, Archives and Local Studies Section, Rotherham, Department of Libraries Museum and Arts, for information and cuttings on Edward John Heseltine; Peter Clifford and Jaqueline Mitchell of Alan Sutton Publishing; and to Jill Hickson.

Acknowledgements

My thanks also go to those who have helped with advice, experience, support and hospitality, and to many others who have helped in diverse ways to supply clues to the missing pieces of the jigsaw of Fanny's life, when often the significance of the information given only became apparent much later. Thank you especially to Robin Appleton, Annette Casey, Bob Cubbage, Norman and Gillian MacSwan, Peter Raby, Patrick and Diana Ridsdill Smith, Ruth Tweedie, and Phoebe Verschoyle.

And last, a very special thank-you to my three children and their partners for looking after affairs in Australia, while I followed the Fanny Trollope trail through England and Europe. This book is for them.

PICTURE CREDITS

Sotheby's, 1. Author, 2, 3, 12, 13, 19, 23–6, 31. *Orley Farm*, 8. *Domestic Manners of the Americans*, 4, 5, 7. National Portrait Gallery, London, 9, 10, 18. Hugh Trollope, 11, 20, 21, 22, 27, 28, 30. Victoria Glendinning, 29. *Vienna and the Austrians*, 14. *Michael Armstrong*, 15. *Charles Chesterfield*, 16, 17.

CHRONOLOGY

1779 10 March Frances (Fanny) Milton born at Stapleton, Bristol.

1801 Fanny moved with her parents to Heckfield.

1803 Went with her sister Mary, to keep house for their brother Henry in Keppel Street, London.

1809 Married Thomas Anthony Trollope.

1810 Thomas Adolphus born.

1811 Henry born.

1812 Arthur William born.

1813 Emily 1 born and died on the same day.

1815 Anthony born. Family moved to Harrow.

1816 Cecilia born.

1818 Emily 2 born.

1823 Trollopes to Paris, met Lafayette, Frances Wright, and the Garnett family.

1824 Arthur William died. The Reverend William Milton died. Trollopes in financial trouble.

1826 Henry sent to Paris.

1827 Fanny to Paris for Julia Garnett's wedding, and to visit Henry. Proposal to accompany Frances Wright to her 'Utopian Colony' in America. 4 November, Fanny, Henry, Cecilia, Emily and Hervieu to America. Mr T. moved to Harrow Weald.

1829 Trollope's Folly.

1831 Fanny returned to Harrow Weald.

1832 March, first book published, *The Domestic Manners of the Americans.*

1833 Family moved back to Julian Hill at Harrow.

1834 Bailiffs moved in, family fled to Bruges. 23 December, Henry died.

1835 23 October, Mr Trollope died. Fanny returned to London.

1836 Moved to Hadley. Emily died in February. To Vienna in July to write travel book.

1838 Moved to 20 York Street, London. Cecilia married John Tilley.

1840 To Paris in the winter/spring. Anthony very ill in London, June, July. Fanny nursed him. To Penrith in the autumn to stay with Cecilia.

1841 Visit to Italy. Built Carlton Hill at Penrith.

1842 Moved into Carlton Hill, stayed less than a year.

1843 Moved to Florence, with Thomas Adolphus.

1844 Anthony married Rose Heseltine.

1847 Cecilia ill. Joined Trollopes in Italy.

1848 Thomas Adolphus married Theodosia Garrow.

1849 Cecilia died in England.

1850 Fanny to Pau.

1851 Moved into Villa Trollope, with Tom, Theo and Mr Garrow.

1856 Last book published, *Fashionable Life, or Paris and London.*

1863 Fanny died in Florence.

Introduction

So many books have been written about Anthony Trollope and so few about his mother, and yet, during her lifetime it was Fanny who always made the headlines.

My first discovery of her was quite by chance; when looking through some family papers, I found an old brochure for the Villa Trollope in Florence, which had once been the home of 'the famous authoress'. My Trollope cousins, the last of whom died in 1964, had not mentioned a connection with Anthony, or his mother; but now I was curious and resolved to explore further. I later discovered that their grandfather, George Barne Trollope, was a second cousin of Anthony's father. What was puzzling, given her renown in her own day, was the apparent lack of interest in her today as a writer.

Fanny commenced writing at the late age of fifty-three because of the desperate need to earn money to support her six children and ailing husband. Her writing continued without fail throughout the illnesses and eventual deaths of her husband and five of their seven children.

A controversial, trail-blazing author, her output was prodigious: she produced 115 highly acclaimed volumes in twenty-five years. Truthful, witty, and hard hitting, she wrote with a fierce passion when she perceived injustice, and a wicked satirical wit when she wished to puncture pretentiousness. Her novels discussed such unmentionable subjects as the rights of unmarried mothers, child exploitation, slavery, and women's emancipation; she also dared to suggest that women should be given the vote, and be allowed to stand for parliament, the church, and the legal profession. Her readers were both amused and scandalized by her novels, but as Victorian morality tightened its grip, Fanny's books fell from favour among the Establishment. She was loved by her readers, who waited with impatience for 'the next Mrs Trollope novel', but she was castigated as vulgar and too daring by most contemporary male critics. Such publicity only increased her sales.

In her lighter works she satirized London literary circles, the power of reviewers, English travellers abroad, and county society. She also created the wonderful Widow Barnaby, 'fair, fat, and forty', a rouged and ringletted social climber, whose outrageous adventures rollicked through nine volumes.

She constantly experimented with different styles of writing: Gothic novels, satires, romances, and a detective story were all part of her repertoire. She was an intrepid traveller, and her travel books contained not only the expected descriptions of majestic panoramas, but also cameo portraits of unusual people she met, and accounts of the daring situations in which she found herself. She was a fierce advocate for social justice and women's rights, and her clever, barely disguised, caricatures of her contemporaries, brought a blast of fresh air into stuffy Victorian drawing rooms. Her influence on her son Anthony's work is strong, not only in the themes such as the church, strong women, and as a chronicler of social conditions but also as the originator of what became known as 'The Trollope Style'.

Why then, today, is she mainly remembered for her travel books, the best known of which was the first book she wrote, *Domestic Manners of the Americans*? It seems that readers' demands changed, and what had seemed daring in her lifetime became old-fashioned. The Victorians favoured the rather more solid values of her son Anthony's books. Fanny was risqué, and a shade too passionate.

Her novels were not republished after 1858; most of them can now only be found buried in the copyright libraries, or at the occasional antiquarian book sale. But fashions change. When read today, the Fanny Trollope of 150 years ago, sounds surprisingly modern, clear thinking and wickedly amusing.

Surely it is now time that this remarkable woman is re-instated as an author in her own right, and that a new generation is given the chance to enjoy 'The latest Mrs Trollope novel'?

TERESA RANSOM
Sydney and Cambridge 1995

CHAPTER ONE

'Her education had been a very strange one'

Bristol and Heckfield. 1779–1803

Frances Milton, known as Fanny, was born at Stapleton, near Bristol, on Wednesday 10 March 1779. Her father was then serving as a Clerk of Holy Orders at St Michael's Church in the heart of the city, and it was there, a week later, on 17 March, that she was christened.[1]

Fanny's paternal grandparents, John and Martha Milton, also lived in Bristol, at 23 Trinity Street. In his will of 1777, John described himself as, 'Gentleman, late distiller'.[2] They had two children: Fanny's father, William, and a girl, Mary, who was later to marry the Reverend George Bent.

William had been given a good education. On 13 September 1757, when he was fourteen, he was admitted to Winchester College, and in 1762 took the Election to New College, Oxford. Places at New College were only awarded as a vacancy occurred, but he did not have to wait long. On 4 March 1763, according to the diary of James Woodforde, who was in his last year at Oxford, 'Milton was admitted Scholar of this Coll: in Clobbery Noel's Place, who died of an Apoplexy.'[3]

James Woodforde's diary of his time at Oxford names William Milton several times, usually in relation to gambling, and reveals endless drinking sprees and riotous behaviour. After three years at Oxford, in 1766 at the age of twenty-three, William Milton was awarded his Bachelor of Arts; he received his Master of Arts four years later in 1770.

In 1773, aged thirty, William was allocated the living of Heckfield, a small village in Hampshire, about 7 miles south of Reading. Woodforde noted in his diary: 'Dec 16th. . . . we had a Meeting of the whole House in the Hall – The chief thing done in it was giving to Milton one of our Fellows the Living of Heckfield in Hants worth 120 pounds per Annum . . . Milton treated with some Wine after Dinner only.'[4]

On 21 May 1774, at the age of thirty-one, the Reverend William Milton took up residence in the Tudor vicarage beside the church.[5] The church, dating back to the twelfth century, still stands, square and nuggety, surrounded by rolling green fields and parklands. Its massive tower built from local rock, was used as a lookout post against any threat of invasion.

William could now afford to marry, and he chose a Bristol girl, Mary, the daughter of Francis and Cecilia Gresley. They were connected to the aristocratic Gresley family of Drakelow in Derbyshire, and Bristol in Somerset. The Gresleys were proud of their Norman ancestors, the earliest of whom was Nigel de Stafford. On a carefully drawn family tree, still in the possession of the family, it can be seen that they had descended through twenty-three generations. This pedigree seems to have become something of a Milton family joke, for in later life, letters from brother Henry to Fanny refer to 'the illustrious Norman blood that flows in our veins'. Fanny also used the influence of 'the highly aristocratic Norman blood which flowed in his [or her] veins', to explain the idiosyncrasies of more than one of the characters in her novels.

William and Mary were married in Bristol at St Thomas's Church, on 23 June 1774,[6] and returned to Heckfield to start their life together. Heckfield was a low-value living, and after only a year, in September 1775, the Reverend Milton installed a curate,[7] and he and his wife returned to Bristol to await the birth of their first child. The Reverend Milton was installed as Clerk of Holy Orders at St Michael's Church in Bristol. The Miltons lived in the village of Stapleton, which was 2½ miles north-east of Bristol beside the village of Fishponds, and it was here that their six children were born. On 29 March 1776, the first child, Mary, was baptized at St Thomas's Church, Bristol,[8] and in 1778 a second daughter, Cecilia, was born. Fanny was the third child. After Fanny's birth in March 1779, three children quickly followed: John, baptized at St Michael's, Bristol on 11 February 1781;[9] Emily baptized, again at St Michael's, on 8 July 1782,[10] and on 20 May 1784, the last child, Henry.[11] Cecilia, John and Emily all died in infancy.

The Bristol Directory gives their address then as Lower Grove Road.[12] No obvious signs of the house now remain, though there are some old houses and stone walls along adjacent Grove Road which leads directly onto Stapleton Common, a large and unspoiled piece of ground bisected by 'the River Frome, flowing through a richly wooded glen occasionally interspersed with precipitous rocks, pennant stone quarries and coal mines. It has a church with six bells, and several good houses.'[13]

The Reverend Milton's right to vote in Bristol was confirmed on 7 September 1780, when 'William Milton Clerk is admitted into the Liberties of this City for that he is the Son of John Milton Distiller and hath taken the Oath of Obedience and paid 0.4.6.'[14] New voters were needed to sway the Parliamentary elections which were to be held in early 1781 to elect a member for the city and county of Bristol. The candidates were George Daubeny and Henry Cruger, and the competition was fierce. 'Milton Rev William AM. Clerk St Michaels' voted for Daubeny. A petition was sent against the result when George Daubeny won by a mere 372 votes out of a total of 6,000 voters. The objectors declared 'That by polling great

Numbers of persons who received Parish Pay, Alms and Charities, and others who had no right to vote, and by many acts of bribery and corruption and other undue, partial and illegal Practices and Proceedings, the said George Daubeny procured a Colourable Majority of Votes.'[15] The petition was rejected.

When Fanny's mother died following the birth of her sixth child Henry, the three surviving children were brought up by their father. Fanny may have been thinking of her own childhood when she wrote later in *Mrs Mathews*:

> Mary King lost her mother while still too young to mourn her. She would probably have been a very different person had this event occurred twenty years later: For decidedly the chief defects in Mary King's character arose from her having been too much accustomed, almost from infancy indeed, to depend upon herself and her own resources upon all occasions which require judgement and decision, either for the regulation of her conduct or her opinions.[16]

In 1786 William's sister, Mary Bent, died and their father, John Milton, added a codicil to his will, signed with a very shaky almost illegible hand, reducing the legacy to Mary's husband George; the money to be held in trust for George and Mary's three children, and George granted the income for life. Fanny was now seven, and her grandfather John Milton, who survived until he was ninety-nine, was living with them in Lower Grove Road, Stapleton.[17]

It seems likely that most of Fanny's education came from her father, who was described as, 'a good scholar with decidedly scholarly tastes, much of a mathematician'.[18] Hannah More, the daughter of Jacob More, the master of the Free School at Fishponds near Stapleton, kept a school for girls with her sisters in Park Street, which Fanny may have attended, but there are no records now available.

Fanny would certainly have been accustomed to meeting her father's intellectual friends and was brought up with an eighteenth-century freedom of thought and speech. A scientific friend of the Miltons, John Garnett, was, according to the Bristol Guide, granted a patent for his invention 'to lessen friction in all kinds of wheels, blocks for ships, grindstones and rollers', and two of his daughters, Julia and Harriet, remained close friends of Fanny's throughout their lives. A description of a scientific gathering in *Tremordyn Cliff*, may have been based on childhood memories:

> In the quietest corner of this splendid room . . . stood a table . . . of some 18 feet in circumference, covered with a soft, rich, crimson carpet, on which were spread various delicate models in brass, of newly invented, or

newly improved instruments. A miniature steam-engine, a small galvanic apparatus, and such curious specimens of newly ground lenses, as might make an astronomer's eyes water to look through them, were among the collection.[19]

The Bristol of Fanny's childhood was a major trading port. Wills' tobacco and Fry's chocolate had their origins there. Some of the staple businesses carried out were pipemaking, pottery, cordwaining, glass manufacture and saddlery. There was also the all-important three-way slave trade, from which vast fortunes were made. Ships sailed from Bristol to Africa, loaded a cargo of slaves, then sailed to the West Indies where the slaves were exchanged for sugar, cotton and tobacco, which were then, in turn, sold to the merchants of Bristol. Reminders of that time linger today in Bristol's Whiteladies Road, and Blackboys Hill. In 1791, when Fanny was twelve, Bristol recorded twenty-two slave traders in port, by 1796 this had dropped to only one. It was reported earlier in 1787 that 'more persons had died in three slave vessels in a given time than in all the other Bristol vessels put together, numerous as they were'.

Travel between Bristol and Heckfield at that time was slow and dangerous, and the Reverend Milton rarely visited his Hampshire parish. In October 1776 the Heckfield parish records have only one entry signed by him, and he did not officiate again at Heckfield church until 1801, although the records have his emendations from time to time. A selection of curates were appointed to carry out the parish duties.

Responsibility for the condition of the roads devolved on to the reluctant local villagers, each of whom was expected to give six days of unpaid labour a year to the levelling and upkeep of the highway. This was seldom done, resulting in deep and impassable ruts in the mud of winter. Roads were often just muddy tracks across the countryside with no signposts to direct the traveller. In some areas turnpike trusts were created for the upkeep of specific stretches of highway, but there was no co-ordination, or supervision, with the result that twenty miles of good road could be followed by a quagmire for the next ten.

The Reverend Milton was much engaged in experiments for improvements to coach designs. He also became involved with the tidal problems of Bristol Harbour. The town relied for its trade on the navigability of the River Avon, but ships could only enter and leave the port at high tide, thereby limiting its use. The question of harbour improvement was raised in October 1791, the Council holding a special meeting to discuss a project 'for floating the ships at the Quay'. A committee was appointed to report, and did so in December, and a meeting of concerned parties was held at the Merchants Hall in Bristol in December 1791, where, among others, William Milton addressed the assembly and read an essay on

'A Plan for Improving the Port and Harbour of Bristol'. He proposed plans for damming the River Frome in order to create a dry dock and a floating harbour, and suggested a scheme to relocate the River Avon. This plan was favourably considered by the Council. However, after lengthy consideration, they recommended another design by Messrs Smeaton and Jessop. 'The subject was soon after allowed to go to sleep again, notwithstanding the frequent occurrence of disasters in the harbour.'[20] This was because far more serious matters began to take precedent. Beyond Bristol, momentous events were taking place.

When Fanny was born, George III was on the throne, and the Tories were in power. In 1783, when Fanny was four, England had, reluctantly, recognized America's Independence, and in doing so, lost its use as a penal colony. When looking for a suitably remote place to send the convicts, the Tories remembered that eighteen years before, in 1770, Captain Cook had discovered Australia. The problem was solved, and in 1788, when Fanny Milton was nine, the first settlers, mainly convicts and soldiers, landed in Botany Bay. In the October of the same year, 'the flying gout', as a contemporary doctor described the king's illness, lodged in his head, and he talked and babbled endlessly. As the king's condition deteriorated, his doctors, fearing he would die, sent for the Prince Regent, but the king tried to throttle him. For two nights in succession the prince sat up waiting for his father's death, fully dressed and resplendent with decorations. However, the king did not die, but was confined in a strait jacket, and not expected to rule again.

William Pitt, the king's champion, thought he would have to resign his Tory leadership if the king died. The Whig leader, Charles Fox, an intimate friend of the despised prince, seeing his chance, insisted that the full prerogatives of the Crown would belong to the prince by right, once the incapacity of the Crown was established. At this critical moment the king recovered, much to the relief of the Tories and most of the population. The Prince Regent was universally disliked for his self-indulgent and extravagant behaviour. He was also believed to have secretly married Mrs Fitzherbert, six years older than him, twice widowed and a Roman Catholic. It was an illegal and unconstitutional union, deeply unpopular, and, as the prince was first in line of succession, potentially disastrous. However, officially at least, the disaster was averted when, in 1795, the prince married Caroline of Brunswick. The young Fanny would no doubt have heard the satirical comments made by her elders, and she used this in a later book, *The Robertses on Their Travels*, when the social climbing Mrs Roberts, decided that an improvement in her name might ease her way into German society and with a flash of inspiration she decided upon, 'Mrs Fitzherbert Roberts'. The hint of a royal connection was observed. She was accepted.

For the next thirty-two years the potentially explosive problem of George III's intermittent madness, as well as the licentious behaviour of his son, threatened the stability of life within England. Europe, too, was about to be plunged into turmoil. In 1789 the Bastille was stormed in Paris, signalling the beginning of the French Revolution. On 10 August 1792, when Fanny was thirteen, the French monarchy was overthrown and the Royal Family imprisoned, an act which sent shudders through the English upper classes. As a result, on 12 December of the same year, at a common council held in St George's Chapel, Bristol, a series of resolutions were passed unanimously. The first and second were expressive of loyalty to the king and constitution and the determination of the council to uphold the laws of the realm; the third stated their intent to detect and bring to justice all authors, publishers and distributors of seditious writings, to suppress all tumults and riots, and to bring to justice all disturbers of tranquillity.[21] The aristocracy closed ranks. In 1793 Louis XVI was guillotined, and England declared war on France.

In Bristol, too, working people were beginning to make their presence felt, and, in defiance of the recent resolution passed by the common council, they rioted against a bridge toll, which had been imposed for an agreed period of twenty-five years when the bridge was first opened in 1768. The first day of free travel was to be 29 September 1793, but, greedy for profit, an advertisement appeared for the re-letting of tolls. On that Saturday an angry mob gathered and stoned the magistrates and militia. The next day, Sunday, was quieter, but on Monday the riots were so bad that the soldiers opened fire, killing eleven people. It was a time of universal unrest, and in 1794, when the harvests were very bad, there were more riots in the High Street market and some meat was stolen.[22]

During the Napoleonic war there was a prison at Fishponds for French prisoners-of-war, where more than 3,000 captured soldiers and sailors were incarcerated. They were kept in the old workhouse at Stapleton, not far from where Fanny lived, and in 1800 a written complaint was made to the Mayor of Bristol about their treatment. 'They were nearly naked, the mud in the unpaved courtyard was inches deep, the bread fusty, the beef carrion, and that only one pound of this bread and half a pound of the beef (bone included) was given every twenty four hours to each prisoner.'[23] Conditions were improved.

There are no contemporary descriptions of Fanny during her years in Bristol, and much of the information we have comes from her novels. Although written much later, they were, as she admitted, almost invariably based on her own experiences. From her sons, Tom and Anthony, we know that she was fluent in Latin, French and Italian, and from her own writing we know that she held some rather unorthodox views on the political and social concerns of the day. As she wrote about one of her heroines:

Her education had been a very strange one; for while it had led her considerably beyond the limits usually fixed, as the *ne plus ultra* of female education in some respects, it had left her very considerably behind-hand in others. She could read Latin with as great facility and enjoyment as either French or English; but as to what might be generally considered as the fittest tone of manners for a young lady to adopt in all the various situations in which accident might place her, she had never received any instruction whatever; and had no guide to direct her, but her own feelings.[24]

By January 1801, the Reverend Milton had moved to Clifton Place, Bristol – now Clifton Road, which runs between Clifton Hill and York Place. Clifton had a hot well, and had become a fashionable spa in the late 1700s, recommended for the treatment of a multitude of complaints. Various cures were offered, including those by the Medical Pneumatic Institution, an experimental centre run by Thomas Beddoes in Dowry Square, Clifton, for the treatment of consumption by the inhaling of laughing gas, or nitrous oxide. Humphry Davy, then a young assistant, built a treatment box, like a sedan chair, and the patient sat inside breathing in the nitrous oxide. The author, Maria Edgeworth, was one of the many who tried the gas when she visited Clifton in 1791, and described it as 'gas which inebriates in the most delightful manner'. The poet Southey declared: 'Davy has invented a pleasure for which the language has no name.'

The artistic and literary set who gathered in Bristol included the poet Samuel Coleridge, who was living with Robert Southey, Mrs Siddons the actress, Hannah More the writer, the artists Francis Danby and Samuel Jackson, and the poet Mathais, who, with his nieces, Marianne and Henrietta Skerrett, became lifelong friends of the Milton family. A local doctor, Andrew Carrick, wrote in a report on the Hotwells:

Three extensive taverns were constantly full, and two spacious ballrooms were profitably kept open. There was a well attended ball, public breakfasts and a promenade every week and often twice a week. The Pump Room was all day long the resort of invalids . . . and from 12 to 2 was generally so crowded there was often some difficulty in getting up to drink the water. The walk adjoining was in the meantime filled with fashionable company . . . the Downs and all the avenues to the Hotwells were filled with strings of carriages, and with parties on horseback and on foot.'

When Fanny wrote *The Widow Barnaby* in 1839, she used familiar locations in Clifton. Mrs Barnaby's cousins, the Peters, lived at 4 Rodney Place, while Mrs Barnaby took lodgings at 1 Sion Row for herself and her orphaned niece Agnes, 'The windows of the room were open, and looked out upon the windmill and the down . . . It was not quite such a drawing room as that of Mrs Peters, to be sure, but it was the most fashionable part of Clifton.' The flamboyant Major Allen, whose company Mrs Barnaby cultivated, had lodgings in Gloucester Row.

It was in this exciting world of assemblies, balls, and among the stimulating conversation of the artistic and literary set that Fanny Milton spent much of her first twenty-two years, and in which she grew up. It was the world in which she was always to feel the most at home.

It is not known why her father decided to resume his responsibilities as the Vicar of Heckfield. He had married again, and perhaps his second wife preferred life in the country; but, on 29 October 1801, the Reverend and Mrs Milton, Mary, Fanny and Henry, left Bristol to take up permanent residence in the quiet vicarage of the little country village of Heckfield.

Heckfield must have seemed rustically quiet for the gregarious Fanny, after the bustle of Clifton's social round. Mary was now twenty-five, Fanny twenty-two and Henry, who was at New College, Oxford, seventeen. Mary Russell Mitford, who was later to become a firm friend of Fanny Milton's, then lived at Grasely only a few miles to the north of Heckfield. It was Mary's mother who first made the acquaintance of the Miltons. Dr and Mrs Mitford had been to a concert in Reading and were invited back to Heckfield Place by the owner, Mr Lefevre. The next day, Friday, they all met again. The gentlemen dedicated the morning to field sports, the ladies walked around the grounds and later took a ride round Lord Rivers' estate, Stratfield Saye, which was to be given, in 1817, by a grateful nation to the Duke of Wellington, the hero of Waterloo.

Mrs Mitford wrote to her daughter Mary at her school at Hans Place in London to tell her about the social goings-on in Hampshire.

> We dressed for dinner, when there was an addition to our numbers of a Mr Milton, his wife and two daughters; the youngest of whom, Miss Fanny Milton is a very lively, pleasant young woman. I do not mean to infer that Miss Milton may not be equally agreeable, but the other took a far greater share in the conversation, and, playing casino a great part of the evening with Mr S. Lefevre, Mr Monck, and your old Mumpsa, it gave me an opportunity of seeing her in a more favourable light than her sister.[25]

Mr Lefevre, the owner of Heckfield Place, was the Member of Parliament for the Borough of Reading, and Bligh Monck the Member for Coley Park. An amusing and intelligent young woman, Fanny seemed to have made an impression on her elders.

What was life like in Heckfield for Fanny and her sister Mary? The rambling

Tudor vicarage, which has changed little since the Miltons lived there, looks out over rolling green fields. An ancient brick wall surrounds neat lawns, and wisteria covers the mellow bricks on the front of the building. The old house has bow windows, low doors, and uneven wooden floors; the crunch of gravel on the path which leads to the extensive coach houses beside the old vicarage is now the only sound to disturb the birds. It is a timeless place.

The Milton girls explored the district on foot and horseback. The country around Heckfield is little changed in the last two hundred years, the Whitewater river winds its way through the valley, with far-ranging views from the low hills on either side.

There was a school kept by a Mr Davis in the building now known as School Farm, and a Dame School for infants held in a thatched cottage on the common. The village bowling green abutted the churchyard on the north boundary, and the stocks and whipping stocks were on the village green.

The three main classes of rural society were all present in Heckfield; poor labourers, independent yeomen farmers and the wealthy landowners. The vicar and churchwardens were responsible to the local justices of the peace for poor relief, the funds were raised by levies on landholdings and then distributed to the needy in the form of 'outdoor relief'. To be poor was a punishable crime, and the pauper could have the humiliation of being harnessed to the parish cart and driven around the parish with a piece of coloured cloth fixed to their sleeve or shoulder, emblazoned with the metal letters P.H. 'Pauper of Heckfield'.[26]

On 30 August 1780 the Vestry had passed a resolution to erect a workhouse in an attempt to combat the soaring poor rate. The site chosen was opposite Coldharbour Copse on the Reading/Basingstoke road, and it was still operating in 1827.[27] In her novel, *Jessie Phillips*, Fanny was later to write a scathing condemnation of the Poor Laws. In the introduction she stated firmly:

> The object the author had in view in the composition of this work, has been to call the attention of her readers to the absolute necessity of some alteration in the law which at present regulates the maintenance and management of the poor. The writer is very far from regretting the existence of the old poor-law. She is well aware that the abuses to which it led in practice were enormous, and that its operation was speedily hurrying a large portion of the country towards bankruptcy. . . . She cannot but think, moreover, that in the administration of the poor . . . a central board of supreme control is inexpedient, and for all good purposes inefficient . . . the author is anxious to declare her detestation of the newly broached doctrine that the poor have no right to a sufficiency of necessary food to sustain the life which God has given them.'[28]

As well as the poor labourers, the Heckfield community consisted mainly of yeoman farmers and craftsmen who were smallholders with grazing and turf-cutting rights on the commons; they were independent men, and largely self-sufficient. The third and smaller group who made up the country village was the landed gentry.

The social life of Heckfield was governed by three leading landowners. Lord Rivers had his large country seat at Stratfield Saye to the north west of the village. He had been a member of the Pitt family, married a rich heiress, and used part of her fortune to make many improvements to his estate.

On the other side of the church from the vicarage, was the former manor house, Heckfield Park. The house, of Queen Anne and Georgian period, was lived in by the brother of Lord Rivers, Lieutenant-General William Augustus Pitt, Governor of Portsmouth, and aide-de-camp to George III, who was known to have visited him at Heckfield.

Two miles to the north-east of the village was Heckfield Place, built as a present for Helena Lefevre by her wealthy industrialist father. In 1789 she married Charles Shaw, the son of a Yorkshire vicar, who took his wife's name and became Charles Shaw Lefevre. It was in this house that Fanny made such an impression in 1802.

Charles Shaw Lefevre was a churchwarden and an MP, but in Heckfield he 'was chiefly remembered for his insatiable appetite for land. He, and his son after him, bought every field, cottage and manor they could lay their hands on, and negotiated exchanges with the neighbouring landowners' until the estate exceeded 4,000 acres.[29] Charles Lefevre bought out those who had grazing and turf-cutting rights on the heath, and as a landowner and MP, was able to have private Acts passed by Parliament which overrode the resistance of individual owners to the enclosure of their lands. The owners were awarded compensation by Parliamentary Commissioners whose word was law. In this way many copyholds, leaseholds and lifeholds were exterminated. It was felt that the use of common land by labourers 'operates on the mind as a sort of independence', as a Mr Bishton wrote in 1794, and independence was the last thing the wealthy wanted to encourage in their labourers. As Lefevre's estate grew, so did his house, and he added larger and more elaborate rooms, installed marble chimney pieces from France, and had a terrace laid out on the north-east side.

It was among this cross section of society that Fanny lived from 1801, and it was from them that she drew the background material for many of her later books.

The Reverend Milton found that he now had time on his hands, and occupied it by pursuing both the fate of his 1791 plans to convert the port of Bristol into a floating harbour, and his quarrel with William Jessop's alternative proposals. Jessop's plans, which do look remarkably like those submitted by William Milton, were approved by an Act of Parliament on

11 August 1803. The Dock-Directors silenced the Reverend Milton's protestations by awarding him a handsome piece of plate, 'in Testimony (as the Inscription purports) of the high Sense they entertain of his Original Suggestion for the Improvement of the Harbour of Bristol'.[30]

Life in the vicarage with the intellectual and somewhat eccentric Reverend Milton meant that his family were very much a part of, and yet apart from, the social manoeuvrings which were so important to the rest of Heckfield. In *Town and Country*, the vicar's daughter talks about her snobbish neighbour:

This lady has been a right good and friendly neighbour to us for above twenty years, but never once during the whole of this time has she ever permitted us to forget for a moment, that, although all men are equal before God – and women too – yet nevertheless, that there would be something rather impious in supposing that this state of things was to begin while we remain on earth; and therefore that, at present, her place is in the manor pew, and mine is in the Vicarage ditto.[31]

Fanny with her quizzical outlook and acute power of observation, was very aware of the power games, and her novels draw a clear picture of class rules. In *Tremordyn Cliff*, Lady Monson of Ashwood, her country estate in the village of Broton:

. . . opened her house for the first public soirée for the autumn, a season which she always spent at Ashwood. Not to be admitted on these occasions was the most fatal stigma that could be attached to any pretender to the privileges of good society throughout Broton or its neighbourhood. In London her ladyship's arrangements were of a different character. Her parties there, if not positively exclusive, were extremely select. . . . To have been equally critical in her judgement of those who wished to be admitted to her circle in the country, would have brought upon her the intolerable nuisance of half-filled rooms. To avoid this, a vast majority of those who called themselves ladies and gentlemen of Broton, received a general invitation to assemble at Ashwood, the first Tuesday evening of every month, from the first of September to the first of February, to remain, as the cards for each season duly specified, from eight to eleven. [Fanny described the setting] . . .
Three handsome drawing-rooms, and a pretty octagon boudoir, all brilliantly lighted, and well supplied with every imaginable device for giving life to conversation, and death to time, were open on this occasion. Two or three card tables were placed in one of the rooms, and various musical instruments in another; but the third, opening upon a conservatory at the far end of which was her ladyship's admired boudoir,

11

was lined with ottomans, before which were ranged unnumbered little tables of most capricious variety of form – some bearing two ivory armies, others sustaining portfolios, filled with choice engravings; and more still sprinkled with albums, annuals, courtly magazines, and books of beauty, tiny sculptures and pretty miniatures of all sorts and sizes.[32]

Country life, with its small circle of exclusives, its petty gossip, and set about with strict rules of etiquette, must have seemed stifling to Fanny after the bustle of Bristol. Ironically, she was saved from it indirectly, by the resumption of the war with Napoleon. In 1803, when Napoleon planned to invade England, Martello towers were built for protection along the south and east coasts. More men were recruited for the War Office, and Henry Milton, who had finished at Oxford, was offered a clerkship at the War Office in London, which he accepted. He suggested that his sisters, Mary and Fanny come and live with him to help him keep house; the offer was accepted with alacrity, and in 1803 they moved into a modest house at 27 Keppel Street near Bloomsbury. Henry's small salary of £90 was augmented by the £50 a year allowance given by William Milton or, as seems more likely, by his wife, to each of his daughters.

The Reverend Milton's second wife had been Miss Partington, a name which cropped up with monotonous regularity in the Milton/Trollope annals. Little is known of this lady, except she appears to be the one who ran the finances of the family, for all matters of the girls' allowances and marriage settlements were referred to her. With three adult women sharing the same house, it is likely that the move to London was welcomed by them all.

CHAPTER TWO

'A fund of fanciful invention'

Keppel Street, London. 1803–1815

Once established in London, Fanny expanded her circle of acquaintances. The Miltons led a busy social life. Frances Eleanor Trollope, Fanny's first biographer – the second wife of her eldest son Tom – wrote about the pleasant circle of friends the Miltons attracted around themselves. 'It would be, perhaps, more accurate to attribute the special attraction to the wit and brightness of Henry Milton and his sister Fanny. Mary was a kind, excellent creature, sufficiently sensible, but not of shining parts.'[1]

Fanny enjoyed theatre, music, and art, and she became an amused observer of manners. In *The Laurringtons* she wrote, 'English gentlemen, before dinner, may generally be observed to keep together in groups, either on the hearth-rug, or round a book-table, or at a window, as time and place may permit; but they rarely, before revivifying themselves by this necessary refreshment, appear to have courage sufficient to enter into conversation with ladies.'[2]

There is only one known portrait of Fanny as a young woman, and very few contemporary descriptions. The portrait is of an intense young woman in a red dress, looking directly at the observer. Her face is handsome rather than beautiful, her eyes are set wide apart and she looks as though she is just about to speak. In later life a certain lord on meeting her son, Anthony, remembered his mother: 'I danced with her when she was Fanny Milton, and I remember she had the neatest foot and ankle I ever saw!' Another friend describing her appearance said, 'When a young woman, she had remarkably beautiful arms. She was somewhat indifferent as to her own personal get up, but very particular that those about her should be well dressed.'

Anthony's wife, Rose, writing of her when she was older said: 'She was rather below the average height, but held herself very upright, and walked with a firm step. Her eyes were bluish grey, set rather far apart; her lips full, with a singularly pleasant smile. She always looked you full in the face when speaking. Her hands and feet were small.'[3]

However, after five years in London – in spite of her small hands and feet – Fanny Milton, at twenty-nine years of age, remained unmarried. She had watched her friends fall in love, but maybe, she, like Agatha in *The*

Robertses felt that, 'for myself I care not a straw whether I marry or not. I cannot endure the idea of making marriage the most important business of life.'[4] Perhaps she also talked too much like Miss Maitland in *The Old World and the New*, who, 'at the age of thirty-three was Miss Maitland still; which was less owing, perhaps, to the blindness or indifference of the male sex to her numerous attractions, than to her inveterate love of conversation, in preference to flirting.'

It was probably just this love of conversation, together with her intelligent vivacity, which attracted Henry Milton's friend, Thomas Anthony Trollope.

Thomas Anthony was thirty-four years old and a barrister at Middle Temple, with chambers at Lincoln's Inn. They had several points in common. Both had fathers who were clergymen; they had both lost their mothers; and they both lived in Keppel Street, Mr Trollope at No. 16, Miss Milton at No. 27.

In July 1808, Thomas Anthony sent Miss Milton a letter, couched in very formal terms. He began, 'My dear Madam' and sent her a copy of Crowe's verses and two little odes in Latin, which, 'he will be obliged if she will give to her brother'. He trusted that, 'she would pardon the liberty which he cannot but acknowledge himself guilty of having taken', and signed himself rather daringly as 'her devoted humble servant'.

Fanny would have understood the hidden meaning for she wrote in *A Fashionable Life*, 'now it almost invariably happens, that when a young gentleman begins lending books to a young lady, something more or less approaching to a flirtation between them is the consequence.'[5] We have a record of this 'flirtation' in the letters which passed between Thomas Anthony and Fanny. Thomas Anthony left his umbrella at the Milton's house, and asked Henry to keep it for him. 'I really hope you will indulge me in the request that it may henceforth be safely deposited in your house, since experience has shown that they are very apt to ramble from mine.'[6] He was invited to dine. The courtship progressed. Books played a large part in the friendship; Fanny sent Thomas Anthony an Italian sonnet, thinking that because he was a Latin scholar he would be able to read it but Thomas Anthony had to admit to failure. They discussed the authenticity of Chatterton's poems, and current books under review.

It was four months later, on 1 November, that Thomas Anthony declared himself. In a pedantically long-winded proposal, he managed to reveal how much he loved her, while hiding his feelings behind a smoke-screen of words.

Is it most expedient for a man to make an avowal of his attachment to a lady *viva voce*, anglice *tête-à-tête*, or by epistolary correspondence? . . . [a page later] I little thought, my dear Madam, that this preface would have run to so considerable a length; since, however, it explains the motive of my now addressing you, it will save me the necessity of a more explicit avowal, and sufficiently declare to you that my future happiness on earth is at your disposal. It is impossible but that I must feel every anxiety till I am favoured with your reply to this note, yet I shall say nothing under the hopes of accelerating it. . . . my chief delight has long since had its source in your society and conversation . . . but let me avoid compliments, which were always my detestation – fit tools only for knaves, and to be employed against fools. . . . my sole object has been to make a declaration which I could no longer conceal.[7]

In between these declarations of love are long, long, paragraphs detailing his income, apologizing for being presumptuous and for his style, and asking if she thought that she could let him know within three weeks. However, he received his answer on the following day, 2 November 1808.

It does not require three weeks consideration, Mr Trollope, to enable me to tell you that the letter you left with me last night was most flattering and gratifying to me. . . . But I fear you are not sufficiently aware that your choice, so flattering to me, is for yourself a very imprudent one. You have every right in an alliance of this kind, to expect a fortune greatly superior to any I shall ever possess.[8]

She told him of her modest expectations. Just £1,000 and a possible annual allowance of £50. She found it hard to express herself quite as she wished. 'There is something of cold formality in what I have written, which is very foreign to what I feel, – but I know not how to mend it.'[9]

The answer from Thomas Anthony arrived immediately; she had made him most happy, and he begged for a personal interview without delay. There were many such meetings, and letters ceased until 2 December 1809 when Fanny returned to Heckfield. She wrote to say that she had been met at Reading at the end of her coach journey by her father's patent cart (one of his many inventions), and had a fine, clear, cold moonlight night for the 8 mile journey to Heckfield. She told him of her proposed settlement:

Mrs Milton, who I told you settled all these things has been telling me what it is their intention to give me. . . . She says my father cannot now give me more than £1,200 stock, and another £100 for clothes; that at his death I am to have the third of the little estate I mentioned to you; and at hers, the third of £2,000. I am afraid, nay I know, this is less than you must have expected, and this vexes me much. . . . Ought not this to make a difference as to the time at which you mean to burden yourself with a poor wife? Indeed I think it ought.[10]

She signed herself Fanny, and then crossed it out and wrote Frances. Her books and most of her business communications were signed Frances; Fanny was her family name.

Thomas Anthony's relations wrote to Fanny, 'a very affectionate letter from your sister Die' (who had married a cousin, the Reverend Henry Trollope). Fanny was to meet, 'your uncle and Mrs Meetkerke', and Sir John and Lady Trollope hoped to make her acquaintance.

Thomas Anthony was earning £700 a year plus a New College Fellowship of £200, which he would lose when he married. He also owned property worth £6,000. It was sufficient for their needs. It seemed that Fanny's small fortune was not to be a stumbling block.

They joked about the Reverend Milton's patent coach; her father had apparently made over to Fanny one-third of the profits from his invention. Thomas Anthony quizzed that she was going to 'reserve it snugly for a little secret pin money'. Fanny replied, 'And so you have found me out! I did hope my share of the patent coach, would have supplied all my little private extravagances and you have been never the wiser.' William Milton's patent coach was later adopted by the Reading Stage Coach Company. However, there is no record of his ever having acquired any wealth from his inventions.

The couple wrote to each other almost every day, Thomas Anthony from London, where he was preparing his house for his future wife, and Fanny from Heckfield where she was making her trousseau, reading Dante, and chatting to him about her daily round.

On 4 May 1809, just three weeks before the wedding, Thomas Anthony wrote:

> But, my dearest love, are you still to learn my character and sentiments? Are you yet to be informed in what detestation I hold all ardent professions, and in what admiration actions that want not the aid of declamation, but boldly speak for themselves? When I see a man vehement in his expressions without any apparent or sufficient cause, I am always inclined to suspect him. From these ideas . . . it may not be improbable that I often seem too cautious of making use of what might be considered a natural and becoming warmth in my declarations; but I confess . . . I always feel afraid of raising doubts to the prejudice of my own sincerity by professing too much, or declaring myself in too vehement a manner.[11]

It was a foretaste of what was to come.

Fanny's reply came fast. 'What you say of professions is very just. . . . But yet one cannot help being pleased (at least women, I believe, cannot) with *expressions* as well as proofs of tenderness from those they love. . . . But I own my heart welcomes a look or word of fondness from those who are dear to me, as cordially as it does more unequivocal proofs of attachment.'[12]

On 23 May 1809, on Thomas Anthony's thirty-fifth birthday, he married Frances Milton in the Norman church of Heckfield. They were married by licence by the Reverend G. Salter, Rector of Stratfield Saye, and the wedding was witnessed by W. Milton, Deletitia Salter, Mary Milton and her brother Henry.[13] As the wedding party walked back to the vicarage they were showered with flower petals by the village children.

When the honeymoon was over, Fanny and Thomas Anthony moved into the house at No. 16 Keppel Street – a part of London largely inhabited by lawyers – and settled down to their married life. After an early breakfast served by the footman at 7 a.m. in the back drawing-room, Thomas Anthony's day was spent in his chambers at No. 23 Old Square, Lincoln's Inn, and he returned from there only in time for a late dinner at five o'clock. His son Tom remembered him as an industrious and laborious man. Fanny was probably remembering his chambers when describing those of Frank Caldwell in *Uncle Walter*:

Nowhere, perhaps, in the whole of our vast metropolis is there to be found so strong a perfume of the past (to borrow a French phrase), as in our Inns of Court, and beyond all others in the Temple. It would be difficult, perhaps, to describe with any very satisfactory degree of accuracy, in what this peculiarly characteristic savour consists. [The room] was on the third floor of the tall pile of buildings which forms the western boundary of this garden terrace . . . this small dingy room, reached by hard climbing up three flights of dark, steep, dirty stairs, with its window commanding in addition to the preciously quiet, but very dingy garden, a countless collection of mud imbedded colliers, was a possession so coveted, and so valuable, that its annual rent was double the entire income of many an independent well-to-do 'rentier' who *flânés* away his elegant leisure hours amid the gay alleys of the Tuileries.[14]

The Trollopes' first child, Thomas Adolphus, was born on 29 April 1810, and, while Thomas Anthony was away in court in Bedford, Fanny took 3½-month-old Tom to Heckfield, to stay with his grandparents. A young barrister working out of London, often found he entailed considerable expense, as he had to travel by private conveyance. He could hire a post-chaise, or ride, but was not allowed to travel by stage coach, or stay in a hotel, in case in so doing, he might meet with an attorney on the same case and so be led into the sin of 'huggery'.

On 10 August Thomas Anthony wrote to Fanny:

I have this moment received your letter, and have been made as happy as I can be . . . at the tidings it contains. – That 'all's well and Tom and his mamma are enjoying themselves in the country' is the source of the greatest pleasure to me. – Yet I should not say the greatest, since I look forward to the happiness of seeing and partaking of this enjoyment with them. – I trust it is not a sin, or at least a venial one, to wish 3 weeks and one day were expired. Then, my Fanny, let time roll on as tardily as he will. . . . I find we are now called upon to attend the Judges in court. I have only, therefore to say God bless you my dearest Fanny, and our darling child. Give him a kiss for me every morning and tell him his Papa sends it to him.[15]

Fanny replied fondly, 'Your letter, my beloved husband, was a cordial to me of the most exhilarating kind'; she told him she had given Tom a kiss, and wondered at how quickly the child's intelligence was increasing; she went on:

My father is perfectly delighted with him, and every day after dinner tries some new trick to try his sagacity. . . . Were I not too wise to be vain, I should certainly become so here. Everybody exclaims that my darling is the loveliest creature they ever beheld, and most add . . . that he is very like his father. Adieu my very dear husband. Adieu. – I will not dictate the moment for your writing, but I shall wish, and wish, and wish, till another comes. Yours wholly and for ever.[16]

Once back in London, Fanny was in her element. She loved to entertain and to be surrounded by her friends. Old Lady Milman, the widow of Sir Francis Milman who had been Queen Charlotte's physician, had two sons, Sir William and the Reverend Henry. Henry, who had the living of St Mary's, Reading, was a poet, and he and his beautiful wife remained lifelong friends of the Trollopes. Friends from Clifton days were the Misses Skerrett, the nieces of the poet Mathais, and the Misses Gabell, the daughters of the headmaster of Winchester. Lady Dyer, the wife of Sir Thomas Dyer of Ovington near Winchester, was another good friend. It was Lady Dyer who introduced several Italian refugees to the Trollopes, including the rather stolid General Guglielmo Pepe, who had a 'kind of simple, dignified, placid manner of enunciating the most astounding platitudes', and who took presents of mandarin oranges and dried figs to the nursery. Mary Russell Mitford, now an author, visited the Trollopes in London and remembered that Fanny, 'used to be such a Radical that her house in London was a perfect emporium of escaped state criminals. I remember asking her at one of her parties how many of her guests would have been shot or guillotined if they had remained in their own country.'[17] As Fanny herself wrote in

Fashionable Life. 'A great part of the enjoyment she found in society, arose from her taking considerably more than a common degree of interest in the characters and peculiarities of those with whom she associated.'[18]

There were dinner parties, where, as Fanny said 'the wise partners never permitted their dinner table to be surrounded by more than twelve, and very rarely permitted it to exceed eight'. There were walks, rides, excursions to the theatre, and the children to play with. Fanny was always entertained.

Social life in London was governed by definite rules. Irrepressible Fanny found the strict rules amusing:

> I have all the routine of ceremony at my fingers' ends; and if you will condescend to learn from me the recondite mysteries of entrances and exits, and when to walk forward, and when to walk backwards, and all the ingenious varieties of bowings and bendings, from the angle which threatens absolute prostration, to the rapid little miniature dip, skilfully imitated from the graceful curtsey of a jointed doll, – if you will first give your whole heart and intellect to this branch of aristocratic learning, you will find all the rest extremely easy. You will have indeed to put your fingers at a particular angle at the distance of about an inch from your lips, and make them perform a sort of pantomimic manoeuvre, which means by being interpreted, a vast variety of both courteous and affectionate greetings.[19]

There were soirées, charades, and fancy-dress balls or masquerades, and as Fanny wrote in *Hargrave*:

> We must keep in mind the important distinction between a fancy-ball and a masquerade. Nothing which I at this moment remember strikes me as so offensively *mauvais ton* as confounding them. In a masquerade-dress, the perfection of a costume consisted in the learned accuracy with which every circumstance of time, station, and personal peculiarity in the character represented, was seized; whether becoming or unbecoming, whether elegant or precisely the reverse, a masquerading dress, to be approved by persons of real taste, must be strictly and severely historical, and nothing else. But at a fancy-ball, thank Heaven! the case is wholly different . . . all the skill of the artist employed must be directed to modify, heighten, or soften, the effect of the costume chosen, with the most studious attention to what becomes the individual, and utter disregard to every thing else.[20]

George Bartley the actor, who in 1829 became the stage-manager of Covent Garden Theatre, and his actress wife Sarah, were friends of Fanny's, and it was probably through them that she met Kean, and later, Macready, who was for a time the actor/manager of Covent Garden. She enjoyed the theatre and loved the fun of charades and private theatricals:

> . . . for certain it is that, from the mighty project of private theatricals, down to the drawing room characters on Twelfth Night – through all the gradations of speaking charades and dumb charades, tableaux vivans, fancy fairs, and costumes quadrilles, the preparation for exhibition is sure to produce more animation, more amusement, and more general gratification, than anything else in the world.[21]

Tom remembered hearing his mother speaking of standing in a queue for four hours to see Mrs Siddons play Lady Macbeth, 'The amount of enthusiasm needed to induce a lady to face (the ordeal) is something scarcely to be understood at the present day.'

During the first eight years of her married life, Fanny was busy bearing children. Contraception was primitive and viewed with suspicion as being rather 'French'. Nice ladies did not practise it. Infant mortality was high, and large families helped to ensure the continuation of the family name. The Trollopes had seven children. After Tom in 1810 came Henry in 1811, Arthur William in 1812, Emily in 1813 (who was born and died on the same day), Anthony in 1815, Cecilia in 1816, and a second Emily in 1818. There was a nurse, Farmer, to care for them; she was a middle-aged woman who ruled the nursery, and whom Tom remembered as 'inspiring more awe than affection. She was an austere and somewhat grim sort of body.' She was also an Anabaptist, which meant nothing to the young Trollopes, but they used to tease her by singing:

> Old Farmer is an Anabap*tist*!
> When she is gone, she will not be missed!

There were also nursemaids, a footman dressed in the the Trollope livery, a cook, and other servants; this was normal staffing for a household of their class.

All the family ate dinner at five, and in the winter the light came from just two tallow candles, which 'partially illumined the table'. The alternative would have been wax lights at half-a-crown a pound, 'an extravagence not to be thought of', said Tom.

Young Tom was adventurous and sturdy, 'as indifferent to weather, wet or dry, wind or shine, as a Shetland pony'. He learnt to read early, taught by his mother who made a great game out of learning. He described her ingenious method:

> Her plan for teaching the letters was as follows. She had a great number

of bone counters with the alphabet in capitals and small letters on either side printed on them; then having invited a charming little girl, the daughter of a neighbour . . . she tossed the counters broadcast over the floor, instituting prizes for him, or her, who should, in crawling races over the floor, soonest bring the letter demanded. Reading thus began to be an amusement to me at an unusually early age.[22]

Fanny loved singing to the children, and Tom remembered one song about an 'unfortunate Miss Bayly', who was seduced by 'a Captain bold of Halifax', a rollicking old ballad which meant nothing to him at the time. 'Nor do I suppose that we had the faintest notion of the nature of the evil inflicted on the unfortunate Miss Bayly.' Fanny could be very entertaining and one attribute was: 'a comic power of description or recitation. There was, moreover, a fund of fanciful invention . . . which seemed to defy the possibility of her ever being at a loss, when seeking the means of amusement, either for herself or for others.'[23]

There was no time to be bored when Fanny was around, 'For so necessary to happiness is the feeling of having something to do, and the consciousness of doing it, that the very idlest people fancy they have an immensity of necessary business to get through, and never awaken to the knowledge of the dismal fact that their whole lives are spent in doing nothing.'[24]

The children often spent time with their grandparents at Heckfield. Grandfather Milton's house must have been a treasure trove of exciting inventions for them, especially for Tom, who remembered him as:

a charming old man, markedly gentleman-like and suave in his manner; very nice in his person; clever unquestionably in a queer, crochety sort of way; and thoroughly minded to do his duty according to his lights in that state of life to which it had pleased God to call him. But he would have had no more idea of attempting anything of the nature of active parochial work or reform . . . than he would have had of scheming to pay the national debt . . . for he was crochety and full of schemes. Especially he was fond of mechanics.[25]

The Reverend Milton spent much time and money on a scheme to prevent the upsetting of stage coaches, and in 1810 he published a *Treatise on the Danger of Travelling in Stage Coaches and a Remedy Proposed*. The large coach house, which stands beside the vicarage, was filled with a collection of models of his inventions. One, especially remembered by Tom, consisted of two wheels, 10 ft high, joined by a number of cross bars. This *rotis volentibus* may have been the test model about which the Reverend Milton wrote two articles for the *Gentleman's Magazine* on the advantages of high wheels: 'the leverage employed being more potent without losing anything in time, the friction less, and the line of traction much more direct and advantageous; the conveyance also on high wheels is smoother and less noisy'.

Those high wheels certainly did use less friction, as young Tom found to his dismay one day when he crept inside the structure and set it in motion by stepping on the cross bars one after the other. Once it had got under way on the steep part of the lawn, the machine only stopped when it smashed into the evergreen hedge. Tom, severely bruised, was advised by his grandfather, 'Never, Tom, put in motion forces which you are unable to control!'

Another eccentricity which Tom remembered were some dinner plates which the Reverend Milton had ordered especially for his own use. He so disliked the contact of a knife's edge with earthenware or porcelain that these plates had a circular depression 2 inches in diameter in the centre, into which the Reverend Milton fitted especially made circles of silver.

A favourite relative with whom the Trollopes went to stay, was Miss Fanny Bent, also an eccentric, who lived in Exeter. She was Fanny Trollope's much-loved first cousin and the daughter of William's sister, Mary. She appeared under various guises in many of Fanny Trollope's books. The detailed description of Miss Christina in *One Fault*, was almost certainly cousin Fanny Bent:

> Her dappled grey hair, which was extremely thick, perfectly straight, and cut as if the edge of a bowl placed upon her head, had guided the shears, was sheltered by a small, black beaver bonnet, which it should seem that she had outgrown; for it hardly reached her ears, and was only kept in the station assigned it by means of strings tied so tightly as to make her little round cherry-cheeks hang like bags over them. Her robe was of stout brown cloth, warm and substantial; but having been exposed to wind and weather during many winters, it had shrunk, till even her short little legs were left most cruelly exposed. Her shoes were such as economical young gentlemen go shooting in; her gloves large, strong, and very dirty; and round her neck she wore a huge tippet of coarse fur with a point behind, and two long much-worn tails before.[26]

When not visiting their relations, Tom, and his younger brother Henry took long walks through London. One of their favourite excursions was to the White Horse Cellar in Piccadilly to see the coaches. There Tom would dream of being 'one of the great-coated companies who were departing to their various destinations by those "Telegraphs," "High Flyers," "Magnets," and "Independents". He fantasized about, 'belonging to some select and specially important and adventurous section of humanity'.

They explored the docks, 'with the outgoing ships bearing, tied to their shrouds, boards indicating their destinations. Here again was unsatisfied longing!'

One especially dangerous adventure was to, 'sundry mysteriously wicked regions where the bandit bands of the great city consorted'; the boys had heard of,

> a certain lane, where it was said all the pocket-handkerchiefs stolen by all the pickpockets in London were to be seen exposed in a sort of unholy market. The name of this place was Saffron Hill. . . . Report had spoken truly. Saffron Hill was a world of pocket-handkerchiefs. From every window, and on lines stretched across the narrow street, they fluttered in all the colours of the rainbow, and of all sizes and qualities.[27]

The boys escaped any misadventure by having neither money, nor any pocket-handkerchief in their possession worth stealing.

The first years of Fanny's marriage were very happy, and Thomas Anthony joined in the parties and theatricals with much enthusiasm. However, after a few years he began to show disturbing signs of the excessive irritability and intolerance which was later to cause such misery to his family. He was allowed by his peers to be a remarkably sound and able Chancery barrister, yet his practice began to dwindle. 'He was unsparing in exposing a fallacy, and would do so in no mitigated phrase . . . but Mr Trollope was never politic in his scourgings. He would demonstrate the folly and incoherence of a rich client, as eagerly as he would scold a poor one.'[28] Tom remembered how 'he became increasingly irritable; never with the effect of causing him to raise a hand against any one of us, but with the effect of making intercourse with him so sure to issue in something unpleasant that, unconsciously, we sought to avoid his presence, and to consider as hours of enjoyment only those that could be passed away from it.'[29]

Thomas Anthony had always suffered very distressingly from bilious headaches, the common treatment for which was calomel, and he and Fanny thought that living out of London might be of help in easing the symptoms. Calomel, also known as 'beautiful black', was a compound of mercury, sulphuric acid, and chloride of sodium. It was prescribed for a wide variety of symptoms, as was opium, with little awareness of the harmful side effects. The Trollopes also needed more space for the ever increasing family, and thought country life would be good for the children. They found Illot's Farm at Harrow, which they leased in 1813, with plans to spend just the summers there. There was, as well, a more practical reason for renting a farm; they hoped to benefit from the higher prices being paid for corn as a result of the international situation. War had broken out in America in 1812 and lasted until 1815, and, because of the continuing war with France and the scarcity of grain, the price of bread rose. Landowners profited from this rise and the middle class was on the ascendant, but there was unrest among the starving poor. There was further unrest when, in 1812, George III's madness became so severe that the detested Prinny was declared Prince Regent. Years later Fanny put the dislike of the fat Prince into her novel, *Town and Country*. The heroine 'was to receive as a guest, the son of George the Third! The eldest son, himself a sovereign! . . . it would be nothing more than right to repay herself for the bore of listening to so much twaddle, by obtaining, either for herself or family, something more precious than the priviledge of being placed always within reach of having the Royal tediousness bestowed especially upon her.' Later the Regent left for, 'one of those dinners which probably robbed England of her fattest monarch some years before his stout stamina would have given way without them.'[30]

In 1813 Napoleon retreated from Moscow, and Emily 1 was born and died on the same day. Napoleon was defeated, and exiled to Elba in 1814, only to escape for the hundred days march and one last defiant stand. The following year, 1815, was the year of Waterloo, a victory which set all England rejoicing. It was also the year in which Anthony Trollope was born, an event, then, of interest to no one but his family.

The advent of this fifth child and the need for more space and country air encouraged the Trollopes to spend more time at the farm. It was decided, in fact, to make Harrow their permanent home and Thomas Anthony would travel from there daily to his London chambers. Towards the end of the year Keppel Street was leased, and the family all moved to the country farmhouse.

CHAPTER THREE

'A lively, brilliant woman of the world'

Harrow. 1815–1827

Illots Farm, on the southern side of Harrow, had 160 acres of land. There were barns, stables, an orchard and a rambling old farmhouse which was later described by Anthony in *Orley Farm*. A variety of crops could be planted on the 21 acres of ploughed land, and 138 acres of meadows provided the main crop of hay. The lease, signed in 1813, was for twenty-one years at a rate of £660 a year. It was there that Cecilia was born in October 1816.

The family was already beginning to outgrow the farmhouse, and, as they now intended to make Harrow their home they decided to build a new and larger dwelling at the top of the hill. An agreement was reached with the landlord, Lord Northwick, that they would lease more land, raise a construction mortgage and put up a handsome house. This mortgage would then be incorporated into the lease of the farm, which was reduced to £360 per annum and the mortgage payments were to be considered as part of the rent. Much money had to be outlaid in order to complete this much grander residence; extra acreage was enclosed, a pond drained, shrubberies planted, and roads relocated. One of the fields incorporated into the grounds was called Julians, and it was after this that the new house was named. The name had good connotations; Thomas Anthony had an uncle, Adolphus Meetkerke, with a fine house and grounds in Hertfordshire, also called Julians. He was elderly with no children, and it was understood by all the family that Thomas Anthony was to be his heir. The family went regularly to visit the Meetkerkes, though Thomas Anthony's practice of arguing fiercely with his uncle, especially about politics, did not endear him to the old man. Every morning Aunt Meetkerke went down to breakfast dressed in a green riding habit, spent most of the day on horseback, and never meddled with the housekeeping. The running of the house was attended to by Miss Anne, Adolphus Meetkerke's sister, 'who always carried a little basket in her hand, in which were the keys and a never changing volume of Miss Austen's *Pride and Prejudice*, which she always recommenced as soon as she had worked her way to the end of it.'[1]

It was partly on the expectation of this inheritance that the Trollopes built their larger house. However, Aunt Meetkerke died unexpectedly on 28 July 1817, and much to the surprise of his relations, Uncle Meetkerke married a young wife the following October. In December 1819 all hopes of inheritance were dashed, when the new wife produced young Adolphus, the first of six children. This must have been a sore blow to Thomas Anthony who, with the birth of Emily 2 in 1818, also had six children to provide for.

The new house, Julians, in which they had lived for less than a year was now seen to be an extravagance for the costs had been higher than anticipated; the Trollopes decided it would be more prudent to lease it. The sum of £500 was spent on improvements to Illots Farm, now renamed Julian Hill, and there the family returned to live. Thomas Anthony retained a London residence, and he wrote to Lord Northwick in 1820 to explain the change of plan: 'The continued ill state of my health has induced me with the advice of my medical friends to return to my residence in town. I have it in contemplation therefore to let my house at Harrow, and to fit up the farmhouse for the summer vacation and other occasional visits to my farm.'

Tom, once he could read, was initiated into the mysteries of Latin by his father. He said he was about six when he was introduced to the *Eton Latin Grammar*, although it may have been earlier than that, as he remembered trying 'to get the due relationship of relative and antecedent into his little head' in the back drawing-room of Keppel Street. All the boys had vivid memories of the detested Latin lessons, when father used, 'to sit with his arm over the back of the pupil's chair, so that his hand might be ready to inflict an instantaneous pull of the hair . . . for every blundered concord or false quantity; the result being to the scholar a nervous state of expectancy, not judiciously calculated to increase intellectual receptivity.'[2]

Thomas Anthony hated to see the boys wasting time, and if he saw them 'idling' would set them another Latin task. He was not popular in his own home, and his increasing irritability made him a person to avoid. Sir Joseph Lexington in *The Three Cousins* was just such a father:

> The tyranny with which he controlled his [son's] actions and regulated every movement of his life, appeared sometimes of so wanton a nature, as to suggest the idea of an absolute aversion, which made the infliction of mortification and restraint a positive pleasure to him. Yet there had been other moments in the life of this miserable enslaved young man, when his existence and his health had appeared as precious to his capricious father as if he had been the honoured lawful heir to all his boasted greatness. Never, however, at any time did he seem to wish for any demonstration of either gratitude or affection in return.[3]

Fanny's disposition, however, as Tom saw it, 'was of the most genial, cheerful, happy *enjoué* nature imaginable. All our happiest hours were spent with her; and to anyone of us a *tête-à-tête* with her was preferable to any other disposal of a holiday hour.'[4]

The boys, like both their father and grandfather before them, were destined for Winchester and New College, Oxford. A public school education could ensure a privileged start in life. As Fanny was to write later: 'History informs us . . . that the public schools of England have been honoured, and in truth immortalized, by the patronage and fellowship of some of the noblest houses in the kingdom. This invests them with a degree of dignity that no mere scholarship could ever bestow.'[5]

Julian Hill was situated just below Harrow School, where, for reasons of economy, Thomas Anthony had decided to send the boys until such time as they could be elected to a place at Winchester. He would have preferred to continue their education himself, but this was impracticable as he drove daily to London to work in his chambers. Harrow School in the meantime was available for their free tuition as local day boys under the care of the Drury family, who were masters at the school as well as family friends.

The headmaster of Harrow at that time was Doctor Butler, 'a gentleman, extremely suave in manner, gentle in dealing with those under his authority and moderate in his ideas of discipline'. He had succeeded Doctor Drury, 'and found the school full of Drurys'. Mark Drury was the second master, Harry Drury the fourth, and William Drury, Mark's son, was the fifth master. Mark Drury was so fat that he could hardly leave his study; he conducted his lessons from there, and it was arranged that Tom, aged eight, would go to the study every day, not for lessons, but to stand behind Mark Drury's chair and pick up what he could in the way of learning. 'I do not think I profited much by my attendance at old Mark's pupil-room. How I hated it all! . . . because I was a "town-boy" . . . and was in consequence an object of scorn and contumely on the part of all the *paying* pupils. I was a charity boy.'[6] Sentiments to be echoed later by Anthony in his autobiography. In 1819 Henry joined Tom at Harrow.

While the children were being educated at school and cared for at home with the help of Farmer, Fanny continued to entertain and to be entertained. Her drawing room became the centre of Harrow social life. Colonel and Mrs Grant and their family lived just behind Julian Hill, and were close friends. Their children were the same ages as the Trollope children. There were many long walks in the country and games with the family. Lady Milman came to visit, so did the Merivale family, who were relations of the Drurys and whose children all went to Harrow. Fanny was very fond of whist, as was Thomas Anthony, but because of his dictatorial manner people tried to avoid playing with him. As one friend said, 'Many men will scold their partners occasionally. But Trollope invariably scolds us all round with the utmost impartiality; and that every deal!'[7] There were parties in London, and, of course, visits to the theatre. At one such evening in February 1822, when the guests included the Italian poet Ugo Foscolo, John Merivale observed, 'Mrs Trollope came in her deepest blue stockings . . . the Siddonian glances which Kean detected the other night in Mrs Trollope were entirely thrown away on Foscolo, who shrugged up his shoulders and observed that she was *very blue.*'

King George III, a white haired, solitary figure, confined in his madness in Windsor Castle, died at last on 29 January 1820. He had suffered a last violent attack of his illness at Christmas, and talked for fifty-eight hours without sleep. Deaf, alone, and ignored by his family, he lost his appetite and became alarmingly thin. The Duke of York was the only member of his family present at his death.

The depised Prince Regent became George IV. Seeking a divorce from his estranged wife, Queen Caroline, the new king had her committed to trial for adultery when she returned to England to claim her place as queen; however, after a sensational trial which dragged on for three months, the queen was acquitted. One of the defence arguments was the production of a copy of the king's will in which he named Mrs Fitzherbert as 'his dear wife'. The combatants called a truce. From France came news, in 1821, of the death of the Emperor Napoleon in lonely exile on the island of Saint Helena.

In Harrow in 1820 there were celebrations when Tom was elected to Winchester, Henry joined him a year later. A letter written by Fanny to Tom at Winchester gives some idea of family activities:

I rode Jack to a very delightful hunt in Wembley Park. We had a delightful gallop, but did not kill the hare, which, to say truth I was not sorry for, as that part of the sport is but savage work. But the gentlemen, I believe, were of a different opinion. The little girls amused me exceedingly. They had been talking and wondering a good deal about Mama's going hunting; and when they saw me equipped and ready to mount, Cecilia said, 'but Mama, you have not got a gun! You must have a gun!' I laughed heartily at this and told her that I was not going shooting but coursing; upon which, with a great air of contempt, and to show off her superior knowledge, Emily said 'No; Mama ought not to take a gun, but she ought to take Neptune.'[8]

Neptune was their large Newfoundland dog, who later bounded through the pages of Fanny's novel *One Fault.*

The vicar of Harrow was a certain Mr Cunningham, a man of mark among the low-church party. He was much disliked by the Drury faction, to whom the Trollopes belonged, and was viewed with suspicion as being too suave and too soft, giving the impression of a certain lack of sincerity. The eighteen-year-old daughter of one of Fanny's friends spoke over-enthusiastically to her one day about the vicar. Fanny, looking her straight in the eyes said, 'Did he kiss you Carrie?'

'Yes, Mrs Trollope. He did give me the kiss of peace. I'm sure there was no harm in that!'

'None at all, Carrie! For I am sure you meant none! But remember, Carrie, that the kiss of peace is apt to change its quality if repeated!'[9]

The Reverend Dr J.W. Cunningham was believed to have been the model for the Reverend W.J. Cartwright in Fanny's later novel, *The Vicar of Wrexhill*, a claim denied by her. Her antipathy towards the Reverend Cunningham might have been exacerbated by the fact that he and his large family now rented her beloved Julians. Dissenters and Evangelicals were looked down upon by the Establishment Church of England. Tom remembered that at Heckfield 'there were two or three Dissenters and their families, generally considered by their neighbours much as so many Chinese settled among them might have been – as unaccountably strange and as objectionable.'[10]

Another scandal which occasioned a great deal of gossip in the Harrow community in 1822, was precipitated by the death, in Italy, of Byron's natural daughter Allegra. Byron was heartbroken, and sent her ashes to his publisher John Murray with a request that she be buried in Harrow Church, under a simple stone marked with her name. Harry Drury, Byron's old tutor and friend when he was a pupil at Harrow, was asked to arrange this. A solemn meeting was held in the vestry, at which the vicar, the Reverend Cunningham, all the masters of Harrow, and sundry parishioners were present. '"Depraved", "profane", "adulterous", "vile", "accursed", in various notes of canting reached the sky.' The words were reported by Fanny in a poem which she wrote and circulated among her friends. It was decided that no stone was allowed to be placed to mark the grave. The reason given by Cunningham was that if he should, 'place at any price, a stone on which the child's name may be read. May it not lead the school boys into vice?'

This poem, *Lines written by a Celebrated Authoress on the Burial of the Daughter of a Celebrated Author*, in sixty-one verses, was written in 1822 after the controversy was over. In Anthony's footnote to his mothers 'Lines', he added 'that there was a fear that it should teach the boys to get bastards'.[11]

It was just this kind of thinking that made Fanny write later in *Uncle Walter*:

It is quite a vulgar error to suppose that the principal or most valuable effect of cant is to deceive others. This is very far from being the case. Those born and bred under its influence, not only speak, but think cant; and it is quite certain that they must do so in order to speak it well. It is like a foreign language. To speak French well, you must think in French. In fact it is this alone that makes our actual system of society possible. All crooked paths are made to look straight, and the rough places are not only plain, but very particularly smooth.[12]

After the summer holidays, when the boys returned to Winchester in September 1823, Fanny and Thomas Anthony went to Paris to visit Fanny's old friends from her Bristol days, the Garnetts. They had migrated to America in 1796, and after John Garnett's death in 1820, his widow and three of her daughters returned to Paris where living was less expensive than England.

The journey from home to Paris took three days. First they drove to London by gig, then by ship from the Tower Stairs to Calais, where they spent the night. The next morning they mounted the diligence to Paris at nine, finding it full of English, and finally jolted into Paris at eight o'clock that evening. It was Fanny's first visit abroad.

The Trollopes spent ten days in Paris sightseeing. Fanny who was now forty-four and the mother of six children, had seen very little of the world. Paris was wonderful. They visited the Louvre – five times – and various private collections, Versailles, the opera and ballet, and met many interesting friends of the Garnetts, including Frances Wright.

Frances Wright was a wealthy young Scotswoman, orphaned at the age of two. She was proud, imperious, and a reformer, and had made a vow in her youth 'to wear ever in her heart the cause of the poor and the helpless; and to aid in all that she could in redressing the grievous wrongs which seemed to prevail in society.' She was attracted by the promise of American freedom, and went there in 1818 at the age of twenty with her younger sister Camilla. She stayed for many weeks with the Garnetts at Whitehouse Farm and returned to Europe in 1820 with plans to emigrate, although 'the crying sin of slavery weighs upon my heart'. In 1821 Frances wrote a book *Views of Society and Manners in America*, which was well received.

Fanny Trollope's brother, Henry Milton, helped the Garnetts with their arrangements to return to Europe, and it was through this connection that Frances Wright met Fanny Trollope. They had become firm friends, and Fanny had introduced her to her circle in London and Harrow. Frances Wright and the Garnetts now welcomed her into their circle in Paris. Fanny always enjoyed the company of younger women; Julia Garnett was thirty, her sister Harriet twenty-nine, and Frances and Camilla Wright were twenty-eight and twenty-seven. They developed a close and intimate friendship, linked by their past connections and family ties. As Fanny wrote in *Town and Country*: 'The genuine liking and affection of the young is a very delicious incense to the old.' The stimulating Paris circle into which Fanny was introduced included General Lafayette, Madame de Segur, the Fenimore Coopers, Madame Récamier, Prosper Mérimée, Stendal, the Macreadys, and

Mary Clarke and her mother. Frances Wright, with her love of freedom and hatred of slavery, became a close friend of General Lafayette, his family thought rather too close. He, at sixty-seven was nearly forty years her senior, and although she publicly stated that she considered him as a father, her letters reveal a desire for a more passionate attachment. It was through this connection that the Trollopes were invited to stay with Lafayette at his country house, La Grange, situated about 40 miles from Paris. Fanny enjoyed their visit and told Tom, 'our apartment is charming. It consists of two rooms and two closets. In the largest room is a very handsome bed in a recess, with rich crimson satin curtains, and a quilt of the same, covering the bed by day. In the smaller room is a small bed for Monsieur, if it were preferred.' Fanny was impressed with Lafayette. 'Nothing could be more interesting than the conversation of this illustrious man; quiet and simple in his manners, open and unconstrained in giving his opinion, gentle and unassuming in listening to the opinions of others.'[13]

During the stay, there was dancing, reading of tragedies and pianoforte playing. The Trollopes were delighted that Lafayette was to be a guest at the farewell party given for them in Paris by Frances Wright. When their visit was over they returned reluctantly to England. Fanny wrote in her journal, 'I know not where to find so intellectual, so amiable a set of beings as those I have been living amongst here.'[14]

Arthur, the Trollopes' third son, went to Harrow with Anthony in 1823, but he was a sickly child and stayed there only a short time. He went to live with his grandfather, William Milton, who by this time was living in Castle Street, Reading. In 1824 Arthur died. His death left Anthony very much the odd one out in the family, sandwiched between his two older brothers and two younger sisters. When Anthony went to Harrow in 1823 as a day-boarder, he was as unhappy as Tom had been before him. 'I was only seven, and I think that boys of seven are now spared among their more considerate seniors. I was never spared; and was not even allowed to run to and fro between our house and the school without a daily purgatory.'[15] He remembered Dr Butler stopping him one day and asking him if it was possible that Harrow School could be disgraced by such a disreputably dirty little boy. After three unsatisfactory years at Harrow, it was decided on the advice of his tutor, Henry Drury, that he might do better at a smaller private school at Sunbury. In his autobiography, Anthony complained that during his two years at Sunbury he 'never had any pocket-money, and seldom had much in the way of clothes'. However, in this he was no different from his brothers, for the two older boys, now at Winchester, were wearing various garments, cricketing flannels and so forth, made by Fanny and the faithful Farmer. Fanny 'flatters herself that they will turn out something worthy of a very good tailor.'[16] In May 1825 in a letter to Tom, Fanny spelt out the problem:

I enclose half a crown from Papa, a proof at once of poverty and kindness. Without the former it would be more, without the latter it would be nothing. All the world are poor as Job, and, rather poorer, for Job put none of his sons to public schools, and had no clients who did not pay him. Next year I fear we shall be poorer still, for assuredly there will be *no hay.*[17]

Fanny's father, the Reverend William Milton, died in Reading on 12 July 1824 in his eighty-first year, shortly after Arthur his much loved grandson. There is a memorial tablet to him in the church at Heckfield which reads: 'Eminent both in literature and science, he added to the exemplary discharge of the duties of a christian minister, the elegant pursuits of the scholar and the active prosecution of extensive designs for the public good.' For Fanny, now forty-five, this was the beginning of many changes.

It was from Cowes, on the Isle of Wight, where Fanny had taken the family for the school holidays, that she wrote to Julia Garnett on 6 August to thank her for her sympathy, 'most sweet, most touching one the words of affection when the heart is heavy with sorrow'. She was aghast at Frances Wright's decision to accompany General Lafayette to America, taking her younger sister Camilla with her. 'It seemed as if she had acted rashly. . . . The very acts that in all other women we should deem wrong, are in her a great, an overpowering duty. The only point in this great and signal devotion of herself to this illustrious old man, which now weighs upon my mind, is the dashing of Camilla. . . . I would have had her the heroine of her own tale' for Camilla 'lives in her light and would droop, would perish, were she withdrawn from it.'[18] Frances Wright was always to sweep others along in her enthusiasms, and had a powerful influence over Camilla.

Thomas Anthony, suffering from severe chronic headaches, with a dwindling law practice, and a debt-ridden farm, was worried about money. In this he was not alone. Inflation and unrealistically high rentals, had driven many to bankruptcy; lists of bankrupts were published daily in the newspapers and journals. Thomas Anthony had a wife and five children to support, and three of his sons were at public school. He was fiercely ambitious for them, and his letters to them at school are extraordinary for their minute and reiterated questions about every detail of their progress at Winchester, their status in their 'part', and the prospects of each individual in the school at the next election for New College. Years later Frances Eleanor Trollope wrote 'The mere reading of these old letters seems to arouse a kind of irritable antagonism. . . . He worries the boys unsparingly.'[19]

In *The Three Cousins* Fanny could have been talking about any one of her three sons, when she wrote of filial love:

. . . this was rendered absolutely impossible by the ceaseless exercise of every species of vexatious authority, as well as by the unmitigated and almost ostentatious display of pretty nearly all the most odious passions of the human heart, how could anything resembling love be the result? In truth, the testimonies of his father's feelings towards him were so utterly contradictory, that he often gave up hope of discovering which were the true and which were the false ones in despair.[20]

Again and again in her books Fanny reveals an intimate knowledge of the problems suffered by her children. 'Her childhood passed in one continuous series of irksome discipline. . . . Words of caution, forbiddance, and restraint, were the only ones addressed to her, excepting when her present importance and future greatness were dealt upon.'[21]

Thomas Anthony's temper could be quite terrifying and his rage sometimes appeared to be perfectly uncontrollable. Fanny tried to protect her children from this turmoil by sending the girls to stay with their friends and relations for extended holidays. Henry, now at Winchester, was causing his parents anxiety by his lack of application. He had a bright intelligence and a warm heart, but he too, 'was of a haughty, exacting, and irritable temper'. In the summer of 1826, fifteen-year-old Henry was removed from the school. His father decided that there was no likelihood of his going to New College and so some other provision must be made for his future. It was decided to place him in a counting house in Paris so that he could learn the language and gain some knowledge of business. The Trollopes would take him there in September and find him a place to live.

In the meantime the family was amusing itself during the summer holidays by acting plays. Fanny wrote to Mary Russell Mitford: 'Our theatre is made in our drawing room, and the object of it was to improve the French pronunciation of our children by getting up scenes from Molière. We have a French friend, who plays with us, and it is really astonishing how much they have got on by his aid.' This was the first mention of Auguste Hervieu the artist, who initially became aquainted with the Trollopes as a drawing master for the girls. Thomas Anthony, also pressed into the *corps dramatique*, talked of the many rehearsals that were necessary, and said: 'Stevens is a good prompter, and thunders capitally; we have not tried our lighting yet.' Fanny, in her element, wrote to Tom:

I wish you had been with us on the night of our *grand representation*. We flatter ourselves that we were extremely successful. I may truly say that we had a full house and the applause was most *flattering*. . . . In the *Femmes Savantes* we fitted up the stage with every kind of thing you can imagine fit to fill the drawing room of a *blue lady* – books, maps, plans of the moon, telescopes, rolls of paper, MSS., etc. Upon the white curtain opposite the windows were fixed engravings, and two little tables loaded with quartos were placed under them. All this, well shewn by the light of the lamps, had a very good effect, and we left the audience several minutes to admire it after the curtain drew up, before we made our entrée. The clapping was *prodigious!*[22]

Fanny was enthusiastic about most things, and especially the theatre. Her good friend Mary Russell Mitford described her as 'a lively, brilliant woman of the world, with a warm blunt, cordial manner, and many accomplishments'. Fanny had been to see a play written by Miss Mitford called *Foscari* and had enjoyed it very much; the play was presented in November 1826. Miss Mitford wrote to her mother on the 4th to tell her,

. . . of the complete success of my play. It was received not merely with rapturous applause, but without the slightest symptom of disapprobation from beginning to end. Mrs Trollope, between joy for my triumph and sympathy with the play, has cried herself half blind. . . . Mrs Storey has been here the greater part of the morning – kinder and warmer-hearted than anyone that ever lived, except dear, dear Mrs Trollope, who has also been with me most part of the day.[23]

Miss Mitford had now written another play *Rienzi* which she had sent to Macready hoping that he would present it for her. She was sadly disappointed when the play was rejected, and enlisted the help of Fanny Trollope who knew both Kean and William Macready. Fanny replied to her plea:

Your tragedy must neither lie on the shelf, nor must it be laid at the feet of 'dear William'. If Kean is about to return this year, I think I can see my way clearly. No, we will not entreat. Do not, however, be afraid of me . . . I know he will make a glorious *Rienzi* . . . but by your leave, dear friend, he must not play out of 'charity'. Trust me, dear William would rather eat his heart than see Kean appear in *Rienzi*.

Macready when cornered by Fanny retreated into an 'ice-case', but she did get from him that 'his movements next year depend entirely on Kean; if he acts in London, Mr Macready will act in America, and vice versa.' On 1 June 1826 Fanny received a letter from Macready in Bath. He asked her to, 'instruct me how I can be of use to her [Miss Mitford] and how I can show you the esteem in which I hold your mediation in such a cause.' The Trollopes were about to go to Paris for the purpose of settling Henry, and Fanny told Miss Mitford that she planned to meet Macready there:

... *seul-à-seul* in the Bois du Boulogne. This is where duels are generally fought – our meeting, I flatter myself, will be of a different kind. .... But, dear friend, if there be the slightest doubt, hesitation, or vacillation of any kind in him I would not, were I you, delay the appearance of this play. *Allez toujours* is what those who know the world best always say to the happy ones of the earth, who are sailing before the wind. *Allez toujours*, and you will reach a station which no woman has ever reached before. You will have possession of the stage.[24]

Macready told Mrs Hofland, a friend, that it was a wonderful tragedy – an extraordinary tragedy, 'for a woman to have written'. Mrs Hofland commented that, 'the men always make that reservation my dear; they cramp us, my dear, and then reproach us with our lameness.' The play was eventually published in 1838, and was a great success, playing to crowded houses. Fanny wrote again to Miss Mitford, 'We shall pass the first fortnight of our stay at Lagrange [sic] the residence of our valued friend, the venerable Lafayette. .... We shall then return to Paris, where we shall stay as long as Mr Trollope's business will permit his absence, but this can only be to the end of October.' Henry was found lodgings with M. Monod, a Swiss protestant clergyman, and remained in Paris. The expense of the accommodation was rather more than they had expected.

Financial affairs at Harrow were going from bad to worse, but in spite of her own problems, Fanny was still trying to help others less fortunate. Auguste Hervieu, who had been employed by the Trollopes as a drawing master, was a young Frenchman whose father, a Colonel in Napoleon's army, was killed in the retreat from Moscow, leaving his son with nothing but debts. Hervieu was trying to earn a living by teaching and painting, and 'this has enabled him (by sometimes going without dinner to buy colours) to paint a picture, which has been received by the committee at Somerset House.' Fanny asked her friend Miss Mitford in a letter written on 22 April 1827, to use her influence to get it spoken of in *The Times*. 'All I would ask is to direct attention to it; for I am quite sure that if it is hung where it can be seen, it cannot be looked at without admiration. The picture will be called in the catalogue "Love and Folly".'[25]

Thomas Anthony had been very anxious about getting Anthony into Winchester, writing to Tom to ask him for every detail as to the numbers of boys who might resign, thereby creating a vacancy. In April such a vacancy occurred, and twelve year old Anthony was admitted to the college. Fanny wrote to Tom explaining to him how fortunate his father must consider himself, in getting three boys into Winchester, although it would not be of much use unless they could also get into New College, Oxford. 'As far as Anthony is concerned this must very much depend on you. I dare say you will often find him idle and plagueing enough. But remember, dear Tom, that, in a family like ours, *everything* gained by one is felt personally and individually by all. He is a good-hearted fellow, and clings to the idea of being Tom's pupil.'[26]

Public schools for the upper class were at that time nothing but ill-regulated boarding houses. Fighting, bullying, poaching, rough practical joking, drunkenness, gambling and disorder of every sort, with no monitorial system, were all considered quite normal. However, a public school education was an entrée to position and society. Tom at the age of seventeen, according to the practice of the college, became Anthony's tutor, but as Anthony said, 'in his capacity of teacher and ruler, he had studied the laws of Draco.' Tom's idea of looking after Anthony was 'as a part of his daily exercise, he thrashed me with a big stick.' Tom exchanged the role of mentor for that of tormentor.

Now with Tom and Anthony to support at Winchester, and Henry in Paris, Thomas Anthony looked for some way of further reducing his expenses. He decided that their beloved Julian Hill would have to be let to pay their bills, and that he, Fanny, and the girls, would move to a dilapidated smaller farm they could rent at Harrow Weald. Anthony later described the building as 'one of those farmhouses which seem always to be in danger of falling into the neighbouring horse-pond. As it crept downwards from house to stables, from stables to barns, from barns to cowsheds, and from cowsheds to dung heaps, one could hardly tell where one began and the other ended.'[27]

The prospect of this move must have filled Fanny with despair. She was to be exiled in Harrow Weald, 4 miles away from her friends and neighbours, with no means of escaping from the trials of Thomas Anthony's temper. With so much less space how could she buffer the girls from his irritability? In September 1827 in response to a miserable letter from Henry, Fanny went to Paris to see what she could do to help him, and to be present at Julia's wedding. She stayed with the Garnetts, Julia was to be married on 23 September to Georg Heinrich Pertz, a German historian she had met the previous year, and who had proposed to her on 3 August while they were both staying with the Trollopes at Harrow. Fanny Trollope, Julia and Harriet Garnett, and Frances Wright were together again.

When Lafayette returned to France, Frances Wright had remained in America to establish an experimental Utopian settlement at Nashoba, with the aim of improving the condition of black slaves. She wrote a paper which she circulated among her friends in Europe, asking them to make it public. Fanny Trollope wrote to Julia Garnett on 17 May 1827, in some consternation. 'Fanny's paper has puzzled me *painfully*. Trollope has read it with attention, and agrees with me in thinking that it would be utter madness to print it here – contempt, ridicule, and reprobation would be the result. . . . Dear, noble, single-hearted Fanny deems not of the light in which her declared opinions against religion would be viewed – I think her perfectly right in her idea that religion should never be tampered with, by lawmakers or schoolmasters – but what is my opinion?' A little earlier in the letter to Julia she said 'Oh how I wish for you! . . . I should like to live among human beings who would not look upon reason as crime, nor on free discussion, as treason and blasphemy.'[28] Frances Wright, having left her sister Camilla in charge of the settlement, had now returned to the old world, not only to recover from a severe attack of American fever, but to try and interest friends and prominent Europeans in her project. She would 'like to rescue out of it [the old world] a few rational beings who are too good for it and would be much happier in the woods.' She had already approached several people, including her close friends the Garnetts, but with disappointing results. Harriet Garnett, who was infatuated by Frances Wright, longed to join the settlement, but Julia was to be married, and refused to let her go alone.

Frances Wright approached Mary Shelley, the writer, who, although intrigued, also declined. Frances Wright was not only searching for recruits for the settlement, but she wanted 'a bosom intimate' or, as she wrote to Mary Shelley on 15 September 'one of her own sex to commune with and sometimes to lean upon in all the confidence of equality and friendship'. This was the moment when Fanny Trollope, herself in a turmoil, arrived in Paris. Tom, writing later of Miss Wright, depicted in a contemporary lithograph wearing Turkish trousers, described her as, 'a very remarkable personage. She was handsome in large and almost masculine style of beauty, with a most commanding presence, a superb figure, and a stature fully masculine.'[29] She was also a very persuasive talker. When Fanny shared her worries about Henry's future, and the problems at Harrow, Frances Wright proposed a solution. Fanny would return with her to Nashoba as her confidante and companion, and Henry would escort his mother and be employed at Nashoba as a teacher. It was a seductive idea. On 7 October 1827, after Julia's wedding, Frances Wright travelled to England sharing the top of the London diligence with Fanny Trollope, and stayed at Harrow. Fanny was swept away by her personality and wrote to Julia on 9 October:

> You know who I travelled with, and will not wonder that even the top of the diligence was delightful. Never was there I am persuaded such a being as Fanny Wright – no never – and I am not the only one who thinks so – some of my friends declare that if worship may be offered, it must be to her – That she is at once all that woman should be – and something more than woman ever was – and I know not what beside – and I for my part applaud and approve all they say. . . . Will it be possible to let this 'angel' . . . will it be possible to let her depart without vowing to follow her? I think not. I feel greatly inclined to say where her country is, there shall be my country.[30]

Fanny's enthusiasm was understandable, her life in Harrow had become impossible, and she could see nothing ahead but increasing gloom and misery. The scheme proposed by Frances Wright would allow her to take herself and the children out of the range of Thomas Anthony's temper in a manner which would be acceptable to society. In a revealing letter to Harriet Garnett, Fanny wrote: 'He is a good, honourable man – but his temper is dreadful – every year increases his irritability – and also its lamentable effect upon the children.'[31]

Anthony and Tom were at boarding school and so protected from the problems at home. The other three children would go with her to America. Henry to be her escort, and the girls her companions. They would all be able to find employment at Nashoba. It was a very tempting prospect.

Fanny, on her return from Paris with Frances Wright, discussed the proposal with Thomas Anthony. Would he come with them for she could not leave without his approval? In her novel the *Old World and the New*, Fanny re-created her own situation. 'My advice is that we shall all leave this country immediately. . . . Were our movements to be regulated by me, we should be sailing, bag and baggage, for the United States of America within a month.'[32] Thomas Anthony was proud to have two sons who had been elected to Winchester College. Tom was seventeen, and was hoping to win a place at Oxford, and Anthony at twelve, had only just been accepted. For a father who was so fanatical about his son's education, this was not the time to leave the country. He did, however, reluctantly give permission for Fanny to go. The most compelling argument in favour of their departure for America, was the far lower cost of living. It cost one quarter of the amount to live in America, as it did to live in England. The situation for Fanny was potentially desperate, and she was very persuasive. As she wrote in a later novel:

> . . . under the influence of more stirring accidents, latent qualities and hitherto unconscious energy, will suddenly appear, as if awakened by some mysterious inspiration newly sent; but such power once awakened, sleeps no more. Her steadfast determination not to quarrel with her husband in any way that might lead to a separation was a far greater proof of the newly awakened energy of character of which I am speaking. The disgrace which such a separation would be likely to bring upon her . . . family, was probably the leading idea in her mind, as she resolved against it.[33]

Fanny's 'unconscious energy', driven by desperation, was beginning to emerge. She tried to explain her sudden departure to the Garnetts: 'My final determination to accompany Fanny [Wright] to Nashoba was brought on by Mr T's telling me on my return to Harrow that he was determined upon letting our house there, for the purpose of retrenching our expenses. He proposes one or two plans of retirement – at which my heart sickened – and I used all my power to persuade him that a year or two passed at Nashoba would repair our affairs more completely than any other.'[34] She left Harrow without saying goodbye to anyone. It must have been quite an entourage. Fanny, Henry, Cecilia and nine-year-old Emily, two servants, a quantity of possessions, including furniture, and, at the last moment, M. Hervieu. At what stage it was decided that he was to be one of the party is unknown, but the proffered position of drawing master at Nashoba would have been a strong inducement. Frances Wright wrote to the Garnetts to explain the secrecy. 'My reason for not writing you, or rather of F.T. sooner was that she requested me not to do it. My own [departure] was positively settled 24 hours before I was on shipboard and her's only 5 days. . . . She expected always something would prevent her voyage and wished it therefore not known or talked about.'[35]

Harriet Garnett, who had yearned to be one of the party, professed shock and horror. 'I can scarcely believe that Mrs T is actually on her way and Trollope alone in his old age in London. . . . But the step once taken there is no return, at least for a woman.'[36]

In Fanny's subsequent novels, this same scene of sudden departure for financial reasons often recurs. It was one with which Fanny was to become all too familiar. As she wrote in *The Old World and the New*:

And now the busy, the important, the most awful moment came on board the bark that was to convey them, very probably for ever, from the land of their birth . . . far, far away from every dear familiar comfort which had hitherto surrounded them, he did feel a sinking at the heart that was very painful.[37]

The sailing ship *Edward* departed from London on 4 November 1827. Auguste Hervieu boarded at the last moment, and they were all under sail, bound for America. Fanny Trollope was setting off along a new path.

CHAPTER FOUR

'Desolation was the only feeling'

AMERICA, Nashoba. 4 November 1827–Autumn 1828

'On the 4th of November, 1827, I sailed from London, accompanied by my son and two daughters; and after a favourable, though somewhat tedious voyage, arrived on Christmas-day at the mouth of the Mississippi.'[1] So began the American adventure. Fanny was now forty-eight years old, Henry sixteen, Cecilia eleven and Emily only nine.

The journey across the Atlantic by sailing ship had taken seven weeks. It was not without some excitement when, at the entrance to the Mexican Gulf, their ship was chased by pirates. 'For some hours our situation was painful enough. The common sailors, having less discretion than the captain, scrupled not to assure us that they should all be barbarously murdered, and that we should be robbed and chained down to our berths *at least*; if not thrown, one upon the other, into the sea.' An English man-of-war appeared and chased off the pirate ship. 'I doubt if the females on board felt more relieved at their escape than did the crew.'

Fanny Trollope was beginning to have her doubts about Frances Wright as she watched her during the voyage and 'persuaded myself that it was my weakness that made me deem Fanny too eccentric, when I saw her sitting upon a coil of rope in the steerage, reading to a sailor occupied in patching his breeches . . . and I often recurred to the idea that had tormented us at Paris, that she was not in her right senses.'[2] Both Frances Wright and Fanny Trollope sent a joint letter to Julia Garnett (now Julia Pertz) from 'on board *Edward* in the Mississippi'. It was dated 26 December 1827. Frances Wright reassured the newly married Julia:

Too well I know thy heart my own Julia to read thy silence amiss. This I shall never do. I fear not least thy love be too little, but rather too much, & cd wish thee for thy peace to wean thy thoughts as much as possible from affections, & places, & opinions calculated to interfere with your happiness. . . . If ever your prospects change, or those you love change or are lost to you (wch Fortune avert!) you know where you have a home. . . . And yet more thou knowest thou hast only to write to thy Fanny come and take me to thee & she will come – were it from the end of the earth to its other farthest extremity.

She told Julia not to hesitate in sharing the contents of the letter with her husband, 'He knows the old & sacred claims of my affection.' In the small space left in the letter, Fanny Trollope told Julia:

> I can hardly believe – the arrangement was so sudden that at times I still fancy that I dream – had I time and paper I would explain to you at large all the motives that have led me to wish, and Mr Trollope to consent to this expedition – but I can now only tell you that some pecuniary claims which came upon us quite unexpectedly, made it very necessary that we should leave our pretty place and large establishment for a year or two at least – and where, or with whom would I pass that interval so much to my satisfaction as in the home, and in the society of our Fanny? *You* at least my Julia will not wonder at my choice – Henry's very earnest wish to visit Nashoba was another very strong reason for my going thither – I have left the people making great eyes at me – but I care but little for this. I expect to be very happy, and very far from care at Nashoba – and this will more than repay me for being the object of a few 'dear me's'! I could make you laugh my Ju could I paint some of the scenes that preceded my departure.[3]

Fanny's first impressions of America were not promising. 'I never beheld a scene so utterly desolate as this entrance of the Mississippi. Had Dante seen it, he might have drawn images of another Bolgia from its horrors.' The ship passed a cluster of huts called the Balize, and then sailed for two days upstream to New Orleans between high mudbanks, seeing the occasional crocodile and passing a succession of planters' villas. They became impatient to touch the soil of the new land, 'having studied the good ship *Edward* from stem to stern, till we knew the name of every sail, and the use of every pulley, we had had enough of her.'

When they reached New Orleans they disembarked, and Fanny was amazed by 'the large proportion of blacks . . . the grace and beauty of the elegant Quadroons; the occasional groups of wild and savage looking Indians; the unwonted aspect of the vegetation; all help to afford that species of amusement which proceeds from looking at what we never saw before.' Fanny and the children explored the forest near the town; it was very hot, and 'the attacks of the mosquitoes incessant, and most tormenting,' but she was amazed to see 'oranges, green peas, and red pepper, growing in the open air at Christmas'. She was also surprised to be formally introduced to a milliner in her own shop, 'the first symptom of American equality'.

The travellers were all impatient to be on their way, first by boat to Memphis, and from thence overland to the settlement at Nashoba. The vast distances of the New World were most comfortably traversed by the river boats, and so, 'On the first of January, 1828, we embarked on board the *Belvidere*, a large and handsome boat', which would stop at Memphis.

> We found the room destined for the use of the ladies dismal enough, as its only windows were below the stern gallery; but both this and the gentlemen's cabin were handsomely fitted up, and the latter well carpeted; but oh! that carpet! I will not, I may not describe its condition; indeed it requires the pen of a Swift to do it justice. I hardly know any annoyance so deeply repugnant to English feelings, as to the incessant remorseless spitting of Americans.

The boat was crowded. In the steerage were the Kentucky flat-boat men who earned their passage upstream by loading wood at every stop to supply the steam-engine. The Trollopes' manservant, William Abbot, was accommodated with this drunken and disorderly mob and warned, 'by no means to detach his watch or money from his person during the night'. The majority of the passengers were men, and were usually addressed by the title of general, colonel or major. Fanny ascribed it to 'a sort of aristocratic longing'. She gave an example of a gentleman inadvertently referred to as Mr M.

'General M. sir' was the correction.

'I beg his pardon, I was not aware of his being in the army.'

'No sir, not in the army, but he was surveyor-general of the district.' came the reply.

The voyage was an unpleasant revelation to Fanny, who was used to the civilized ways of London and Paris.

> The total want of all the usual courtesies of the table, the voracious rapidity with which the viands were seized and devoured; the strange uncouth phrases and pronunciation; the loathsome spitting, from the contamination of which it was absolutely impossible to protect our dresses; the frightful manner of feeding with their knives, till the whole blade seemed to enter their mouth; and the still more frightful manner of cleaning the teeth afterwards with a pocket knife, soon forced us to feel that we were not surrounded by the generals, colonels, and majors of the old world; and that the dinner-hour was to be anything rather than an hour of enjoyment.

The English party marvelled at the scenery, the monotonous flatness of the Mississippi broken only by the luxuriant foliage of palmetto, ilex and bright orange trees. They passed sugar cane and cotton plantations, although, as they went further north the country became more desolate, 'but for one or two clusters of wooden houses, calling themselves towns, and borrowing some pompous name, generally from Greece or Rome, we might have thought ourselves the first of the human race who had ever penetrated into this territory of bears and alligators.' There were a few wretched dwellings to be seen, of wood cutters and their families, which were raised on wooden piles to keep them above the winter flooding. 'The squalid look of the miserable wives and children of these men was dreadful. Their complexion is of a bluish white, that suggests the idea of dropsy.' A desolate cow and a few pigs could be seen standing knee-deep in water. Fanny heard a terrible tale of the inhabitants of one hut, newly erected close to the lair of some crocodiles, where the wife and five young children were all devoured by these reptiles during the night.

At long last they arrived at Memphis; 'but this pleasure was considerably abated by the hour of our arrival, which was midnight, and by the rain, which was falling in torrents.' They disembarked and found they must climb from the wharf up to the town perched at the top of a high bluff. The only access was a steep ascent via a newly constructed road, 'which beguiled us into its almost bottomless mud. . . . Shoes and gloves were lost in the mire, for we were glad to avail ourselves of all our limbs; and we reached the grand hotel in the most deplorable state.' Once there, where Miss Wright was well known, they were welcomed and given the best rooms.

The next day the rain prevented them making the hazardous journey through the forest to Nashoba, and they were forced to spend another day at the hotel. Fanny was longing to have a meal in the privacy of their room, but this was not to be; 'This, Miss Wright said, was impossible; the lady of the house would consider the proposal as a personal affront.' And so, when the great bell was sounded, they proceeded to the dining room. The table was laid for fifty persons.

> The company consisted of all the shopkeepers of the little town. . . . They ate in perfect silence, and with such astonishing rapidity that their dinner was over literally before ours was begun. . . . No women were present except ourselves and the hostess; the good women of Memphis being well content to let their lords partake of Mrs Anderson's turkeys and venison, (without their having the trouble of cooking for them) whilst they regale themselves on mush and milk at home.

The Trollopes were eager to see the promised Nashoba, and the next morning set off in 'a clumsy sort of caravan drawn by two horses,' for the 15-mile expedition through the forest. Unhappily for them, their negro driver took a short cut through a stream instead of over the rickety bridge; the cart broke an axle, and they had to return to Memphis. Frances Wright was anxious to see her sister Camilla, who, during her absence, had unexpectedly married one of the overseers, Whitby, and there had been some gossip of it having been an unwilling union. Not wishing to endure the delay, she set off once more on horseback, accompanied by the faithful William Abbot.

The following day the Trollopes attempted the journey again, but this time in a high-hung Deerborn which was able to pass over the 3 ft high tree stumps left where the forest had been cut away to open a passage.

> The forest became thicker and more dreary-looking every mile we advanced; but our ever-grinning negro declared that it was a right good road, and that we should be sure to get to Nashoba; And so we did . . . and one glance sufficed to convince me that every idea I had formed of the place was as far as possible from the truth. Desolation was the only feeling – the only word that presented itself: but it was not spoken. I think, however, that Miss Wright was aware of the painful impression the sight of her forest home produced on me, and I doubt not that the conviction reached us both at the same moment, that we had erred in thinking that a few months passed together at this spot could be productive of pleasure to either.

In *The Old World and the New*, Fanny described the first sight of such desolation on a new settler, who, like herself, 'felt his heart sink within him as he stood . . . and looked around him upon a portion of the wilderness . . . it was his children whose young limbs were to be strained in the performance of the endless tasks which must be performed ere they could be permitted to eat their hard earned daily bread.'[4] Fanny was totally disillusioned with the hitherto loved and admired Miss Wright, and appalled at the predicament into which she had led her family, servants and Hervieu.

> When we arrived at Nashoba, they were without milk, without beverage of any kind, *except rain water*, the River Wolf being too distant to send to constantly. Wheaten bread they used very sparingly, and, to us, the Indian corn bread was uneatable. They had no vegetables but rice and a few potatoes we brought with us, no meat but pork, no butter, no cheese. I shared her bedroom. It had no ceiling, and the floor consisted of planks laid loosely upon piles that raised it some feet from the earth. The rain had access through the wooden roof, and the chimney, which was of logs slightly plastered with mud, caught fire at least a dozen times a day. . . . I found her amiable sister, Mrs Whitby, in very bad health, which she confessed she attributed to the climate! This so much alarmed me for my children, that I decided upon leaving the place with as little delay as possible, and did so at the end of ten days.

The volatile Auguste Hervieu was even more devastated. He had joined himself to the expedition on the understanding that he would be drawing-master in the Nashoba school. 'As soon as he arrived, he asked, "Where is the school?" and was answered, "It is not yet formed." I think I never saw a man in such a rage. He wept with passion and grief mixed, I believe.' Fanny in her novel, *The Refugee*, gave an insight into what was expected of Hervieu. 'It was signified . . . that he was to hew down a tree, cut it into rails, and fix it as a zig-zag or serpentine fence. The poor Frenchman, whose visions had been of scientific lecturers, amateur concerts, private theatricals, and universal philanthropy, was startled.'[5] Hervieu returned to Memphis, and managed to pay his expenses by painting portraits of the local inhabitants.

Fanny found herself in a predicament. She was marooned in the wilds of Tennessee in the company of a woman whose sanity she was beginning to doubt, with three children, two servants, and no money. What to do now? Firstly she must obtain a loan, and for this she applied to the Nashoba trustees. A loan of $300 was granted to Mrs Trollope, 'to assist her in removing from Nashoba to some place in the western world better suited to her future plans for herself and her children.' It was ten days before this could be arranged; it must have seemed like an eternity. The Nashoba journal recorded on the 27 January 1828, 'Frances Trollope and family with their manservant William Abbot and Esther Rust, her maid, and Auguste Hervieu, left us for Memphis.'

Exactly when the decision to reside in Cincinnati was made, is not known. In an early letter to her Harrow acquaintances she had declared her intentions of staying with friends in Nashoba and New York and visiting Niagara. After the disaster of Nashoba, where it seems she had planned to spend two years, Fanny had to make drastic new plans.

If she were to travel from Memphis towards New York, the route was north up the Mississippi river, then east into the Ohio river via Cincinnati. Fanny wrote to the New York banker Charles Wilkes, who was handling the Trollopes' financial investment in Nashoba, to say that she had gone with her children to Cincinnati to wait for her husband. It seems from her letters that the plan had always been for Thomas Anthony to join them towards the end of the first year. In the meantime, she decided to send Henry to New Harmony, an educational establishment in the state of Indiana, based on the Utopian ideals of Robert Owen. Industry, peace, and plenty were the principles upon which the school was said to be conducted. Unbeknown to Fanny Trollope the running of the school had fallen into the grasping hands of a French lady, the intimate friend of the founder's son, who was only interested in the principle of plenty. She threw out all educational aspects; increased the industrial activities of the pupils in the fields; and enjoyed a plenteous golden harvest from their labours. Henry was there for two miserable months, until in March, with Hervieu's help, he was able to rejoin his family in Cincinnati. On his return from New Harmony Henry tried to help with the finances by offering 'to give lessons in the Latin language to gentlemen in their own houses. . . . Terms: 50 cents for lessons of one hour.' It seems there were no takers.

The Trollopes arrived in Cincinnati on the 10 February 1828, and were impressed by the noble landing place, with space for mooring at least fifteen steam-boats at one time, and disappointed by the lack of domes, towers and steeples in the city. Before the party had left Memphis they had heard nothing but good of Cincinnati, of its beauty, wealth, and unequalled prosperity.

> But, alas! the flatness of reality after the imagination has been busy! I hardly know what I expected to find in this city, fresh risen from the bosom of the wilderness, but certainly it was not a little town, about the size of Salisbury, without even an attempt at beauty in any of its edifices, and with only just enough of the air of a city to make it noisy and bustling. . . . I believe the number of inhabitants exceeds twenty thousand.

They repaired to the Washington Hotel, and having had dinner, 'went forth to seek a house for our permanent accommodation'. Before long they found a dwelling and returned to the hotel. Not wishing to take their evening meal with the three score and ten gentlemen of the dining-room, nor with the half dozen ladies of the bar-room, Fanny ordered tea in her own chamber. The landlord was outraged; 'we have no family tea-drinkings here, and you must live either with me and my wife, or not at all in my house.' Fanny apologized, explaining that they were strangers. 'Our manners are very good manners, and we don't wish any changes from England', was the curt reply.

The next day they moved into the new dwelling 'which looked neat and comfortable enough', but which lacked most of the basic essentials, 'that Europeans conceive necessary to decency and comfort'.

> No pump, no cistern, no drain of any kind, no dustman's cart, or any other visible means of getting rid of the rubbish, which vanishes with such celerity in London, that one has no time to think of its existence; but which accumulated so rapidly at Cincinnati, that I sent for my landlord to know in what manner refuse of all kinds was to be disposed of. 'Your Help will just have to fix them all into the middle of the street; but you must mind, old woman, that it is the middle. I expect you don't know as we have got a law what forbids throwing such things at the sides of the streets; they must just all be cast right into the middle, and the pigs soon takes them off.'

The refuse problem was solved, and as Fanny remarked of the pigs, 'it is as well they are so numerous, and so active in their capacity of scavengers.'

After the Trollopes' arrival in Cincinnati there is no further record of William Abbot and Esther Rust, the servants who had come with them from Harrow. They must have felt very out of place in America, where 'all men are equal, and women too; and that it was a sin and a shame for a free-born American to be treated like a servant.' As Fanny explained, 'The greatest difficulty in organizing a family establishment in Ohio, is getting servants, or, as it is there called, "getting help". The whole class of young women, whose bread depends upon their labour, are taught to believe that the most abject poverty is preferable to domestic service. Hundreds of half-naked girls work in the paper-mills . . . for less than half the wages they would receive in service; but they think their equality is compromised by the latter.' Fanny with great difficulty found a girl, who came on the condition that her 'mother's slave Phillis must come over once a week from t'other side the water, to help me clean.' She left after two months when Fanny refused to lend her the money to buy a silk dress to go to a ball, stating, 'Then 'tis not worth my while to stay any longer.'

On her arrival in Cincinnati Fanny had written to Thomas Anthony to tell him of their change of plans and their financial predicament. The posts were erratic, and by May Fanny was in great distress, for she had not received one answer to her pleas for money. In desperation she wrote to her sons:

> I cannot express to you the dreadful anxiety to which this silence gives birth. Is your father ill? Is he dead? Have his affairs fallen into such confusion that he has not been able to procure the money to send us a remittance? Wherever you may be, my dearest Tom, when you receive this, I entreat you to write to me immediately. Our situation here would be dreadful, were it not for M. Hervieu's grateful, and generous kindness. It is more than a month that we have not had a mouthful of food that he has not paid for. How are you both my darling boys? Oh, what could I do – alas, I have nothing to *give*, but what would I not give to have you both for half an hour! Dear Tom, dear Anthony, do not forget us![6]

At the end of June she heard from Thomas Anthony that he planned to join them immediately. However, beset by his own financial worries, he did not arrive until November. What the family would have done without the support of Auguste Hervieu is hard to imagine. He was thirty-five, with no family of his own, and seems to have adopted the Trollope family as his special charge. He made a tolerable living by his painting, and with this money was able to support them through their worst trials in America. On 15 March 1828, Hervieu was invited to join Frederick Eckstein, a German painter, as a second teacher in the Academy of Fine Arts. Three weeks later he parted from him over a disagreement about discipline, and opened his own school in his lodgings which were not far from the Western Museum.

The Western Museum had a newly appointed director, a French naturalist called Joseph Dorfeuille. The museum was almost bankrupt as the exhibited offerings of dusty mammoth bones, fossils and other assorted specimens were of little interest to the average Cincinnatian. Dorfeuille decided that what the people wanted was novelty, and to provide this, bought a job lot of wax figures. He had them repaired by a young man called Hiram Powers, and opened an exhibition on 5 January 1828. It was a moderate success. Through the French connection, Dorfeuille met Hervieu, and so, through him, the Trollopes. It was to be a profitable meeting. The combination of talents was formidable, albeit inexperienced: Dorfeuille, the scientist cum showman; Fanny Trollope, forty-nine, presenter of drawing-room dramas and writer of satirical verse; Hervieu, thirty-five, artist, who specialized in panoramic scenes; Hiram Powers, eighteen, mechanical genius and would-be sculptor; and Henry Trollope, seventeen, speaker of Latin, Greek and French. Between them they created *The Invisible Girl*, which opened in April 1828. Fanny Trollope wrote the announcements.

THE INVISIBLE GIRL, AT THE WESTERN MUSEUM, is now ready to deliver her RESPONSES to visitors. The chamber prepared for the audience is fitted up as one of those theatres of probation in the *Egyptian Mysteries*, in which the candidate for initiation was subjected to her incipient trials. The light is admitted *through tranparencies* painted by MR HERVIEU.

The gloomy chamber also exhihibited a group of the weird sisters returning to the cauldron of Hecate with the various ingredients of her horrible incantation, a group of banditti, and spectral figures and curious animals. In the centre of the room was a cloud:

from which a female arm projects, holding gracefully a small glass trumpet; the whole is entirely unconnected with any part of the wall or ceiling.
Parties of 12 persons, and no more, can be admitted at a time to the presence of the Oracle – and each visitor is allowed to propound three questions. . . . The *profoundest silence* to be observed during the delivery of the responses.[7]

The figures and the mechanics were supplied by Hiram Powers, and the voice of the Oracle was that of Henry Trollope, whose ability to speak in strange tongues awed and impressed the onlookers. The show was a huge success and ran for a solid eight weeks.

The team was encouraged by this enthusiastic response and decided to create something more ambitious. Fanny Trollope, still desperately waiting to hear from her husband, decided, appropriately enough, that a re-creation of the Infernal Regions from Dante's *Divina Commedia* would give scope for invention. The idea fired the imagination of Powers. Once again, Fanny Trollope drew up the programme, provided the explanatory English translations and suggested the composition of tableaux; Hervieu painted the transparent back-drops of Purgatorio and Paradiso, and Powers designed and executed the figures. And, once again, the show which opened in July 1828, drew huge crowds. The advertisements promised: 'The World to come, as described by Dante, and comprising, Hell, Purgatory, and Paradise, will be exhibited in a room adjoining the Western Museum on the 4th of July, and days following. Admittance 25 cents.'

A Bostonian, Linus S. Everett, visiting the exhibition soon after it opened, gave the following description:

> In the centre is seated his Infernal Highness as large as life. This diabolical personage sits on a throne of darkness of sufficient elevation to give him a commanding view of the abyss on either side. His body is clad in a sable robe which, however, discloses that all-essential appendage – a cloven foot. In his left hand he holds a pitchfork, like a weaver's beam; while his right is pointed towards an inscription directly in front, *Whoever enters here leaves hope behind!* His head is adorned with a huge crown, and his face (which by the way is not the most pleasant) is woefully ornamented with a hoary beard, made of horses' tails! To give importance to this King of Hell, his neck is so constructed as to admit of his giving a nod of recognition to the spectator; and his glaring eye-balls are made to roll most horribly by means of some machinery in the room below. . . . On the right hand of the devil above described, and on the left of the spectator, is seen one department of this hell, which is denominated the *hell of ice*; a most heretical place, where the damned, instead of being burned in fire and brimstone, are *frozen* in eternal death! . . . I observed a beautiful child, represented as in the greatest agony, frozen fast to the foot of the infernal throne. But what added much to the *effect*, was the condition of a poor old negro just entering upon a state of perpetual freezing; a sad predicament, truly, for one so constitutionally fond of a warm climate! In the corners of this part of hell, were to be seen several *imps* waiting the orders of his Majesty. . . . On the left of the devil, which is to the right of the beholder, is the *hell of fire*. In this department, are seen the skeletons of persons, thrown into various positions, the sockets of their eyes, their nostrils &c. &c. filled with some bright substance resembling fire; presenting to the eye one of the most loathsome and disgusting scenes that imagination can portray![8]

Later advertisements talked of unearthly sounds, horrid groans, and terrible shrieks, 'produced by some instruments of discord in the appartment below, resembling the imaginary groans of the damned!'

It is interesting to observe that when Fanny was writing later of her experiences in Cincinnati, she made no mention of her own involvement in Dorfeuille's 'pandemonium'. In fact, she spoke slightingly of the display of wax figures as, 'this barbarous branch of art'. However, she did describe Dorfeuille's exhibition with more enthusiasm:

. . . in which he has congregated all the images of horror that his fertile fancy could devise; dwarfs, that by machinery grow into giants before the eyes of the spectator; imps of ebony with eyes of flame; monstrous reptiles devouring youth and beauty; lakes of fire, and mountains of ice; in short, wax, paint, and springs have done wonders.

To give the scheme some more effect, [said Fanny] he makes it visible only through a grate of massive iron bars, among which are arranged wires connected with an electrical machine in a neighbouring chamber; should any daring hand or foot obtrude itself within the bars, it receives a smart shock, that often passes through many of the crowd, and the cause being unknown, the effect is exceedingly comic; terror, astonishment, curiosity, are all set in action, and all contribute to make 'Dorfeuille's Hell' one of the most amusing exhibitions imaginable.

Fanny quite deliberately distanced herself from the exhibitions. For a lady to be associated with public entertainment indicated that she was no longer a lady; hence the reticence. Fanny, writing about a lecture given in Cincinnati by Frances Wright, stated the current thinking. 'That a lady of fortune, family and education, whose youth had been passed in the most refined circles of private life, should present herself to the people as a public lecturer, would naturally excite surprise anywhere; but in America, where women are guarded by a seven-fold shield of habitual insignificance, it caused an effect that can hardly be described. I shared the surprise, but not the wonder.' Frances Wright had given up the settlement at Nashoba, and was now giving public lectures, arguing for freedom and equality for all people. As she grew in recognition, she became increasingly reviled, being called among other names, the 'High Priestess of Infidelity'. Fanny Trollope, writing later to Julia, said:

You will expect me, my dear Julia and Harriet to say something of F.W. – but it is impossible to say anything that will not give you pain. She has taken her slaves to Cuba, where it is said their fate will be most wretched. On her route she attempted to lecture in N. Orleans but was assailed by such a clamour that she could not proceed. Yet still in her paper she

boasts of continued success. . . . I saw Fanny at Cincinnati about three
months ago – every time I see her I am struck by the increase of that dry,
cold, masculine, dictatorial manner that has been growing upon [her]
since she commenced her public lectures – Oh how unlike the Fanny of
former days![9]

Meanwhile, the 'Infernal Regions' continued to draw huge crowds, and
was still running in 1861, thirty-three years later. There is no indication that
these diversions brought Fanny any urgently needed income. This was a
pressing matter to which she gave much thought. Thomas Anthony was
expected at any time, and in the meantime she must think up a scheme
which would provide both for her family's immediate needs and for Henry's
future. For herself, there was the possibility of writing a book of her
experiences, based on a journal she had been keeping.

However, the present needs must be addressed first. Towards the end of
May of that first year, the whole family began to suffer from the excessive
heat. Henry became sick with a bilious complaint and was prescribed large
quantities of calomel and repeated and violent bleeding. For some days
Fanny feared for his life, but he managed to survive both the illness and the
treatment, although he took many weeks to recover fully. She wrote home
'You would hardly know Henry and me, we are both grown so thin. This
climate is a very strange one.'[10] Cincinnati was an unhealthy town, and
Fanny resolved to move to a dwelling in the country, but for a considerable
time found it impossible to find anywhere available. At length she obtained
a cottage in a village called Mohawk, about a mile and a half outside the
town, and there they moved. 'We found ourselves much more comfortable
here than in the city. The house was pretty and commodious, our sitting
rooms were cool and airy; we had got rid of the detestable mosquitoes, and
we had an ice house that never failed.' They also received milk from their
own cow, and picked home grown tomatoes. There they waited for the
arrival of Thomas Anthony, and made plans for the future. Fanny was
determined to settle Henry in America. 'We heard on every side, that of all
the known places on "the globe called earth", Cincinnati was the most
favourable for a young man to settle in; and I only awaited the arrival of Mr
T. to fix our son there, intending to continue with him till he should feel
himself sufficiently established.'

They found themselves among more congenial neighbours in the
country. One family that they saw frequently was that of a 'Dr Price, a very
competent physician with a large practice, a foolish, friendly little wife, and
a pair of pretty daughters.'[11] Fanny enjoyed her conversations with another
neighbour, Timothy Flint: 'He is the only person I remember to have known
with first rate power of satire, and even of sarcasm, whose kindness of
nature and manner remained perfectly uninjured.' Timothy Flint, writing

of Frances Trollope after the publication of her book on America, was, however, more truthful than kind. He described her as, 'a short, plump figure, with a ruddy, round, Saxon face of bright complexion'. Her appearance was 'singularly unladylike' and she lacked taste in her manner of dressing. At times, however, 'she was as much finer and more expensively dressed than other ladies, as she was ordinarily inferior to them in her costume.' She was also 'robust and masculine' in her habits and took long walks regardless of the weather. He described her voice as 'shrill and piercing', but says she was 'as voluble as a French woman' and that she 'knew more about plays, English, French, and Italian, than any person with whom we are acquainted . . . and was, moreover, acquainted, as we knew from her correspondence, with the most distinguished men and women of genius in England.' He admired her as 'a woman of uncommon cleverness, a first rate talker'.[12]

The *Cincinnati Mirror* remembered her as, '*A Bas Bleu*, a learned lady, short, thick and vulgar-looking some forty or fifty years old . . . she might be seen ever and anon, in a green calash and a long plaid cloak dragging at her heels, and walking with these colossean strides unattainable by any but Englishwomen.'[13]

Fanny's life, until her arrival in America, had been that of wife, mother, and hostess, in a society where everyone knew their place and understood the rules. In America, obsessed with 'equality', the rules were different. She 'was extremely likely to make very egregious blunders on many of the social laws amid which she lived, without always being sufficiently instructed to understand them.' One of the cardinal sins she committed – apart from striding out in all weathers – was having the temerity to arrive in Cincinnati without any letters of introduction, which were as essential to a traveller then as a passport is now. It seems certain from this, that Cincinnati was not part of her original plan. Once there, however, she wrote to General Lafayette asking him to send her some introductory letters, which he did in November 1828; hoping that the letter would reach her, as he had been told that it was her intention, 'to move with your family to New York. . . . Should you be still in Ohio, my correspondence with N. must, at a long distance of time I fear, have answered your purpose. In New York you are surrounded with friends.' Fanny wrote home, 'Such an introduction is worth something in this country. I am very much pleased by these letters of Lafayette. They contain *in fact*, the first certain assurance that we are not a set of very accomplished swindlers!'[14]

Another neighbour who may well have influenced Fanny's next venture, was Mr Bullock, the famous proprietor of the Egyptian Hall of Mystery, a museum in Piccadilly. This museum, built to much acclaim in 1812 when Fanny was still living in London, followed the Regency love for the flamboyant and exotic. Mr Bullock and his wife, now settled in America, lived about 2 miles below Cincinnati on the Kentucky side of the River Ohio, and had bought a large estate with a noble house upon it. 'It is impossible to help feeling that Mr Bullock is rather out of his element in this remote spot,' wrote Fanny, 'and the gems of art he has brought with him, show as strangely there, as would a bower of roses in Siberia, or a Cincinnati fashionable at Almack's . . . his frank, and truly English hospitality, and his enlightened and enquiring mind, seem sadly wasted there.' How much did Fanny see of Mr and Mrs Bullock one wonders, and how much were her plans for her own Emporium, influenced by Bullock's Egyptian Hall in London?

One of the given reasons for the journey to America, was to find some useful, and remunerative, employment for Henry. When the scheme to become part of the colony at Nashoba failed so suddenly, followed by an equal failure to make Henry part of the colony at New Harmony, Fanny was left with a problem for which she was not prepared, with only her protégé Hervieu to turn to for advice. As she wrote later in *Fashionable Life*: 'Doubt and uncertainty, though they may sometimes have the flickering light of hope to cheer them, are far more destructive to *tranquillity* than heavier sorrows, which are looked at, seen, and known, *distinctly*.'[15]

Now, burdened with the full responsibility for Henry's future, and the immediate support of herself and the two girls, Fanny Trollope decided on a brave, and bold, venture. She would build a bazaar.

CHAPTER FIVE

'A pretty sharp lesson in economy'

AMERICA, Trollope's Folly. Autumn 1828–5 August 1831

Fanny was convinced that what Cincinnati lacked was a cultural centre, where the sexes could mingle, as they had been doing for years in Libraries and Assembly Rooms in England. There was nowhere like that in Cincinnati. The segregation of the sexes was considered mandatory. Fanny on one occasion had suggested to a young lady that a picnic party might be agreeable, but she was aghast: 'We are not used to such things here, and I know it is considered very indelicate for ladies and gentlemen to sit down together on the grass.' Fanny found this attitude incomprehensible.

> I never saw any people who appeared to live so much without amusement as the Cincinnatians. Billiards are forbidden by law, so are cards. They have no public balls, excepting, I think, six, during the Christmas holidays. They have no concerts. They have no dinner parties. They have a theatre, which is, in fact, the only public amusement in this triste little town; but they seem to care little about it, and either from economy or distaste, it is very poorly attended. Ladies are rarely seen there. . . . It is in the churches and chapels of the town that the ladies are to be seen in full costume. . . . Were it not for the churches, indeed, I think there might be a general bonfire of best bonnets, for I never could discover any other use for them.

American parties were no better.

> Whatever may be the talents of the persons who meet together in society, the very shape, form, and arrangement of the meeting is sufficient to paralyse conversation. The women invariably herd together at one part of the room, and the men at the other. . . . The gentlemen spit, talk of elections and the price of produce, and spit again. The ladies look at each other's dresses till they know every pin by heart; talk of Parson Somebody's last sermon on the day of judgement, on Dr T'otherbody's new pill for dyspepsia, till the 'tea' is announced, when they all console themselves together for whatever they may have suffered in keeping awake, by taking more tea, coffee, hot cake and custard, hoe cake, johnny

cake, waffle cake and dodger cake, pickled peaches and preserved cucumbers, ham, turkey, hung beef, apple sauce and pickled oysters than ever were prepared in any other country of the known world . . . and then they arise 'en masse', cloak, bonnet, shawl, and exit.

Fanny hoped that she might improve this miserable state of affairs, and so, encouraged by her remarkable successes with *The Invisible Girl*, and the *Infernal Regions*, she decided that she would build a centre to encourage the Arts and to provide a respectable place for the two sexes to mingle in congenial and cultural surroundings. A form of social intercourse seldom practised, as Fanny discovered when she attended a ball in honour of General Washington's birthday.

The arrangements for the supper were very singular, but eminently characteristic of the country. The gentlemen had a splendid entertainment spread for them in another large room of the hotel, while the poor ladies had each a plate put into their hands, as they pensively promenaded the ballroom during their absence; and shortly afterwards servants appeared bearing trays of sweetmeats, cakes and creams. The fair creatures then sat down on a row of chairs placed round the walls, and each making a table of her knees, began eating her sweet, but sad and sulky, repast. . . . This arrangement was owing neither to economy nor want of a room large enough to accommodate the whole party, but purely because the gentlemen liked it better. [She went on to say] With the exception of dancing . . . all the enjoyments of the men are found in the absence of women. Is it to be imagined . . . that women were made for no other purpose than to fabricate sweetmeats and gingerbread, construct shirts, darn stockings, and become mothers of possible presidents? Assuredly not. Should the women of America ever discover what their power might be, and compare it with what it is, much improvement might be hoped for.

Fanny, for the time being, could only help with what she saw as the immediate problem. If the people lacked 'amusement', then she would provide them with the kind of congenial surroundings so common in England at fashionable spas like Bath, Cheltenham, and in Bristol in the Clifton of her youth. Fanny set to work to design an Emporium.

Hervieu must have played a large part in these plans, as the Exhibition Gallery was designed to hang his huge panorama entitled 'La Fayette Landing in Cincinnati'. The idea was that Fanny Trollope would stay in Cincinnati until the Bazaar was up and running, her plan being 'to remain here with Henry for about two years, by which time we think he will be settled in the establishment', and then return to England, leaving it under his supervision. This was to be Henry's future. The money for the venture was to come largely from Fanny's inheritance from her father, only just released from probate in 1827.

They were now in daily expectation of the arrival of Thomas Anthony, 'but day after day and week after week passed by. . . . At last when we had almost ceased to look out for him, on the road which led from the town, he arrived, late at night, by that which leads across the country from Pittsburgh. The pleasure we felt at seeing him was greatly increased by his bringing with him our eldest son, which was a happiness we had not hoped for.' It was October 1828, and Tom, now eighteen, had finished his schooling at Winchester, and so was free to accompany his father, while waiting for a vacancy at New College, Oxford. Unfortunate Anthony, his summer holidays over, was sent back to Winchester where he was a boarder.

Thomas Anthony and Tom had travelled steerage on the boat from England for reasons of economy. Conditions on board were so appalling that Tom spent the whole voyage on deck, while Mr Trollope stayed in the stinking conditions in his bunk below, prostrated by his usual sick headache. Now, at last, they had arrived overland from the American north-east. That autumn, the family explored the countryside and visited their neighbours and places of interest. Tom and his father went to 'visit an establishment of "Shaking Quakers".' Tom was dismissive. 'There was an air of unmistakable stupidity over the whole establishment. Nobody laughed. Nobody seemed to converse. There was excellent lodging, clothing, and food in plenty till they died! And that was all.'[1]

They went to the theatre, where Fanny was appalled by the behaviour of the audience, but was impressed

by the excellent acting of Mr and Mrs Alexander Drake, the managers. . . . It was painful to see these excellent performers playing to a miserable house, not a third full, and the audience probably not including half a dozen persons who would prefer their playing to that of the vilest strollers. In proof of this, I saw them, as managers, give place to paltry third-rate actors from London, who would immediately draw crowded houses, and be overwhelmed with applause. The theatre was really not a bad one, though the very poor receipts rendered it impossible to keep it in high order, but an annoyance infinitely greater than decorations indifferently clean, was the style and manner of the audience. Men came into the lower tier of boxes without their coats; and I have seen shirt sleeves tucked up to the shoulder; the spitting was incessant, and the mixed smell of onions and whisky was enough to make one feel even the Drakes' acting dearly bought, by the obligation of enduring its accompaniments. The bearing and attitudes of the men are perfectly indescribable. . . . The noises, too, were perpetual, and of the most unpleasant kind; the applause is expressed by cries and thumping with the feet, instead of clapping.

The Trollopes were frequently invited to dances at the house of Dr and Mrs Price and their two pretty daughters. And there they also got up a performance of *The Merry Wives of Windsor*, and Tom played the part of Falstaff. Fanny found the opinions of one 'serious gentleman', worth noting. He was said to be a scholar and a man of reading.

At the name of Dryden he smiled, and the smile spoke as plainly as a smile could speak, 'How the old woman twaddles!'
'We only know Dryden by quotations, madam, and these, indeed, are found only in books that have long since had their day.'
'And Shakespeare, sir?'
'Shakespeare, Madam, is obscene, and, thank God, WE are sufficiently advanced to have found it out!' . . .
That was the most literary conversation I was ever present at in Cincinnati.

Tom and Henry were pleased to be in each other's company again, and went on many long rambles together. Fanny talked over the proposed plans for the Bazaar with her husband. The site for the building was chosen, the finances arranged, plans were drawn up, and, on 20 January 1829, a deed for the property on Third Street near Broadway was executed. Thomas Anthony paid $1,665 of Fanny's money for the land, with a mortgage held by Mr Longworth, a viticulturist. Laws prohibited married women from holding or disposing of property so the deeds had to be signed by the husband.

Almost immediately after this transaction, Thomas Anthony and Tom returned home to England, visiting Niagara Falls on the way, and leaving Fanny, Henry, Hervieu, Cecilia and Emily to organize the building of the Bazaar. On that fateful 20 January, Fanny wrote to her old friend Mary Russell Mitford, whose book *Our Village* had been appearing in American newspapers to much acclaim, and implored:

Write to me, dear friend, I entreat you, in this remote but very pretty nest, where I am sitting to hatch golden eggs for my son Henry. A letter from you would be like the first warm bright sunbeam after a long dreary winter. . . . I do sometimes languish for that fine full flow of London talk which Johnson describes. . . . Henry's prospects here are, I think, very good, but eighteen is too young to be left, too young to be judged of fixedly. I believe him to be very steady but I must watch by him for a year or two longer. . . . Oh, my dear friend, had I but the tenth of an inch of the nib of your pen, what pictures might I draw of the people here – so very queer, so very unlike any other thing in heaven above or earth below. But it may not be. I can look and I can laugh, but the power of describing is not given to above a dozen in a century.[2]

The designs for the proposed building seem to have been inspired by a cross between the Regent's Brighton Pavilion, and Bullock's Egyptian Hall in London. Cincinnati had seen nothing like it. When built, the Bazaar covered an area 38 by 100 ft, and varied in height from 52 to 85 ft. The front, facing Third Street, was 'taken in part from the Mosque of St Athanase, in Egypt', and was formed of 'three large arabesque windows with arches, supported by four Moorish stone pilasters with capitals'. Above these were 'large and beautifully wrought free stone ornaments', and above that again, a wall that terminated in 'Gothic battlements, each of which supports a stone sphere'. The front, facing south towards the Ohio river, was even more splendid. The chief feature was an Egyptian colonnade formed of four massive columns modelled after those 'in the temple of Appollinopolis at Eftou'. The four columns rose three stories, and their entablature constituted a fourth story. Above this rose a rotunda, 'twenty-four feet in height to its curvilinear roof and this was to be topped by a large Turkish crescent.' This amazing edifice was to house an Exchange Coffee House, and an elegant Saloon, where ices and other refreshments were to 'lend their allurements to the fascinations of architectural novelty', a bar room, an exhibition gallery, an immense ballroom, and a circular structure intended for 'Panoramic Exhibitions'. A small proportion of the building was to be used for the sale of 'fancy goods'. The Bazaar was to be lit by gas, traditionally the first building in Cincinnati to be lit in this way.

The interior decorations were painted by the indefatigable Hervieu. The ballroom, 38 by 60 ft, was painted in the style of the Alhambra, the palace of the Moorish kings at Granada in Spain. The windowless side walls were decorated with false columns, in between which were painted windows looking upon a variety of Spanish scenery and draped with crimson curtains. The art of perspective was again used in the music gallery so that it appeared to lead to an upper apartment from which it was divided by a damask curtain, and Hervieu had the interior of the rotunda covered with canvas with the intention of executing a 1,500 ft panoramic exhibition. Culture would come to Cincinnati.

No one could accuse Fanny Trollope of lacking vision or courage. The proposed Bazaar sounds remarkably like some of our modern art centres. What she did lack, however, was the necessary entrepreneurial experience, and, even more importantly, the support of the citizens of Cincinnati. This unknown English woman was travelling with young children, without her husband, and in the questionable company of a young French artist; who *did* she think she was? America was the land of the free, and as for the English:

> Think only what a deplorable oppressed country they come from, and what a glory of a paradise they find here. There is not on the face of the earth such another, and 'tis no great wonder that they should feel a little envy at the sight. . . . Surely we ask no more of no man, let him come from what country he will, than just to own that we are first and foremost; and after that, we grant him freedom to keep the rest of his thoughts to himself.[3]

With no support, Fanny's vision became a nightmare. Unscrupulous contractors charged exorbitant fees for even the most basic goods. At the opening, the gas pipes emitted smoke and an unpleasant smell, the contractor went off with the money, and the work had to be re-done by someone else. Thomas Anthony had sent out $2,000 of Fanny's money on his return to England, but it was insufficient to finish the building, which then had to be completed on credit. Worse still, he spent far too much of her precious money on unwanted fancy goods. Fanny's letter to Julia Pertz written on 22 August 1831 after her return to Harrow, told the whole story:

> When Mr Trollope was with us, he agreed to advance $6,000 for the purpose of erecting a building in which Henry and Mr Hervieu were to be engaged in partnership. They had formed a plan, too long to be detailed here, but which promised every success. Mr T. thought that to this plan he would add that of a *Bazaar*, the letting the stands of which, he calculated would be very profitable. It was objected that the people having never seen such a thing, would not be likely to take to it. To this he replied that he would *teach them* what it was, by sending out things to fit out the room at first. This frightened me, as I knew we none of us understood anything of buying and selling – but he was determined on making the experiment. I then entreated him to limit his purchases to £150 and I made out a list of such articles as I thought would be easily disposed of, in some manner or other – he went to England engaging to send out the funds for the building – he *did* send $2,000, and the building proceeded rapidly – and then (imagine my dismay) he sent out $4,000 worth of the most trumpery goods that probably ever were shipped. Mr H. Wilkes to whom they were consigned, assured his father that they never could sell for as much as the duties upon them amounted to. Mr Trollope wrote at the same time, to say that he had exerted himself extremely to procure those goods, and that he flattered himself that they would sell well, and speedily, and *so enable me to pay for the completion of the building.* Meanwhile *this* had been finished on *credit*, and the workmen

were becoming clamorous for payment. The sight of those dreadful and utterly unsaleable goods, and the consciousness of the money to be paid, was *certainly* the cause of the fever which seized me a few days after their arrival. I was eleven weeks in my room, and a great part of the time delirious. Poor Henry was obliged to sell these things, or most of them, at auction for what he could get, in order to pacify the workmen. The bills came in, infinitely higher than we calculated upon – and after an ineffectual attempt to let the bazaar, *everything* was seized by the creditors, and had not Hervieu's labour enabled him to furnish us with money to live upon – I know not how we should have escaped *starving* in that land of plenty.[4]

The dream was shattered.

When she had sufficiently recovered from her dangerous bout of malaria, which confined her to her bed, Fanny and Hervieu made a valiant effort to recover something from the wreckage. They were penniless, 'every dollar they had brought with them had been borrowed, or vested, or subscribed, or begged away; and she literally had not wherewithal to pay the inland postage of a letter.'[5]

Fanny with the aid of the actors from the local theatre, the Drakes, resolved to stage entertainments. On 21 November 1829, this advertisement appeared in the Cincinnati press:

MUSICAL FANTASIA

On Thursday ev'g, 26th, the Great Room at the Bazaar will be open for music, songs, and recitation. This species of amusement, so popular of late years, both in Paris and London, has not hitherto been introduced in America, and it is hoped the present attempt will be favourably received. Mr and Mrs A. Drake have kindly promised their services on the occasion. Between the acts tea and coffee will be served in the saloon.

Doors to be opened at half past six.

Admittance $1, tea & coffee included.

Children half price.

Joe Cowell, a comedian, who was one of the performers, wrote an account of the evening. He described how Mrs Trollope had fastened a green baize curtain across the raised platform at one end of the ballroom. Behind this the entertainers of the evening huddled together as there were no backstage entrances, and it would be improper for the artists to enter through the audience.

Mrs Drake, the tragic actress, was to deliver 'O'Connors Child', 'The Scolding Wife', and 'half a hundred more fashionable recitations'. She and her husband, Alexander Drake, were also to act scenes from selected classics, including that of Sir Peter and Lady Teazle in *The School for Scandal*. The orchestra consisted of a violin and a violoncello. The audience of about thirty people entered and a bell was rung, and then rung again. Mrs Drake opened the green curtain, 'Her majestic form and white satin train, which Drake had spread out and placed on the floor at its full extent . . . taking possession entirely of the stage. She gave three queenlike curtsies to the right, left, and centre (which was entirely vacant), but there was no response from the audience. The fact is, it was not fashionable to take notice of anything.' At the intermission Fanny took Cowell aside, and, undaunted, told him her plans for the future of the Bazaar:

'Now you see, Mr Cowell, I'll have the dais enlarged, and made on a declivity; and then I'll have beautiful scenes painted in oil colours, so that they can be washed every morning and kept clean. I have a wonderfully talented French painter, whom I brought with me, but the people here don't appreciate him, and this will help to bring him into notice. And then I'll have a hole cut here', describing a square on the floor with her toe; 'and then a geometrical staircase for the artistes to ascend perpendicularly', twirling round and round her finger, 'instead of having to walk through the audience part of the area. Or,' said she, after a pause, 'I'll tell you what will be as well, and not so costly. I'll have some canvas nailed along the ceiling, on this side, to form a passage to lead to the stage; Mr. Hervieu can paint it like damask, with a large gold border, and it would have a fine effect!'

However, all her enthusiastic planning was to no avail. A second evening was even more poorly attended than the first, and on 19 December 1829, Hervieu, as master of ceremonies, regretfully announced that the entertainments were at an end. 'Painting, Poetry, and Music, were put in requisition at the great room of the Bazaar, to gratify their taste, and to win their favour – but it has failed', reported the *Cincinnati Gazette*.[6]

The creditors closed in, and all the Trollopes' possessions, so lovingly brought out from England, were seized to pay their bills. Fanny in her anti-slavery book, *Jonathan Jefferson Whitlaw*, describes just such an event, with an all too intimate knowledge:

His ignorance of business had led him to conceive that the $6,000 he had placed in the bank was all he risked; but his name was in the firm, and house, lands, stock, and furniture, were all seized and sold by auction, towards clearing the large demands of the creditors. . . . He and his two . . . helpless children, were left utterly and literally destitute; and it was only by the sale of some articles of wearing apparel which they were permitted to retain, that their existence was for some time supported.[7]

As Fanny philosophized, 'When serious cares and serious business beset us, the nonsense and fal-lalery of life seems to wither, crumble, and fall away, leaving us in the grand simplicity of reality.'[8]

Fanny, writing later to Tom, told their story.

Everything from the time you left us, went wrong, in spite of exertions – nay hard labour, on our part that would pain you to hear of . . . the fact was that *every bed had been seized*, and that we – your sisters and myself were sleeping together in one small bed at Major L's and boarding there, as well as Henry and Hervieu who both lay on the floor in the kitchen, *for the value of my parlour carpet*. In one letter, in answer to one of mine in which I stated our situation, your father writes, 'How is it possible that you are dependent on Hervieu for your living, when I have sent you out goods to the amount of £2,000?' Is it not strange, Tom, that he does not yet know that these goods never brought *one penny* into my hands? The proceeds of those we sold, went to the workmen and servants, and the *rest were seized*. I trust my letters have reached him, and that he now knows this fact, but I would have you recall it to his memory.[9]

Eventually the Bazaar building, known locally as Trollope's Folly, was turned over to a group of trustees of whom Thomas Anthony was one. Frederick Marryat wrote after he saw it; 'It is composed of many varieties of architecture; but I think the order under which it must be classed is the PREPOSTEROUS.' The building was subsequently taken over by the Presbyterian Society, to be used for preaching and prayer meetings – one hopes they were not subverted by the flamboyance. Later it became the home of a restaurant, a Masonic Hall, a Dancing Academy, and a Ballroom. In 1834 the Trustees sold it for $4,667, from which the Trollopes got not a penny. In 1840 it became a Physico Medical Institute; later, a hospital for soldiers in the Civil War, and it ended its chequered career as a shelter for disreputable women. Finally, in 1881, Trollope's Folly was torn down to make way for an apartment building.[10]

Back at the house in Mohawk, the problems continued to mount. Henry was the next member of the family to collapse. While his mother had been so dangerously ill with malaria, Henry had manfully struggled to run the Bazaar and sort out the mess. Now he, too, became seriously ill.

Fanny wrote to Julia:

No sooner was the physician dismissed and we thought him recovered, he fell ill again worse than ever – we recovered him, and after about six weeks interval, he took the ague and fever so severely that he soon looked like a walking corpse. Everyone said that his native air was all that was left to try for him. . . . Henry was far from steady, and I flatter myself that he is much more likely to become so, after all he has suffered. – He proposes, if his health is restored, to apply with diligence to the law, the profession his father originally wished him to adopt. By no means the least embarrassing part of my situation was the not having funds sufficient to enable us all to start for England.[11]

It was impossible to leave Cincinnati straight away. It was midwinter, the river was frozen, and there was no money. But get away they must, and as soon as possible. Thomas Anthony had written to say he would join them in Cincinnati in May 1830, but that he had 'made such large disbursements for Henry, and also for placing Tom at Oxford that he shall bring no more money than will convey him to us'. He expected Fanny to pay for their 'long projected tour through the union, and also for his return, either with us or without us, as providence might dictate'. Fanny decided that under these circumstances all she could do was to give Henry the money to take him to London as soon as they could get away, 'leaving myself and my dear girls with less than sufficient to pay what few bills I had in the town'. Hervieu once again came to the rescue, as Fanny explained to Julia, 'having it in his power to be useful to us, is the greatest pleasure he could have.' Supported by Hervieu, they survived the winter, and when the ice began to break and it was safe to travel they set off by steamboat. 'We quitted Cincinnati the beginning of March, 1830, and I believe there was not one of our party who did not experience a sensation of pleasure in leaving it . . . we left naught to regret at Cincinnati. The only regret was that we had ever entered it for we had wasted health, time, and money there.' They left on board the *Lady Franklin*, the steamboat which was to take them upstream to Wheeling, a three-day voyage. It was a comfortable journey, though, as always in America, the sexes were separated at all times except for meals. Fanny speculated that this is encouraged by the men as 'no boat left New Orleans without having as cabin passengers one or two gentlemen from that city whose profession it was to drill the fifty-two elements of a pack of cards to profitable duty. This doubtless is an additional reason for the strict exclusion of the ladies from their society.'

Wheeling was the point at which most travellers disembarked in order 'to take the stages which travel the mountain road to the Atlantic cities.' Their destination was Washington, where Hervieu planned once again to set up as a portrait painter. The Trollopes had to wait two days at Wheeling for places on the American stage-coach, which was high with no step and the entrance was by a ladder, which was then removed leaving them marooned 5 ft above the ground. 'The coach had three rows of seats, each calculated to hold three persons, and as we were only six . . . we were for some miles tossed about like a few potatoes in a wheelbarrow.' The journey, although rough, took them through the beautiful Allegheny mountains, and eventually after several adventurous days of travel, the party arrived at Baltimore. Fanny, writing in April to Tom, who increasingly became her confidant, said, 'Nothing, my dearest Tom, but the state of mind I was in when Henry left me, could excuse my not writing to you by him. I will not now dwell on all that has happened. You will doubtless learn it soon enough from Henry. I trust the return to his native air will restore his health, which was dreadfully shaken in the climate of Cincinnati.'[12]

Henry left in early March, and the record of his arrival home comes from Tom's diary of Monday 19 April 1830. 'At half-past twelve last night I was awakened by a knocking at the door, and having got up and gone down, I found Henry at the door, who had just arrived by the coach from Liverpool, and walked down here. I gave him my bed, and passed the rest of the night in a large chair. He came across in a British trader, the *Dalhousie Castle*. All today has, of course, been consumed in talking to him.'[13]

Henry, ill, and with no money, had walked the 16 miles from London to Harrow Weald.

The Trollopes went by boat from Baltimore to Washington, where they stayed with some friends for a few days, and were able to attend some of the debates in Congress. Fanny, who had been horrified by the inhumane treatment of slaves which she had observed in the Southern States, and saddened by the expulsion of the Indians 'from their own, their native lands', could observe:

no single feature in their [the American], national character, that could justify their eternal boast of liberality and the love of freedom. They inveigh against the governments of Europe, because, they say, they favour the powerful and oppress the weak. You may hear this declaimed upon in Congress . . . listen to it, and then look at them at home; you will see them with one hand hoisting the cap of liberty, and with the other flogging their slaves. You will see them one hour lecturing their mob on the indefeasible rights of man, and the next driving from their homes the children of the soil, whom they have bound themselves to protect by the most solemn treaties.

Fanny was later to write four powerful novels set in America, in which she expanded on these beliefs.

In the meanwhile, the cost to the impoverished family of remaining in Washington was too high, and Fanny arranged for herself and the two girls to stay 10 miles out of Washington at Stonington, the home of Mrs Annie Stone, the eldest of the Garnett sisters. Annie Stone was herself short of money, and much regretted that she had to charge her old friend boarding fees of $8.25 per week, which, as always, were paid by Hervieu. Fanny was by now entirely dependent on Hervieu for the support of herself and her two daughters. She had resolved on writing the story of her own adventures, in the hope that on her longed-for return to England, it would earn her some money. She had kept notebooks of her experiences since she first arrived in America, and now she began to turn these into a book. She needed to visit other places, especially the famed Niagara Falls, but that would have to be on the way home. First she needed to recuperate at Annie Stone's house, and she told Tom:

> Nothing can exceed her kindness, and with her we have found a home, the tranquillity of which has done much towards the recovery of my health both of mind and of body. But you must expect, my dear Tom, if Heaven indeed permits my safe return, to see a very old lady! My eyes have greatly failed me since my illness. I can do nothing without spectacles, and can no longer walk as I did. But I am infinitely better than when I came here. . . . I wish with all my soul that you could see and hear poor Hervieu! He seems only to live in the hope of helping us. He has set his heart on getting us home without drawing on your father's diminished purse. God send us safe home, and he will, I know, be repaid, not only in money, but by the gratitude and affection of my husband and children. But sometimes my heart sinks when I think of our present dependence. Poor Cecilia is literally without shoes, and I mean to sell one or two small articles to-morrow to procure some for her, and for Emily. I sit still and write, write, write, – so old shoes last me a long time. As to any other articles of dress, we should any of us as soon think of buying diamonds!
>
> Your dear sisters have had a pretty sharp lesson in economy. They mend, – and mend, – and mend. They are, indeed, treasures to me, and their devoted affection outweighs all my misfortunes. . . . I wish not that you should be ignorant of our life since we parted. . . . Be not unhappy about us nevertheless, dearest . . . you know enough of composition to be aware that nothing more completely and agreeably occupies the mind; and Hope – that quits us the last, perhaps, of all our friends – tells me that it is *possible* my book may succeed. It will have great advantages from Hervieu's drawings. If it *should* succeed, a second book would bring money. If I can but get home next spring, I feel as if I should still find the means of being happy and comfortable. My poor dear Anthony will have outgrown our recollection! Tell him not to outgrow his affection for us. No day passes, – hardly an hour – without our talking of you all. I hope a letter from your father is on the way. . . . God bless you, my dearest Tom.[14]

Fanny wrote to Mary Russell Mitford from Stonington Park on 28 July 1830. She sent her sympathy on the death of Mary's mother, and hoped that it would not be many months before she would see her again. 'I have nothing now to detain me but the waiting to know Mr Trollope's final decision as to the necessity of his once more crossing the Atlantic to arrange himself the final settlement of our untoward speculation at Cincinnati. . . . I, too, am writing a book, my dear Miss Mitford, which, let its success among others be what it may, has helped to amuse me at many moments that would have passed heavily without it.' Fanny apologized for not having written before, 'But I had long ago determined that my American letters should not ruin my European friends.' Of her sons she told Mary, '*Trollope senior* is a most kind and constant correspondent, but *Trollope junior* (your admirer) is a most idle personage, and rarely does more than give me a scrap in one of his father's sheets of foolscap.' Of America she said; 'I would not pass the remnant of my days here, even if I could have all my family around me. America is a glorious country for Americans, but a very so so one for Europeans.'[15]

While staying in Maryland Fanny had time to observe the treatment of the slaves, and she wrote about it at length. She was horrified at the indifference shown to them by their owners, although admitted that even that was preferable to the brutality meted out by the plantation owners in the South. Slaves were bred, like livestock, for sale to the Southern plantation owners. She described how Mrs Smith in *The Refugee* was: '. . . as usual, hard at work, though surrounded by many young slaves, to whom she continued to assign various tasks. . . . It was a sort of breeding farm, and to bring this profitable stock into marketable condition, it was necessary to teach them in some degree the use of their hands.'[16] Apart from this training they were kept in deliberate ignorance, 'By the law of Virginia it is penal to teach any slave to read, and it is penal to be aiding and abetting in the act of instructing them.'

One of the first British or American novels protesting against American slavery was written by Fanny Trollope in 1836. Called *Jonathan Jefferson Whitlaw*, and based on her own knowledge of New Orleans and Natchez, it is a powerful story of brutality, rape, and murder, in and around a slave plantation. It was published before public awareness had made slavery an international issue and was a pioneering book. Officially slavery was abolished throughout the British Empire in 1833, but only in 1838 were all the British slaves legally freed. Slavery was abolished in America much later.

The Trollope family spent the summer of 1830 at Maryland. In spite of money worries, it was a peaceful and enjoyable time in the midst of a proliferation of wild flowers, fruits and 'an atmosphere of butterflies, so gaudy in hue, and so varied in form, that I often thought they looked like flowers on the wing.' In late August 1830, Fanny and the girls journeyed to Philadelphia, where they visited the sights. Fanny was struck by the difference between this American city after sunset, and those of Europe. In Philadelphia, 'scarcely a sound is heard; hardly a voice or wheel breaks the stillness. The streets are entirely dark, except where a stray lamp marks an hotel or the like; no shops are open . . . scarcely a step is heard, and for a note of music, or the sound of mirth, I listened in vain.'

Fanny noted the lack of influence of American women in society, especially married women, who are doomed to sit at home all day; 'I believe they clear-starch a little, and iron a little, and sit in a rocking chair, and sew a great deal. . . . It is after marriage . . . that the lamentable insignificance of the American woman appears.' They returned to Stonington, but once again Fanny was struck down by the American fever, and once again confined to her bed. 'It was declared that a change of air was necessary, and it was arranged for me (for I was perfectly incapable of settling anything for myself), that I should go to Alexandria, a pretty town at the distance of about 15 miles, which had the reputation of possessing a skilful physician.' She found the accommodation at Alexandria warm and comfortable, and there they spent the winter while she slowly recovered. On 12 February 1831 they watched a solar eclipse, and 'during the following months, I occupied myself partly in revising my notes, and arranging these pages; and partly in making myself acquainted, as much as possible, with the literature of the country.'

Fanny wrote to Julia from Alexandria on 10 April 1831, and gave her news of the girls. 'Cecilia is half an inch taller than I am, and is really a very pretty girl, but I dress her like a little Quaker, and make as much a child of her as *a tall fourteen* will permit. Emily is very small, and looks as much within her age, as Cecilia does beyond hers – they are both the very best girls that ever a mother had.'[17]

Fanny was still waiting impatiently for some financial help from Thomas Anthony, but he was bedevilled by his own problems and could send no remittances. 'At length, in spite of the lingering pace necessarily attending consultations, and arrangements across the Atlantic, our plans were finally settled. The coming spring was to show us New York and Niagara, and the early summer was to convey us home.'

The Trollopes and Hervieu went by river from Baltimore to Philadelphia, and then changed for Trenton. Here they left their 'smoothly gliding comfortable boat, for the most detestable stage-coach that ever Christian built to dislocate the joints of his fellow-men'. Then, finally, into another boat which was to take them down the Ruraton river to New York. 'We seemed to enter the harbour of New York upon waves of liquid gold, and as we darted past the green isles which rise from its bosom, like guardian sentinels of the fair city, the setting sun stretched his horizontal beams farther and farther at each moment, as if to point out to us some new glory in the landscape. . . . Situated on an island, which I think it will one day cover, it rises like Venice, from the sea.'

In New York Fanny visited the theatres, where she found the same loathsome habits; 'Several gentlemen without their coats, and a general air of contempt for the decencies of life, certainly more than usually revolting.' She visited all the exhibitions, and dined out, a rare treat. 'At night the shops, which are open till very late, are brilliantly illuminated with gas, and all the population seem as much alive as in London or Paris. This makes the solemn stillness of the evening hours in Philadelphia more remarkable.' On 29 May 1831, Fanny wrote to Mary Russell Mitford from New York:

> I write to you, my dear friend, almost on the eve of departure, and would rather have done so on the eve of my arrival in my own dear land, were it not that I wish to propitiate your assistance in the business that must occupy me immediately on my arrival. . . . You know, I believe, that I have looked and listened since I have been here with a view to publication, and you know also, dear friend – for how can you help it? – that I am as utterly unknown in the world of letters as your dog May was before you immortalized him. What I would ask is a letter of introduction to your publisher as would enable me to present myself before him without feeling as if I had dropped upon him from the moon. . . . I am well aware that it is difficult to bring a first effort to the light, but I think your powerful name will help me much. We are just about to start for Niagara, and shall leave New York for London immediately on our return thence.[18]

The next day, on the 30 May, they set off for Niagara. They went by boat up the Hudson, passing West Point, Albany, and so to Utica. Here they took a carriage for Trenton Falls where they descended on a perilous path to view, 'a world of cataracts, all leaping forward together in most magnificent confusion'. Setting off again by stage-coach and river boat, they came to Lockport where they had to spend a night. Fanny was not impressed: 'Lockport is, beyond all comparison, the strangest-looking place I ever beheld. As fast as half a dozen trees were cut down, a *factory* was raised up; stumps still contest the ground with pillars, and porticoes are seen to struggle with rocks. It looks as though the demon of machinery, having invaded the peaceful realms of nature, had fixed on Lockport as the battle ground on which they should strive for mastery.' The next day they set off again.

> At length we reached Niagara. It was the brightest day that June could give; and almost any day would have seemed bright that brought me to the object which for years I had languished to look upon. . . . It is not for me to attempt a description of Niagara; I feel I have no powers for it. . . . As for myself, I can only say, that wonder, terror, and delight completely overwhelmed me. I wept with a strange mixture of pleasure and pain. We passed four delightful days of excitement and fatigue; we drenched ourselves with spray; we cut our feet on the rocks; we blistered our faces

in the sun; we looked up the cataract, and down the cataract; we perched ourselves on every pinnacle we could find; we dipped our fingers in the flood at a few yards distance from its thundering fall; in short, we strove to fill as many niches of memory with Niagara as possible, and I think the images will be within the power of recall for ever.

Fanny was observed at Niagara by Captain Hamilton, a visiting Englishman. 'She was then travelling with her two daughters, merely girls, and a Frenchman. In what capacity the latter attended her, Hamilton could not make out, but from the odd appearance of matters, and her apparent poverty, which hardly admitted her and her daughters being decently dressed, it was conclusive against her being taken notice of by respectable ladies, or treated as one herself.'[19]

The party left Niagara on 10 June 1831 and returned to New York, where they spent a last, happy two weeks. 'But the time was come to bid it adieu! The important business of securing our homeward passage was to be performed.' They packed up their 'trumpery' as the paraphernalia of ladies is sometimes called, and among the rest, Fanny's 'six hundred pages of griffonage'. She confessed, 'I suspect that what I have written will make it evident that I do not like America.' She spoke of the population generally:

. . . as seen in town and country, among the rich and the poor, in the slave states and the free states. I do not like them. I do not like their principles, I do not like their manners, I do not like their opinions. . . . A single word indicative of doubt, that any thing, or every thing, in that country is not the very best in the world, produces an effect which must be seen and felt to be understood. If the citizens of the United States were indeed the devoted patriots they call themselves, they would surely not thus incrust themselves in the hard, dry, stubborn persuasion, that they are the first and best of the human race, that nothing is to be learnt but what they are able to teach, and that nothing is worth having which they do not possess.

As always, the difficulties of getting enough money together to pay for their passage home had been almost insurmountable. Fanny told her friend Julia of her husband's attitude. Thomas Anthony had said:

He had no more money to send – That he was ruined by the transaction which *we* had managed wretchedly – That he felt himself under the greatest obligations to Hervieu, and that he should be glad to see us home, as soon as we could find the means of coming! Painting is a poor business in America – but this excellent and devoted friend continued to support us by it, for *two years*. Mr Trollope constantly continued to write very kindly, but always assuring us he had *no* money to send. With all the exertions Hervieu could make, he never could get enough before hand, to realize a sum sufficient to bring us home. I wrote to Mr Trollope and told him that for my dear girls' sake I was *determined* upon returning to England – and that if he was unable to furnish me with the means, I would apply to his family for them. This brought £80.[20]

Thus with this and the money which Hervieu had painstakingly saved, they paid for their passage. Fanny, Cecilia, Emily and Hervieu, were finally able to escape from America. In July 1831, they sailed from New York in a ship bound for England, and docked at Woolwich on 5 August 1831. Fanny Trollope had been away for three and a half years.

CHAPTER SIX

'Heaven grant it may pay me!'

Harrow Weald. August 1831–September 1832
Julian Hill. September 1832–April 1834

While Fanny, Henry, Cecilia and Emily had been in America, Tom and Anthony remained in England to complete their education at Winchester.

Tom, once he reached the age of eighteen was ready to go on to New College, Oxford, but as no vacancy was immediately available he had accompanied his father to America in the October of 1828. Anthony, now thirteen, was left as a boarder at Winchester to continue his education: 'Then another and a different horror fell to my fate. My college bills had not been paid, and the school tradesmen who administered to the wants of the boys were told not to extend their credit to me. . . . My schoolfellows of course knew that it was so, and I became a Pariah. . . . But, ah! how well I remember all the agonies of my young heart.'[1]

Almost certainly from lack of funds, and also sheer mismanagement, Thomas Anthony had made no provision for his youngest son. It was a humiliation Anthony never forgot. Worse was to come. When his father, returning from America, was confronted with the unpaid bills, Anthony was removed from the school.

> When I left Winchester, I had three more years of school before me, having as yet endured nine. My father at this time having left my mother and sisters with my younger brother in America, took himself to live at a wretched tumble-down farmhouse on the second farm he had hired! And I was taken there with him . . . It was nearly three miles from Harrow, at Harrow Weald, but in the parish; and from this house I was again sent to that school as a day boarder. Perhaps the eighteen months which I passed in this condition, walking to and fro on those miserable dirty lanes, was the worst period of my life.[2]

Anthony, scruffy at the best of times, now had a daily walk of 12 miles, as he travelled the muddy lanes four times a day. He was a sizar, a charity boy, at a fashionable school, 'a condition never premeditated. What right had a wretched farmer's boy, reeking from a dunghill, to sit next to the sons of peers, – or worse still, next to the sons of big tradesmen who had made their ten thousand a year? . . . My tutor took me without the fee; but when I heard him declare the fact in the pupil-room before the boys, I hardly felt grateful for the charity.'[3]

Life at home must have been very bleak for young Anthony. Tom was now at Oxford, and Henry, after returning from America in the spring of 1830, had been entered at Caius College, Cambridge. Thomas Anthony, his father, 'spent nearly half his time in bed, suffering agony from sick headaches'. When not in bed he shut himself in the parlour, working on his *Encyclopaedia Ecclesiastica.*

> It was his ambition to describe all ecclesiastical terms, including the denominations of every fraternity of monks and every convent of nuns, with all their orders and subdivisions. . . . No father was ever more anxious for the education of his children, though I think none ever knew less how to go about the work. Of amusement, as far as I can remember, he never recognized the need. . . . In those days he never punished me, though I think I grieved him much by my idleness; but in passion he knew not what he did, and he has knocked me down with the great folio Bible which he always used.[4]

Tom agreed with this:

> Concomitantly with continued increase in the frequency and intensity of his headaches, my father's irritability of temper had increased to a degree which made him a very difficult person to live with. For simple assent to his utterances of an argumentative nature did not satisfy him; he would be argued with. Yet argument produced irritability leading to scenes of painful violence, which I had reason to fear hastened the return of his suffering. . . . The terrible irritability of his temper, which sometimes in his later years reached a pitch that made one fear his reason was, or would become, unhinged, was undoubtedly due to the shattering of his nervous system caused by the habitual use of calomel.[5]

Anthony was unwillingly pressed into helping in the kitchen garden, or, in the holidays, in the hay-field; 'but I passed my most jocund hours in the kitchen, making innocent love to the bailiff's daughter.'

His father was always in debt; the house had a leaking roof and rotting timbers; the table was poorer than that of the bailiff's; and the furniture was mean and scanty. Anthony, locked in his own misery, had reason to resent his mother's absence. He was not aware of how unwilling an exile it had become.

On 5 August 1831 Fanny, now fifty-two, with Cecilia, fifteen, Emily, thirteen, and the faithful Hervieu, landed at Woolwich. From there they proceeded directly to Harrow Weald, and Fanny wrote to Miss Mitford: 'How delightfully English everything looks! I cannot describe to you the pleasure of returning to Europe after an absence of nearly four years.'

While the family had been in America, England had undergone a period of change. A new king had come to the throne; George IV had died in 1830 and now his brother William IV, the sailor king, ruled. In 1829 the first regular London police force had been created by Peel. There was much unrest in the country, as poor harvests in 1828 and 1829 caused the price of bread to rise steeply. Rents were still high, and landholders like Thomas Anthony were in serious financial trouble. Henry had written to Lord Northwick, on Thomas Anthony's behalf, on 31 January 1831 in response to a demand for payment, to say that his father had no money to pay his bills; he was very harassed and not well.[6] Fanny was disturbed by the changes she found on her return, and wrote to Julia on 22 August,

Mr T. assures me that his affairs are in the greatest disorder – that he has lost more than 500 sterling per ann. by his farms for many years past; that he has endeavoured to redeem this by many speculations, *all* of which have failed. . . . God knows what will become of us all – Tom is doing very well at Oxford – Henry and Anthony are perfectly without destination – they are both excellent scholars – but Latin and Greek are very *unmarketable.* We are living at a miserable house at the Harrow Weald farm – my pretty cottage Julia is let. . . . My friends all declare themselves delighted at my return – but if I can give no more parties – I shall not long count many friends – This I should care nothing about, could I see my dear boys placed in situations where their talents and good conduct might enable them to gain their bread – But I must cease this strain dearest.[7]

Fanny was saddened to hear of Camilla Wright's death, 'at lodgings in Paris quite alone.' It seems to have been a gloomy homecoming. It was not long, however, before Fanny began to improve the 'miserable farm'. As Tom said:

It had once been a very good house, probably the residence of the owner of the small farm on which it was situated. But it . . . was assuredly shabby enough, and had been forlorn enough, as I had known it in my vacations, when inhabited only by my father, my brother Anthony, and myself. But my mother was one of those people who carry sunshine with them. The place did not seem the same . . . and a very short time elapsed before my mother had got round her one or two nice girl guests to help her in brightening it.[8]

It has been impossible to be definite about the location of the old farmhouse; one building named by some biographers was demolished in the 1930s. However, local lore has it that the old house still exists, incongruously tucked into a modern housing estate in Harrow Weald.

At the bottom of a leafy cobbled lane, and hidden from the road, sprawls Harrow Weald House Farm, a rambling, higgledy-piggledy sixteenth-century building. Black beams criss-cross the white exterior. Roses now grow over the low porch which protects the massive front door. Much has been added over the centuries, but the basic structure, consisting of two main rooms with thick oak beams, huge open fireplaces and a large high barn at the back, is unchanged. The bedrooms and the priest's hole are up the winding stairs. Now beautifully restored, one has to look deep to see the gloomy semi-ruin it once was.

Realizing that her husband was in dire financial straits, and that their only help would be from friends and relatives, Fanny dispatched her manuscript with all speed to Whittaker and Treacher, the publishers, on the recommendation of Mary Russell Mitford. In September it was being read by Captain Basil Hall, himself the author of a controversial book on America. On 25 November Fanny wrote to Julia:

> If the delays of the law are tormenting, those of booksellers are at least equally so. – Capt. Basil Hall to whom my little volumes were sent for *judgement*, has been most kind and serviceable to me, and by his means the thing is now en route – I remember the time dearest, when if I had made such an attempt my only thought would have been 'what will be said of it?' but now Alas! my only anxiety is, what will be paid for it? – This same poverty has a mighty lowering effect on ones sublimities.[9]

Captain Hall had estimated that, if the entire edition of 1,250 copies was sold, Fanny would earn £270, 'which in these bad times would be an important sum to us'. Fanny hoped that, '*if* my book should take, and *if* it should be favourably reviewed in the quarterly (the *Edinburgh*, if it does anything, will abuse it) I should offer the publisher to travel into Germany'. She hoped that by this means she could visit Julia, although 'these thoughts are at present only moonshine'. She gave her news of the children. 'Cecilia is at Offham where they seem to be very kind to her – Tom is at Oxford – Henry with a Barrister in London. Anthony at Harrow (where he has just got a prize) and Emily as usual about 24 inches from my elbow.' Fanny was already hard at work on a second book. Originally titled *The American Exile*, it was a fictionalized, and therefore considerably less censored, version of her own experiences in America. *The Refugee in America* becomes a far more interesting book if read in conjunction with *Domestic Manners of the Americans*. By February 1832 Fanny had completed the first volume. In order to give her more privacy to write, the family had set aside a little room, probably the priest's hole, which they nicknamed 'the Sacred Den'. She wrote to Tom, now back at Oxford:

12th of October   The Sacred Den
Yesterday the whole Milman family mounted the stairs to my room, clamorously calling for 'More book! More book!' Imagine me, if you please, looking extremely modest, but being vastly delighted. . . . All this is very encouraging.[10]

We get a glimpse of the importance of this room in a few of her novels. In *Tremordyn Cliff* she writes; 'The hours devoted to this occupation [writing her journal] were always stolen from the night. A little boudoir, occupying one floor of a turret to which her bedroom opened, was the scene of this nightly confession. . . . So sacred had she taught her attendants to consider this retreat, that none ever ventured to enter it.'[11] And in *Mrs Mathews*, a later book, she writes:

Several very commodious shelves had found themselves places in the odd corners of her sacred den for the accommodation of their contents. [It was] that secret bower in which the chief materials of her life's history were to be found. It is certain that the first aspect of this oddly-shaped and oddly-furnished apartment, as well as the queer, narrow twisting little staircase which led to it, was not much calculated to excite admiration.[12]

Fanny now started her day at four in the morning so that she could write in the comparative peace of the early dawn, and be ready for the family at breakfast time. The negotiations for *Domestic Manners* slowly came to fruition. Captain Hall advised her not to sign the agreement until she had communicated with him. Fanny wrote to Tom: 'I have done nothing to my new book, nor shall I till the other is gone to press. I always feel that I have still something more to do to it.'[13]

Fanny wrote to Mary Russell Mitford on 16 September 1831, telling her that Whittaker 'was willing to print it, dividing the profits with me. I suppose, however, that this is as favourable an offer as a person so utterly unknown can expect. *But,* as we have been losing money on both sides of the Atlantic, a little money *in esse* would have been more agreeable than the hopes he gives *in posse.*'[14]

Just before Christmas the agreement for her book was signed. It was in the publisher's hands. Fanny confided in Tom:

I quake a little, but if I can get even a little money, I will not mind abuse, – nor labour. . . . While my head is at work upon story-telling and money-making, I often encourage my energy, and solace my fatigue by thinking that if I should succeed in getting up one step of the literary ladder, it would incontestably help you immediately to the second.[15]

While waiting for the book to be published, Fanny had some hope that her husband might get a London magistracy. His uncle, Adolphus Meetkerke, had solicited Lord Melbourne for the position on his nephew's behalf. Alas, it was not to be.

A few early copies of *Domestic Manners* were sent to the reviewers, and the early reports were promising. 'Lockhart [editor of the *Quarterly Review*] has read the first volume of Mrs Trollope's book, with which he is very much amused. He said it was the cleverest woman's book he had read for a long time.'[16]

Thomas Anthony too, had some good news. He went along to see the publisher John Murray in his rooms, to be told that his ecclesiastical manuscript had been perused by one of Murray's readers and approved. Murray went on to ask: 'By the bye! – Trollope – who the devil is Mrs Trollope? Her book is the cleverest thing I ever read. I have read it through. So spirited!'

Trollope replied, 'The lady is my wife.'

'Why did she not bring it to me? asked Murray, 'It will sell like wildfire! She ought to have brought it to me. But I will help all I can. You must introduce me to her.'

Fanny writing on 13 February 1832, to tell Tom of this encounter, declared, 'There, my son, what do you think of that? May I not say like Lord Byron, "I awoke one morning and found myself famous"?'[17] She was still working on *The Refugee*, and had completed one volume and two long chapters of the second. If her critics were right, then she surmised:

> . . . let it be as bad as it will, – I shall get something for it. It is strange to observe how circumstances can change ones character. I remember the time when a glowing review in the *Quarterly*, and the being read before publication, and approved, by the set above mentioned, would have made me as proud as a peacock. But now – I only count the possible pence. Apropos of which I may tell you that on Lockhart's report I bought a quarter of a pound of green tea, and on Murray's behalf a pound of fresh butter, and at this moment – past eleven p.m. – I am sipping my favourite nectar with all appurtenances, in solitary comfort by the light of a wax candle.[18]

The book should have been published in February 1832, but Fanny told Julia, 'The agitation of the times, with the Bristol and Manchester riots, so occupied the minds of the people that nothing but home politics could find place in the January number [of the *Quarterly*] and I was *postponed*.' The book was kept back until after the review appeared in March. On 19 March 1832, just after Fanny's fifty-third birthday, *Domestic Manners of the Americans* was released. It was to change her life.

In the first year the book went into four editions in England, and four American editions. '*Domestic Manners of the Americans* made the Old World laugh, and the New World howl with rage', wrote John C. Jeaffreson. However, not all the Old World laughed.

In England, now in political turmoil on the eve of the passing of the contentious electoral Reform Bill, there were fierce divisions between the radical Whigs and the conservative Tories. In March 1831 a Bill had been introduced by Lord John Russell, and defeated in Committee. Parliament was dissolved by Lord Grey. At the general election which followed, a vast majority of seats was won by the reformers. In October of the same year the Reform Bill was passed by the Commons, but thrown out by the Lords. Popular opinion exploded against bishops and peers, leading to the Radical riots in Bristol and Manchester, but, under the threat of a national uprising, the Bill was eventually passed in April 1832. Nomination was replaced by popular election, and seats were taken away from nomination boroughs. The Franchise was opened to all 'Ten Pound Householders', and there were to be no secret ballots. The sovereignty of the people had been established, and the middle class began to have their say.

This was the political climate at the time of publication of *Domestic Manners of the Americans*. The Tories hailed the book as a dire warning of the pitfalls of equality. The pro-American Whigs and Radicals railed against it as lies. The Whig *Edinburgh Review* devoted forty-seven pages to spluttering attack. It began by referring to her companion, Hervieu:

> The scene opens with a matron, her son, and two daughters. On looking narrowly into the background, whom else do we discover? No Mr Trollope, the centre of a family group. . . . First appears her friend Mr H. This is pretty good for a beginning. After that farewell to the virtue of common sense, what ever other discretion may be retained. . . . Mrs Trollope seems not to be in the least aware that she has assumed a most difficult task. Her mode of treating it, and the consequence given to her conclusions, require that we should speak our mind with more sincerity and plainness than is agreeable when a lady is in the case. . . . In doing this, we are sorry to be obliged to state, that she has neither the talent nor the attainments, – neither the temper nor the opportunities, which so comprehensive and delicate an undertaking imperatively requires. . . . She was not sent out by the English people, nor has she been adopted by them since her return.

The *New Monthly Magazine* in its April review, proclaimed; 'This is a work, which, though its author be clever, and itself amusing, has, nevertheless, singularly disgusted us.' In a later review in the November issue of the same magazine, the reviewer became almost incoherent with rage:

> Mrs Trollope makes great pretensions to superior delicacy and refinement, but the texture of her mind is essentially gross. There are stories in her book which offend modesty, and in her spite against prudery she indulges in something far less to be endured. . . . So subtle is her enmity, that it mildews every sentence; her commendations imply censure; when she smiles she calumniates, and in her pleasantry she inflicts a wound. . . . Woman in her own sphere is always mighty; but when she descends from her elevation, and ceases to respect herself . . . conventional courtesy ought not to screen her from admonition and reproof.

The Americans, too, were outraged and insulted by her perceptions of their country. Fanny Kemble, who was then in America, said, 'Mercy on me how sore all these people are about Mrs Trollope's book and how glad I am I did not read it. She must have spoken the truth, for lies do not rankle so.'[19]

An English subaltern, E.T. Coke, who was in New York when the book first appeared, observed:

> The Tariff and Bank Bill were alike forgotten, and the tug-of-war was hard, whether the *Domestic Manners*, or the cholera, which burst upon them simultaneously, should be the more engrossing topic of conversation. At every corner of the street, at every door of every petty retailer of information for the people, a large placard met the eye with, 'For sale here, with plates, *Domestic Manners of the Americans*, by Mrs Trollope'. At every table d'hôte, on board of every steamboat, in every stage-coach, and in all societies, the first question was, 'Have you read Mrs Trollope?' And one half of the people would be seen with a red or blue half-bound volume in their hand, which you might vouch for being the odious work; and the more it was abused the more rapidly did the printers issue new editions.[20]

Fanny Trollope was soon one of the best known, and most hated, authors in America. She was lampooned on the stage, displayed as a wax effigy in New York, and insulted in cartoons. Several reviewers doubted that such a 'vulgar' book could have been written by a woman. Even her old friend Timothy Flint jested about how such passions could lead to conflict:

> We first fight the wordy war of tongue and pen. The emergency comes, and evil passions, and concentrated and long-gathered bitternesses concur

1.   *Frances Trollope.*
*Fanny as a young married woman aged about thirty-five. The painting by R.A. Bacon shows Fanny
in a red dress with a rustic background. (Sotheby's)*

2.   *Heckfield Vicarage.*
Situated beside the church and facing what used to be the village green, the house has changed little since Fanny lived there in 1801. (Author photo)

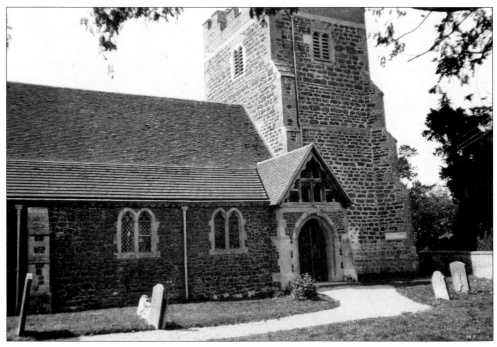

3.   *Heckfield Church.*
Thomas Anthony Trollope married Frances Milton in the old Norman church on 23 May 1809. Fanny's father, the Reverend William Milton, is buried in the churchyard. (Author photo)

4.   *The* Belvidere.
The New Orleans steamboat which carried the Trollope party from the mouth of the Mississippi to Memphis. The vast distances of the New World were most comfortably traversed by the river boats. (Illustration by Hervieu for Domestic Manners of the Americans)

5.   *Nashoba.*
*Hervieu's sketch of the settlement at Nashoba. 'Desolation was the only feeling.' (*Domestic Manners of the Americans)

6. *Trollope's Folly.*
Mrs Trollope's Emporium for the
entertainment of the people of Cincinnati. An
Egyptian, Moorish, Turkish extravagance. A
contemporary print of the Bazaar.

7. *Cincinnati Ballroom.*
'The gentlemen had a splendid entertainment spread for them in another large room of the hotel,
while the poor ladies had each a plate put into their hands . . . and each making a table of her knees,
began eating her sweet, but sad and sulky repast.' (Illustration by Hervieu for **Domestic Manners**
of the Americans*)*

8.   *Julian Hill.*
Julian Hill was the model for this drawing of
Orley Farm by Millais, for the book of that
name by Anthony Trollope.

9.   *Thomas Adolphus Trollope in 1832 aged twenty-two.*
The would-be author. 'I find myself writing and sending off a surprising number of "articles" on all
sorts of subjects.' Painted by Hervieu (National Portrait Gallery)

10.   Anthony in 1832, aged seventeen.
'Some salutary changes were made to my
wardrobe.' These two portraits were in the
possession of Muriel Trollope, Anthony's
granddaughter. The conditional
identification was made by Michael Sadlier
after her death. Painted by Hervieu
(National Portrait Gallery)

11.   Cecilia in 1838, aged twenty-two
Painted when she was engaged to John Tilley.
They were married in February 1839. Painted
by Hervieu (Hugh Trollope)

12.   *The house at Hadley.*
It was in this house that Fanny wrote some of her best books. The house looks out over the goose green, and was rented by Fanny from January 1836 to the end of 1838. Anthony lived here with his mother for much of that time. (Author photo)

13.   *Emily's grave.*
Emily died from consumption at Hadley in February 1836, aged eighteen. She is buried in the graveyard of Hadley Church, only about a hundred yards from the house on Hadley Green. (Author photo)

14.   Vienna – La crème de la crème.

'Instead of tacitly demonstrating their exclusive pretensions merely by such little social impertinences as none but themselves would practise, they honestly bring forward their claims by loudly and distinctly proclaiming "Nous sommes la crème!" Nay, a few spirits, more honest and more candid still, take up the strain at least an octave higher, and say, "Nous sommes la crème de la crème."'
(Illustration by Hervieu from Vienna and the Austrians)

15.   Factory boys eating pig swill.

'Seven or eight boys had already made their way to the sort of rude farmyard upon which this door opened, one and all of whom were intent upon purloining from a filthy trough just replenished for the morning meal of two stout hogs, a variety of morsels which, as Michael's new acquaintance assured him, were "dainty eating for the starving prentices of Deep Valley Mill."' (Illustrations by Hervieu for Michael Armstrong) with reasons of state, and the passions of a dominant party, to engender a war, and we redden the ocean and the land with human blood, that is spilled because Mrs Trollope had no letters of recommendation, and was a short dumpling figure – a war of a frock and a petticoat.[21]

Why did this book, written by a middle-aged Englishwoman about her travels, cause such a furore that at one stage it almost created an international incident? Mark Twain had one answer. In the introduction to *Life on the Mississippi* (part of which was cut), he said: 'Of all these tourists I like Dame Trollope best. She found a "civilization" here, which you, reader, could not have endured; and which you would not have regarded as a civilization at all. Mrs Trollope spoke of this civilization in plain terms – plain and unsugared, but honest and without malice, and without hate.'

Her son Tom said of the book:

It was emphatically the book of the season, was talked of everywhere, and read by all sorts and conditions of men and women. It was highly praised by all the conservative organs of the press, and vehemently abused by all those of the opposite party. Edition after edition was sold, and the pecuniary results were large enough to avert from the family of the successful authoress the results of her husband's ruined fortunes.[22]

Eight months after she had struggled home from America, Fanny was launched on a profession which was to supply the needs of her family for as long as she was able to work. Hervieu, as promised, was given £100, half the proceeds of the second edition of *Domestic Manners*. He had drawn the illustrations for the book, but the Trollopes owed him far more than that. There was some gossip about Hervieu's relationship with Fanny. When they first went to America, Marianne Skerrett wrote to Julia, 'I wish to see them all again (excepting one, I can't say I want to see Mr Hervieu back).' But whatever her friends thought privately, there is no evidence that he was anything but a good and faithful friend.

First Fanny took care of the basic and most pressing needs. She paid for the coal and candles used in her own room in the winter. 'Half a year's rent and taxes paid in advance; a good bed and pillows, bolsters, sopha, and a chest of drawers bought at a sale.' She hoped in the future to buy a cow and some malt for brewing, and to find £180 needed for Henry, to enter him at the Temple.

Tom and Emily went to stay with cousin Fanny Bent at Exeter, Henry was already down there. In April, leaving Thomas Anthony at Harrow Weald, Fanny took Cecilia with her to London where they took lodgings in Thayer Street off Manchester Square.

In London, Fanny dined with Mr Murray, and was 'abundantly complimented'. She was introduced to 'half the poets, painters, wits and wonders that were in town. And there again I was beflattered most outrageously'. On 25 April she wrote to Tom at Exeter: 'You would laugh did you know to what an extent I am lionized.' A friend, Captain Hamilton, had told her, 'that Southey and Wordsworth are both delighted. . . . In short I am bepraised so violently that – I am afraid my poor little novel will disappoint everybody.' In a much later novel, *A Clever Woman*, the heroine echoes Fanny's sentiments: 'Never till last night was I conscious of the pleasure of talking, where I was both looked at and listened to, as being decidedly something out of the common way.'

At one dinner party a gentleman called Albert Pell reported that he had seen Mrs Opie (herself a writer) and Mrs Trollope together; the former, 'in the neatest possible cap and shawl, sitting upright and rather silent. Mrs Trollope not at all prim, neat or silent.'[23] Fanny was already becoming known for her outspokenness. She was invited to a Sunday evening party at the Misses Berrys, and wrote to Tom:

> They are ladies famous for their conversation parties; and a very 'good' set were assembled there. I dare not, even to you, repeat all the things that were said to me. A few, however, you shall have! The Countess of Morley told me she was certain that if I drove through London proclaiming who I was, I should have the horses taken off and be drawn in triumph from one end of town to the other! The Honourable Mr Somebody declared that my thunderstorm was the finest thing in prose or verse. Lady Charlotte Lindsay implored me to go on writing – never was anything so delightful. Lady Louisa Stewart told me that I had quite put English out of fashion, and that everyone was talking Yankee talk. In short I was overpowered! . . . How strange all this seems![24]

Fanny, in a whirl of engagements, began to worry about getting her expected novel completed. She could 'scarcely find an hour in each day to give to it'. When she wrote to Mary Russell Mitford in April 1832, the fatigue was beginning to show:

> I never felt less in good humour with people in my life than I have done since I was so be-puffed and be-praised. I am, however thankful for the *money* I have gained by it; it has been very useful for us. My dear Henry . . . is to be immediately entered at the Temple by means of it – so *vive la plume!*
>
> What does one do to get business with the mags and annuals? Does one say, as at playing *ecarté*, 'I propose,' or must one wait to be asked? Remember, dear, that I have five children.[25]

There was still unrest about the Reform Bill and the Whig Ministry. William IV was abused by all, wrote Fanny to Tom, and the most seditious placards were circulated. Riots were expected in London. The windows of Apsley House, the London home of the Duke of Wellington, were broken by the mob, and he had iron shutters installed for protection. Fanny told Tom, 'I have been living among high Tories, and have the honour of meeting sundry peers, but their apathy and despair provoke me beyond expression.'[26]

By September 1832, enough money had been earned by Fanny to cancel the sub-lease of Julian Hill. They were able to return to their much-loved home and circle of friends. Anthony said it was an Eden compared to Harrow Weald. 'The three miles became half a mile, and probably some salutary changes were made to my wardrobe.'

In October of 1832, the family had started a weekly magazine called *The Magpie*, which described itself as 'A weekly Magazine of Literature, Politics, Science, and Art'. All the family participated. The contributions were in manuscript form, and pasted into a folio scrapbook. Henry was the editor, and the team, which included Mrs Grant and one of the Drurys, would meet from time to time to hear it read aloud. Even Fanny managed a few lines, and signing herself 'Grub Street', warned the editor *never* on any account to employ weary and hackneyed writers!

Tom, the only member of the family who had been accepted at Oxford, began to talk of becoming an author. His mother, who was far more in touch with reality, advised him: 'Whether you apply for a Fellowship, a pupil, a living, a London lectureship, an article in the *Quarterly*, or an engagement with a bookseller, a good degree will aid you at first in setting out, beyond anything else whatever. Be firm to this object.'[27]

Fanny had finished *The Refugee* in June of 1832, writing, 'Heaven grant it may pay me! I really have worked very hard at it.' In July this second book was sold to Messrs. Whittaker and Treacher for the sum of £400. This was encouraging, but she still felt far from secure, the money from her first book had gone fast. She resolved, 'should my little fame expire directly, and no further returns reward my labours, I shall burn my pen, and immediately seek a situation where I may earn something.'[28] However, all seemed to be well and *The Refugee* was a 'decided success'.

Fanny had her portrait painted by Hervieu, and it was shown in an exhibition at Somerset House in 1833; today it hangs in the National Portrait Gallery in London. One critic wrote of the picture, 'This is the portrait of the sarcastic Mrs Trollope. The painter has not flattered her good looks. He has had vinegar in his brush, too.' The family thought this was hilarious. Cecilia wrote to Tom: 'Mamma now goes by the name, at home, of old Madam Vinegar!' Hervieu also painted miniatures of Tom and Anthony in 1832.

Fanny had continued to write for there were many bills to be paid. In 1833 she produced a little book of satirical verse entitled *The Mother's Manual: or Illustrations of Matrimonial Economy. An Essay in Verse*. A slim, one-volume book, illustrated by Hervieu, it is a tongue-in-cheek dissertation on how to marry your daughters well, even if they lack the advantages of beauty and fortune. In it Lady Hook gives advice to Mrs Philtre, the mother of three unmarried girls:

Few have yet learned how far, by care and skill,
A well-taught girl may marry whom she will.

When you ask me what means are most fit to obtain,
Any man you're especially anxious to gain,
I reply – you must study him, ere you prepare,
For his conquest alone, a particular snare,
Lest he see your design, and shall learn to beware.
[However, learning will not catch a man, they must learn to be witty]
My girls were sure to make a famous hit,
By passing their rhymed nonsense off for wit.

By the end of the book all three daughters have, by a variety of subterfuges, successfully captured a husband. The book was published in London by Treutel and Wurtz and Richter, and was probably written more for Fanny's friends, than for the public. It was the only published book of verse she wrote and highlights, in a mocking way, the almost desperate need for women to get married.

The Abbess, her next novel, was in a different style. Gothic novels were in fashion. Mr Walpole, Mrs Radcliffe, Miss Austen, had all written successful Gothic romances. Why not Mrs Trollope? She set to work. Influenza raged in England that year, and all the family succumbed. Fanny became sick, and was very feverish, but tried to finish *The Abbess*. She wrote: 'I have never, at any period of my work, felt so pressed – I may add, so oppressed – as at present. I think I have fever still hanging about me.'[29] Mr H. the apothecary, was savage with his treatments. Henry had fourteen leeches applied to him; Anthony was bled until he fainted; Cecilia became hysterical from weakness; and Hervieu, having taken a powerful mixture of pills and potions, was found wandering in the fields, a rush of blood to the head having produced delirium.

The Abbess is a wonderful tale of theological intrigue, set mainly in medieval Italy. A war of wits between the Abbot of St Andrea, Father Isidore, and the Abbess of Sant' Catherina, Geraldine d'Albano, it involves brooding passion, secret loves, forbidden religious practices, and, after a chilling trial for heresy, the walling up alive of a beautiful nun, discovered to be pregnant, who has been forcibly separated from her lover. After a daring rescue, and many dramatic twists, all ends happily. Although melodramatic, it is a surprisingly engrossing book, as a contemporary reviewer in *The Spectator* wrote:

> *The Abbess* is manufactured by a not unskilful bookmaker: the taste of the circulating library is remarkably well hit; there is no doubt but that it will extremely well suit the wants of the ladies who have been long pining for a genuine bit of romance, such as they used to be supplied with in the days of their youth – those 'deep' times when Mrs Radcliffe made them hide their heads under the bedclothes, and converted every sound into a warning and every sight into a ghost. . . . Some of the scenes indicate skill in the workmanship, which must put the American idea of Mrs Trollope's not being her own composer, and having employed Captain Hall to invent her book of *American Manners*, altogether to shame.[30]

The book safely completed and in her publisher's hands, Fanny set off with her old travelling companions, Henry and Hervieu (Tom was back at university and Anthony at school), for the promised tour of Belgium and Western Germany, and the longed-for visit to her old friend Julia. Another travel book would be the result, and she could visit other old friends.

The trio left London on 1 June 1833, and stopped first at Ostend where they stayed with the British consul and his wife, Mr and Mrs Fauche. Mrs Fauche, a handsome lady with a beautiful singing voice, had arranged some amateur theatricals in which Henry and Hervieu both performed. During the fighting of a burlesque duel, Henry was wounded quite severely in the thigh and was confined to bed for ten days. As usual Fanny was chief nurse, 'her son desiring her almost constant presence at his bedside'.

At the same time, in Harrow, Thomas Anthony was taken seriously ill with what appeared to be a seizure. He recovered, after being subjected to the usual treatment of bleeding and cupping. The local apothecary, the same inept Mr H., assured Cecilia, who was looking after him, that there was no danger of a recurrence of the attack; however, Thomas Anthony had another lesser attack a few weeks later. Fanny didn't receive this disturbing news until it was too late to return, Cecilia's letter to her went astray, and by the time it reached her, there had been later letters saying all was now well.

Once Henry had recovered enough to walk with crutches, the travellers went on by canal to Bruges, where the Fauches introduced them to many of their Bruges acquaintances. They visited Waterloo and viewed the battlefield. Their French guide asked them if Wellington was loved in England, '*N'est-ce-pas?*' 'My cheeks tingled as I remembered the windows of Apsley House', wrote Fanny.[31]

Journeying on, dauntless as ever, they climbed, with donkeys, to the top of the Brocken Mountains in Germany, and were met with beautiful and wild views and great winds. They slept the night in a mountain hut. The next morning there was such a gale blowing that Fanny mounted her donkey in the stables: '. . . and there I was tied, and pinned, till it was declared impossible for any morsel of drapery to be taken at disadvantage by the storm.' However, on setting out she nearly got blown away, and so the tying was re-done 'with stronger tackle'.[32]

They travelled on towards Baden Baden, and visited the dungeons of the Alt Schloss, unlit except for candles, and learnt how the 'Secret Tribunal' was able to convey political prisoners from the judgement chambers to the dungeons by means of a concealed opening like a huge chimney in the centre of the circular stone staircase. The prisoner was placed in this tiny room containing only one chair; when he sat down, the floor dropped away, the chair descended to the dungeons, and the victim was heard of no more. The party visited the question chamber, 'and so strongly did visions of the past rise up before me, that, with the strange clinging to horror which makes so puzzling a part of our nature, I remained gazing on these traces of vengeance and of woe.' Their guide showed them the oubliette, a black hole into which prisoners were thrown. 'The horror of this vault, removed all fear I should not find the dungeons terrible enough. It is quite impossible that stone walls can convey a feeling of more hopeless desolation.'[33] Fanny was to use this setting, with telling effect, in her anti-Jesuit novel, *Father Eustace*, written in 1847.

Fanny also visited the gaming tables in Baden Baden, not to play, but, with her passion for people, to watch the players. One figure who drew her attention was that of:

> . . . a pale, anxious old woman; who seemed no longer to have strength to conceal her eager agitation under the air of callous indifference, which all practised players endeavour to assume. She trembled, till her shaking hand could hardly grasp the instrument with which she pushed or withdrew her pieces; the dew of agony stood on her wrinkled brow. . . . I was assured she was a person of rank; and my informant added, but I trust she was mistaken, that she was an English woman.[34]

Another woman sounds very like the prototype for Mrs Barnaby, who became the heroine of three of Fanny's most successful novels. She was rather more than thirty, rouged, presumed respectable, and accompanied by one or two gentlemen:

> This talking, laughing, flirting lady was constantly accompanied by a little girl of about seventeen, who made ones heart ache. She was the most quiet, modest, unobtrusive being I ever looked at. The simple elegance of

her dress formed as remarkable a contrast to that of her companion, as her person and manner. No one spoke to her; no one noticed her; in the ball-room she sat silently beside her laughing friend; she never danced; she never smiled. At the gaming table where her flighty chaperone often played, she stood close behind her, with the same gentle look of immovable gravity. Who could have had the barbarity to consign her to such cruel care?[35]

Fanny was constantly gathering information to be used in later novels, and this young girl was re-incarnated as Agnes, Mrs Barnaby's niece. In the introduction to *Belgium and Western Germany*, Fanny confessed: 'I have an inveterate habit of suffering all I see to make a deep impression on my memory, and the result of this is, a sort of mosaic, by no means very grand in outline or skilful in drawing; but each morsel of colour has the deep reality of truth, in which there is ever some value.[36]

At the beginning of September, Fanny, Henry and Hervieu visited Dr and Mrs Pertz in Hanover, where Thomas Anthony joined them. Julia, the devoted friend to whom Fanny had written so often, had much news to exchange with her. The visit was all too short, and on 15 September they returned to Harrow, after a slow and roundabout journey, during which Hervieu was not allowed to travel through Holland with them, because the Dutch and Belgians were at loggerheads, and Hervieu carried a Belgian passport.

The journey around Belgium and Western Germany, for which Fanny paid, had been rather more expensive than she had expected. The book had to be made ready for publication with all speed. Fanny had her suspicions that Whittaker and Treacher, her current publisher, had brought out a further edition of *The Refugee* without telling her, or paying royalties. She was not pleased, and decided to take her 'Belgium' book to John Murray, the publisher who had been so enthusiastic about *Domestic Manners of the Americans*. He was interested, but would only offer her half profits. This would cause her some difficulties, as she wrote to Julia: 'I particularly wished a payment in ready money on account of Tom's taking his degree next month at Oxford – at which time all arrears are paid – I stated my difficulty – or rather my objection to this mode of dealing – but he assured me that for many years past he had practised no other.'[37]

Fanny refused the offer, she felt she could not afford to accept it, and went back to Whittaker who only offered her £200. 'On this I desired my son to call for the manuscript and inform Mr Whittaker that I declined his proposal. He then informed my son that he was willing to pay £200 for 1,000 copies, and £50, for all printed after. . . . He also proposed half profits – and finally begged that the question might be left open.'

Fanny was annoyed and returned to John Murray, but it was only in July

1834 that he finally published the work. As Fanny asked Julia, 'Is not this bungling business of mine a torment? You will say and I feel that it is – yet you can hardly guess how much so.'[38]

The Trollopes had been in financial strife for some time, and by now, with mounting arrears in rent payments, the family was struggling for survival. Thomas Anthony in his bull-headed way, had given his wife little idea of the 'difficulties which might have been easily met and mastered, if Mr Trollope had been more open with us all', and she only discovered the magnitude of the problem when Lord Northwick's agent called on the day after Christmas, demanding payment. The agent, Quilton, reported to Lord Northwick on 27 December, that he 'had found him in bed but saw Mrs Trollope who promised to communicate my message which was I must have settlement of those bills without further delay – I have just now seen him who is going to town tomorrow with every expectation of recovering money.'

Two days later when no money had been paid, he wrote, '. . . this he promised last week and many times before which makes me have no confidence in him and what would be best to do with him I know not.'[39] Fanny told Julia 'We had no idea that a years rent of the *pernicious* farm which for twenty years has been so losing a concern for him, was due to Lord Northwick – *I* could have paid this at almost any other period since my first publication – but now it is impossible – my last summer's tour was very costly and my five children's private expenses as well as my own have swallowed the rest of what remained from furnishing Julian Hill.'[40]

It was at this stage that Fanny began to press with some urgency for the publication of her book on Belgium. The delays must have had a nightmare quality. Anthony and Henry then both became ill. Fanny wrote again to Julia:

> I have never had so much sickness in my family as this year – For about ten days we were very seriously alarmed for Anthony – and since that more seriously still for my poor Henry who has been, and yet is, very ill – He is grown pale and thin beyond what you can imagine and has a cough that tears him to pieces. But our medical man assures me that as yet he perceives no danger and that if he will not leave the house until the east winds are over, and warm weather settled in, he thinks he will recover the attack upon his lungs.[41]

Tom seems to have been the only member of the family not ill during that time, though Cecilia escaped the worst of it as she spent Christmas in Lincolnshire with her uncle and aunt, Henry and Diana Trollope. Fanny, as usual, nursed the invalids.

In February 1834 the Cincinnati Bazaar was sold. Nicholas Longworth,

Fanny Trollope's erstwhile friend in Cincinnati, held the mortgage on the building. He had obtained a court order for the seizure of the building in January 1834, and the sale was on 18 February. The purchaser was the same Nicholas Longworth, who 'was more widely known as a real estate entrepreneur . . . than as a patron of the arts.' Thomas Anthony, who was a shareholder in the company, got nothing.

Fanny decided that, once again, they must go abroad where their expenses would be much less. Germany was their first choice, as she told Julia, 'This farm is ruinous and we hope to get rid of it – If we succeed in this we shall *all* greatly prefer a year in Germany to taking a house elsewhere', for they could save money and the children learn the language. The plans then changed and she contacted her friend Mrs Fauche, to enlist her help in finding the family a home in Bruges. However, before making a final decision, Fanny planned to take them all to Belgium in the summer, to allow them to see and approve the house. Tom would have finished at Oxford; Anthony, who had not obtained a place at university, would have finished at Harrow, and by then there might be be some money from her Belgium book. As it happened, disaster struck too early. Lord Northwick's agent reported on 11 April 1834:

> I have made many and repeated applications to Mr Trollope for payment of the large arrears due from him to your lordship. . . . I am fearful that Mr Trollope's affairs are in sad disorder, but as he has not now nor for a long time past any live or dead stock upon his premises, I think the most prudent course to pursue will be to seize at the proper time and sell the present growing crops and permit Mr Trollope to let his farm.[42]

Thomas Anthony owed Lord Northwick more than £500, an impossible sum to realize. Fanny accepted the inevitable, and took immediate steps to try and salvage something from the disaster. She had already had all her possessions seized by the creditors in Cincinnati, and now once again, 'everything on the farm went to pay this sum – and the furniture I had so recently purchased among the rest.'[43] Some of the furniture was delivered to her friends the Grants, and Colonel Grant arranged to have it shipped out of the country for her.

The morning of the 18 April 1834, was the day when the bailiffs swooped. Quilton, Lord Northwick's agent, was told by Thomas Anthony that, 'he was going to Cheltenham . . . but I understood Col. Grant that he was gone to London in order to go a Broad.'[44] Thomas Anthony, who would have been sent to a debtors' prison if he had stayed, was driven by Anthony to London and from there dispatched by boat to stay with the Fauche family in Brussels until the others could join him. Anthony told the story in his autobiography, and wrote of his father: 'He had been ill, and must still have been very ill indeed when he submitted to be driven by any one. . . . It was not within his nature to be communicative, and to the last he never told me why he was going to Ostend.'[45]

Poor, sad Thomas Anthony looms in the background of his family's life as a shadowy burden. Suffering disabling headaches, morose, sometimes violent, autocratic, argumentative, impossible to live with, financially inept, and yet fiercely ambitious for his difficult sons, who must in the end have disappointed him sadly, he is a tragic figure.

On his return to Harrow, Anthony discovered the reason for the sudden flight. He was stopped on the road by a man who had been a former gardener of the family, who warned him that if he went on, the horse and gig would be seized by the bailiffs. Anthony then drove to the village and sold the outfit to the ironmonger for £17, but was given no money, as the ironmonger claimed the whole amount as owing to him. Anthony remarked drily, 'I fancy that the ironmonger was the only gainer by my smartness.' He went on, 'When I got back to the house a scene of devastation was in progress, which still was not without its amusement.' The two Grant girls in collusion with Cecilia and Emily, then just fifteen and seventeen, were salvaging as much of the glass and household silver and as many books as they could. 'These things, and things like them, were being carried down surreptitiously through a gap between the two gardens onto the premises of our friend Colonel Grant.'[46] Anthony joined them in their depredations. Lord Northwick's agent, seeing what was happening, abruptly terminated the removal, and summoned the auctioneer to appraise the articles. Twelve pounds was demanded, and duly paid, and the transfer was allowed to continue. Julian Hill was now occupied by bailiffs.

This was a scene which Fanny used in several of her novels. In *Charles Chesterfield*, young Clara Meddows was left with huge debts after Sir George, her father, was killed in a duel and the bailiffs moved in. Her aunt told her that 'the best remedy for that . . . is to go abroad directly.' However, Clara demurred and argued:

> If we cannot pay the whole, let whatever is left be divided fairly and honestly amongst all who have claims, and for God's sake let the trades people be the first paid! . . . Of all the difficulties which surrounded her, the one which pressed most painfully on her feelings was that she anticipated in paying the trades people, who had hazarded the fruits of their time and industry by trusting the honour of her family, and furnished them with the means of daily existence from believing in their honesty.[47]

The Widow Barnaby, in the novel of the same name, was not so lucky when she ran into debt; she was dragged off by the Sheriff's Officers and thrown into the Fleet Prison. Again and again in her books, Fanny drew on her own experiences.

After they had been thrown out of Julian Hill, 'for a few days the whole family bivouacked under the Colonel's hospitable roof, cared for and comforted by that dearest of all women, his wife', said Anthony. 'Then we followed my father to Belgium.'[48]

Not quite the whole family went, and neither did Hervieu accompany them this time. Tom, who was preparing for his final examinations at Oxford, was kept in ignorance of the events until after they had left Harrow, and Henry, who had not recovered from his bout of influenza, and who was showing marked symptoms of consumption, was declared by the apothecary not well enough to travel. Fanny sent the girls off with Anthony to Bruges, and took Henry down to Devon, where he was to be left in the care of cousin Fanny Bent.

There wasn't even time to sign the agreement for her Belgium book. She spent a night with the Grants on her return journey from Devon to Bruges, and wrote to John Murray to tell him that Mr Trollope had decided to take his family abroad for some time. As she could not sign the agreement before her departure, she requested that he would have the kindness to send the estimate of the expenses of publication, and the terms of agreement to her brother, Henry Milton, 'who is authorized to execute the agreement for me'.[49] She did not give him the reasons. She did not even have time to correct the proofs, a job which her brother Henry did for her, and in the confusion her preface was omitted and so were some of Hervieu's plates.

Fanny, by now aged fifty-five, was once again to pick up the pieces. She set off wearily for Bruges to establish a new home for the family.

CHAPTER SEVEN

'Met with resolution, and endured with courage'

Bruges. April 1834–December 1835

Before she finally left for Bruges, Fanny tried to discover how much money remained from both her marriage settlement and the property in Keppel Street, for, according to law, Thomas Anthony was responsible for all his wife's possessions. Her brother Henry Milton helped her with the investigations, and the results were alarming. Frances Eleanor described the situation:

> Mr Trollope's legal knowledge and acumen would have been vigilantly exercised on behalf of his clients, but in the case of his own family affairs they seem to have slept as though under some malignant spell. It appeared that not only had Mrs Trollope's marriage settlement not been registered, but two gentlemen who, with Henry Milton, were her trustees, had never signed it! Moreover, title deeds of property in Keppel St. and elsewhere were found to have been lodged as security in the hands of various persons, without due acknowledgement being received for them.[1]

Some of the losses were irreparable, but enough was salvaged to give Fanny an annual income of £250. This was to keep herself, her husband and the five children aged between sixteen and twenty-four. Fanny wrote to Tom, who had finished taking his finals at Oxford: 'We are, in truth, arrived at the corner I have so often talked about, and if we can but turn it, things must be better with us than we have seen them for years. Two hundred and fifty pounds in a cheap country, with my own management, and the hope of gaining more by my own means, yours, and Henry's, cannot be called a dreary prospect. Courage! and you will do well.'[2]

The rest of the family appeared to accept without question that Fanny would work to support them, and, apart from occasional private tutoring by Tom and Henry, little attempt was made to assist her. Anthony acknowledged this later. 'Now and again there would arise a feeling that it was hard upon my mother that she should have to do so much for us, that we should be idle while she was forced to work so constantly; but we should probably have thought more of that had she not taken to work as though it were the recognised condition of life for an old lady of fifty-five.'[3] As she was to write in *Fashionable Life*, when the heroine was advised to endure her misfortune with patience, 'I do not *intend* to bear it patiently. I think it must be met with resolution, and endured with courage.'[4]

The family moved into the apartment in Bruges which had been selected with the help of their friend Mrs Fauche. Bruges had been chosen for two advantages; cheapness of living and easy access to London. They were not alone in their predicament:

She had heard . . . that multitudes of ruined families went abroad every year, and found that, ruined as they were, they could do perfectly well upon the continent, and this, of course, gave her a very delightful feeling of confidence in the certain sufficiency of her own resources. But she had not heard it exactly stated how many of this multitude had sunk, and slunk, and dwindled away, becoming absorbed, as it were, into more or less width of space, and more or less length of time, till every familiar eye had ceased to follow them.[5]

Not a great deal was salvaged from the house at Julian Hill, although throughout her various troubles Fanny had managed to keep a few precious possessions, 'pretty-pretties', as Anthony called them. She had also bought back out of her own money some indispensable household articles at the appraiser's valuation, and there was, of course, the small amount of furniture saved by Colonel Grant (ostensibly in payment of debts), which he had shipped out of the country for her. She wrote to tell him how she was: 'plotting and planning from morning to night how to make one table and two chairs do the work of a dozen'. She made light of the problems. 'Each of us have already learned to fix ourselves in some selected corner of our different rooms, and believe ourselves at home. – The old desks have found new tables to rest upon, and the few favourite volumes that could not leave us, are made to fill their narrow limits in orderly rows that seem to say – "here we are to dwell together."'[6]

Thomas Anthony's brother, Henry, a clergyman in Lincolnshire, was a constant friend and support to his sister-in-law and her children. When they had to flee to Belgium he lent Fanny £100, this sum to be repaid out of her earnings. It was repaid, and as Frances Eleanor remarked in her biography, 'And, indeed, unless from that source, it is difficult to conjecture how it could ever have been repaid at all!' Anthony agreed:

At this time, and until my father's death, everything was done with money earned by my mother. She now again furnished the house, – this being the third that she had put in order since she came back from America two years and a half ago. There were six of us went into this new banishment. My brother Henry had left Cambridge and was ill. My younger sister was ill. And though as yet we hardly told each other that it was so, we began to feel that that desolating fiend, consumption, was among us. . . . I was an idle, desolate hanger-on, that most hopeless of human beings, a hobble-dehoy of nineteen, without any idea of a career, or a profession, or a trade. . . . But as to my future life I had not even an aspiration. There were two sick men in the house, and hers were the hands that tended them. The novels went on, of course. We had already learned that they would be forthcoming at stated intervals, – and they always were forthcoming. The doctor's vials and the ink bottle held equal places in my mother's rooms. I have written many novels in many circumstances; but I doubt much whether I could write one when my whole heart was by the bedside of a dying son. Her power of dividing herself into two parts, and keeping her intellect by itself clear from the troubles of the world, and fit for the duty it had to do, I never saw equalled.[7]

Henry, who was still very ill, remained in England in the care of Fanny Bent. Fanny T. told Tom: 'I *must* send Fanny Bent money to pay Henry's expenses at Dawlish. And whether we shall have enough to find us bread till the June rents come in, I am very doubtful.' At the end of May, Tom joined them in Bruges, having finished his time at Oxford, but returned to London in June with the 'intention of giving classical teaching to any who were willing to pay about ten shillings an hour for it'. He had taken rooms in Little Marlborough Street, 'in a house kept by a tailor and his mother'. He was able to send his mother good reports of *Belgium and Western Germany*, which had just been published by John Murray. The book was selling well, but she would have to wait for payment.

Before they had left Harrow, Fanny had begun a new novel, *Tremordyn Cliff*, but it was July before she felt able to start writing again; as she told Tom, 'The day before yesterday I opened my MS. again for the first time since Friday 18th April, – on which day we turned our back for ever upon Julian Hill, and I now feel sufficiently inclined to work upon it. But I am shocked and surprised to discover my great want of tools. My paper has almost entirely dwindled away for the letters of the family, and I find not more than half a dozen little pens in my box.'[8] She asked Tom to bring a ream of writing paper and a supply of pens.

Henry, who seemed to have benefited from his three months with cousin Fanny Bent at Dawlish, joined the rest of his family at Château d'Hondt towards the middle of July. Fanny asked him to bring with him six pounds of wax ends, as those she could buy in Bruges were wretchedly bad and very dear; also a supply of old Brown Windsor soap. Tom saw Henry in London on his way to Bruges and was shocked at his appearance – he thought he looked dangerously ill. Henry was, in fact, in the last stages of consumption. However, when he arrived at the Château d'Hondt, his disease went into remission, and Fanny thought there might be hope. In a desperate scheme to save his life, she planned to send him, in the care of Tom, to the West Indies. 'The means for this must come from Murray [the publisher]. His letter tells me that half the impression is sold, and that as soon as the whole is disposed of, he will let me draw on him. My hopes and fears for this make me sick at heart. Yet I do, and will trust that I shall not be doomed to see this precious hope pass away from me.'[9]

Fanny, who would have sacrificed all she possessed to help any of her children, had nothing left to give. Tom made enquiries about the cost of travel to Jamaica and Madeira, and found that the fare to Jamaica was £46, and that to Madeira £35. It was money which Fanny did not have. At the end of July the destination was changed:

After many consultations, and collecting the best information I can get on the subject, we are led to think that sailing about from port to port in the Mediterranean, and passing the winter months on its shores, would be better for Henry than the West Indies. . . . Now that I believe Henry's only hope of life hangs on the change of climate, you may guess with what anxiety I look for every indication that may give me a hope of finding the means of giving it him. . . . My mind is in no good state for composition, but I do my best.[10]

Fanny's daily routine at this stage was exhausting. Henry was a demanding and difficult patient who left her little time for writing; but nevertheless, as the money from the current novel, *Tremordyn Cliff*, was needed for Henry's winter abroad, it must be finished with all speed. Again she wrote to Tom, 'I wait to hear from you that something near one hundred pounds is due from Murray, and when I know this, I will write to him stating the simple fact, and asking his permission to draw for that sum. . . . Learn if possible how the sale goes on. It is dreadful to think that dear Henry's life may perhaps depend upon it!'[11]

In August her worst fears for Henry were realized. The Belgian physician told her that it was too late for a sea cure, and so the Mediterranean trip was abandoned. The novel that she was writing during this heartbreaking time, *Tremordyn Cliff*, had as one of its central characters, a young man who was dying of tuberculosis. Fanny wrote her own anguish into the story.

'Lord Tremordyn is in a situation of great danger, madam. He may survive this attack, but others must be expected.'
'I must know all, sir, – I must know how long – he is likely to remain with me.'

'Your ladyship must prepare yourself to endure much uncertainty on this part,' replied Nouvert. 'Everything will depend on the degree of care he can be persuaded to take of himself. If it were possible to guard him from every powerful emotion, whether of sorrow or joy – from all fatigue of mind and body, and from every inclemency both of climate and season – he might live for years, my lady. But at his age we find it almost impossible to obtain this. Compose yourself, I entreat you madam.'[12]

Fanny wrote despairingly to Tom. 'There are still moments when I think it possible he may recover. But my fears predominate. My life is too sad, and the calls upon me too incessant, to let me write much. But I must submit to this. There is no help for it.'[13]

At the end of August she had some more cheerful news. John Murray, junior, surprised her by a visit to the Château d'Hondt. He brought with him a copy of the *Quarterly Review* which contained a good review of *Belgium and Western Germany*. He took coffee with them, 'and gave us a delightful quantity of literary gossip, all fresh from the mint'. He also spoke of a second edition of the Belgium book.

Fanny's dear friend, Lady Dyer, had also lent her money which was now due to be repaid, but Lady Dyer insisted that the discharge of this debt must be postponed until money matters were easier. Henry, knowing of the availability of the money, begged to be allowed to consult a leading London physician, and in September Fanny agreed, eager to do anything in her power to help him. Fanny writing to Tom to ask him to obtain lodgings for Henry, Emily and herself, was apologetic about the expense, but explained, 'Anything which relieved the tedium of the poor fellow's lingering complaint, would be a blessing.'[14]

They arrived in London on 8 September 1834, and settled into Northumberland Street, Marylebone. A Doctor Harrison was consulted, who paid several visits and examined Henry very thoroughly. He also examined Emily, and even brought in a fellow physician for a second opinion. They both regretfully agreed that there was no hope for Henry, and Emily's health was in a precarious state. He absolutely refused to take a fee.

Fanny's only confidant for this sad news was Tom. As Thomas Anthony became increasingly incapacitated, she leant more and more on her eldest son for support. She told him, 'A kind friend had offered to provide free passages to Madeira. Alas! the first consultation with the medical authorities put an end to all such schemes.' She decided that it would be better for Henry and Emily to be kept in ignorance of the prognosis.

One piece of good news came from Mr Murray the publisher, who paid her a considerable sum of money for the Belgium book. A second edition was published.

On 26 September Fanny returned to Bruges with the two invalids, Henry and Emily. Once back at the Château d'Hondt, she suffered from an acute attack of rheumatism in her shoulders; she was very ill, and barely able to write. She scribbled to Tom, 'My shoulders are in such very severe pain that I can hardly guide my pen', and she asked him to let her friends in Harrow know that this was the reason why she had failed to answer their letters.

Family friends were using every influence to find employment for Anthony, and eventually he had an offer of a commission in an Austrian cavalry regiment if he could first learn German and French. He was allowed a year to do this, and so that it could be accomplished without expense to his parents, he undertook the duties of a classical usher in a school then kept by William Drury in Brussels. The Drurys, too, had suffered financial problems in 1827, and were now living on the Continent. 'To Brussels I went', wrote Anthony, 'and my heart still sinks within me as I reflect that anyone should have intrusted to me the tuition of thirty boys.'[15]

In October Fanny's brother, Henry Milton, invited Cecilia to stay with him and his family in Fulham, London, and she, too, left Bruges. Fanny must have been thankful to get her to a cheerful, friendly environment, and away from possible infection.

On 27 October Fanny wrote to Tom:

The more I feel pressed for the want of money, the more I fret over the ever-recurring impediments to my getting on with *Tremordyn Cliff*. But indeed I do my best, – not to put the impediments aside, for that would be impossible, or, at any rate, what I ought not to do – but I try to get on in spite of them. I have taken to sit up, under the awakening influence of coffee, for about three hours every other night. If I can keep this up it will greatly help me. Henry is very uncertain in his hours. Sometimes he lies in bed very late, and then I scribble away; but when he gets up, it is over for the day. . . . Emily is very little with him. She comes up for half an hour after he has taken his tea, and stays while I read aloud two chapters in the Bible. This was his request. I place her at the side of the fire next me, and at a good distance from his place.

He now lives entirely upstairs, in the room that was the girls'. I sit alone with him from four o'clock – his dinner hour – till nine. This makes a long, long evening. For some time I did not even go downstairs to tea; but now I do, which is a great relief, though it lasts but for a few minutes. . . . You will wonder to hear that he has taken to carpentering, and has bought various tools.[16]

Not only was she nursing Henry and Emily, and trying to write a book, but Thomas Anthony's condition was steadily deteriorating. In one of her later novels Fanny considered the nature of a woman's strength:

People who have taken the trouble of studying perhaps the most powerful, though not the most obvious, peculiarity in the female character, cannot but have perceived that a very strong and resolute power of self-control is at their command, when circumstances call upon them to exert it. It is needless to enter into the philosophy of the subject; but it might be easily shown, that this sort of passive power often very effectually supplies their want of strength, both moral and physical, in other respects.[17]

Anthony, struggling with his duties as a classical usher at the school in Brussels, was given a reprieve after he had been there only six weeks. On 28 October, 'a letter reached me, offering me a clerkship in the General Post Office, and I accepted it. Among my mother's dearest friends she reckoned Mrs Freeling, the wife of Clayton Freeling, whose father, Sir Francis Freeling, then ruled the Post Office. She had heard of my desolate position, and had begged from her father-in-law the offer of a berth in his own office.'[18] Fanny declared, 'I am happier in receiving this news than I thought anything just now could make me. . . . Indeed we have no cause to complain of our friends; for our sorrows have drawn them nearer, and not sent them away from us.'[19]

Fanny's associations with the Freelings stemmed from her childhood in Bristol, when Francis Freeling, then a young lad employed at the Bristol post office, was chosen to accompany the first mail coach service from Bristol to London on 2 August 1784. The post office clerks in London had mutinied against the new plan as impossible to execute, but as the journey took a mere sixteen hours instead of the usual thirty or forty hours, Francis Freeling proved them wrong. This marked the beginning of the fast mail-coach service.

Anthony set off for London and a career in the post office with his mother's blessing, and stopped at Bruges on the way, only to find the number of invalids had been increased. Emily, too, was now worse.

Of course she was doomed. . . . And my father was very ill, – ill to dying, though I did not know it. And my mother had decreed to send my elder sister away to England, thinking that the vicinity of so much sickness might be injurious to her. All this happened in the autumn of 1834; and then my mother was left alone in a big house ouside the town, with two Belgian women-servants, to nurse these dying patients – the patients being her husband and children – and to write novels for the sustenance of the family![20]

Tom agreed:

This was the task in which with agonised mind she never faltered from about nine o'clock every morning till eight o'clock in the evening. Then with wearied body and mind attuned to such thoughts as one may imagine, she had to sit down to her desk to write her novel with all the verve at her command, to please lighthearted readers, till two or three in the morning. This by the help of green tea and sometimes laudanum, she did daily and nightly . . . and lived after it to be eighty-three![21]

In *Tremordyn Cliff*, parts of which almost became her diary during this exhausting time, Fanny wrote: 'A bottle of laudanum always stood on her toilette; Lady Augusta, however, was too careful of her health to use it habitually; nevertheless, she now swallowed sufficient to ensure sleep, after a day of such violent and harassing emotions as made tranquil repose highly necessary.'[22]

In December Fanny wrote to Tom:

This is my night for writing, – not letters, but novel; so do not wonder at my scrawling with more rapidity than precision. Tell my dear, dear friend at Harrow [Mrs Grant] whose kindness to you binds me to her for ever, that I will write to her next week. But tell her also that in spite of everything I go on with my book, which makes the indulgence of scribbling even to her, a thing that must be taken only now and then; – though Heaven knows I love her better than all my heroines. . . . Poor Henry grows daily more exigent as to my time. It is so hard to refuse him in his sad state when he wishes to have me with him. But I do go on, though not so fast as I wish. And I *do* take care of myself, dear Tom; – all the more because my children wish it. My working nights are far from disagreeable, and I sleep the night after, like a top. I have great hopes that my dear kind cousin Fanny Bent will come to me. Think what a comfort this would be! Emily is getting well fast, and if we were quite less sad in our circumstances would, I feel sure, be quite herself again. Henry is *very* bad. Poor dear, dear fellow! It is heartbreaking to watch him. God bless you, my beloved son. Write to me often. It is such a comfort.[23]

At nine in the morning on 23 December 1834, two days before Christmas, Henry died. The staunch companion who had battled for Fanny in those disastrous days at Cincinnati, and shared with her the fun of the *Invisible Girl*, had gone. He was the most unsettled of her children, and had struggled against his father's rigid control and authority to the detriment of his own schooling. The confrontations between Henry and his father were often so savage that Fanny, trying to mediate, had to take laudanum to allow her to sleep. Unable to find a career, in spite of all his parents' endeavours, and bedevilled by his father's impossible aspirations for him, he seemed to be most happy when fossicking for geological specimens. Fanny had fought for him all his difficult life, but she could not save him now. She described such a death in *Tremordyn Cliff*.

> The bed was steeped in blood, which had flowed, even to the floor – but now had ceased to flow. Stretched on this ghastly couch, his head fallen from the pillow, his hands clenched, and his features disfigured by the crimson tide that had choked him, lay Lord Tremordyn – the young, the beautiful, the good. Life was quite extinct and even the inexperienced eyes of his poor wife, who had never looked on death before, could not mistake the fearful glare, the rigid stiffness, the awful strangeness that was left, where she had ever seen the soft, sweet smile of happy love.[24]

To Tom she wrote:

> It is over. My poor Henry breathed his last about nine o'clock this morning. I wish Cecilia to return to us *immediately*, and I would wish you to bring her over. After all I have suffered – and it has been *very much* – I need the comfort of your presence. Make as little delay as possible, – and this very much for Emily's sake. Nothing will do her so much good as having you both here. The doctor declares her well, but delicate and nervous. . . . We want the comfort of seeing you and Cecilia, dearest Tom. We have suffered greatly. Give our most affectionate love to dear, dear Anthony. Tell him I will write to him in a day or two, but *cannot* do it now. God bless you.[25]

Henry was buried in the Protestant section of the cemetery at Bruges, but Tom arrived too late for the funeral. It must have been a miserable Christmas. Tom stayed in Bruges until April, and early in 1835, to try and allay some of Fanny's anxieties about Thomas Anthony's health, he consulted a Dr Herbout, an old army doctor. 'His opinion was that my father's condition, though not satisfactory, did not indicate any cause for immediate alarm.' However, he was probably not the most suitable doctor to consult, as Tom added in his memoirs, 'It is probable that he was more of a surgeon than a physician.'[26]

Fanny was having problems finding a publisher. She had argued with Whittaker and Treacher; and John Murray, though happy with the sales of the Belgium book, was not interested in her novel. It was not easy for her to negotiate from Bruges, and much of this was done for her by her brother, Henry Milton. Without publication, the family had no income; it was a difficult time. Eventually a publisher was found, and a complex agreement drawn up on 10 March 1835, between Mrs Trollope of Northumberland Street, and Mr Bentley, for a novel entitled *The Rivals* (the title was later changed to *Tremordyn Cliff*). There were to be, 'three volumes of the usual number of pages'. The first edition was to consist of one thousand copies and Fanny was to be paid £250 by promissory note 'at nine months from the date hereof'; Bentley might reprint at his own discretion if he felt it necessary; and appropriate payments would be made when the sales reached certain levels. Agreements were also made for two further books, *Paris and the Parisians* and *Jonathan Jefferson Whitlaw*.

When Bentley delayed the publication of *Tremordyn Cliff*, she explained her position: 'Circumstances have rendered what I gain by my pen an object of importance to my family; I therefore may not indulge, as persons differently situated might do, in writing books only to beguile their idle hours, while enjoying the blessing of indifference as to the time and manner of their publication.'[27]

Tom remained in Bruges until the first week in April and travelled round Belgium while his mother was writing in order to pay the family bills. He made frequent visits to Ostend to see Mrs Fauche and her beautiful daughter and to 'vary the monotony of the Château d'Hondt'. For one week of this time in Bruges, he accompanied Cousin Fanny Bent, 'The very plain, Quaker-like, middle-aged old maid, absolutely new to Continental ways and manners . . . in a little tour through those parts of Belgium which I had not already seen.'[28]

When Tom returned to Bruges in April he found a letter waiting for him offering him a mastership at King Edward's Grammar School at Birmingham. 'The salary of the mastership offered me was £200 a year, with, of course prospects of advancement. I at once determined to accept it, and, with the promptitude which in those days characterized me . . . I decided to leave Bruges for Birmingham on the morrow.'[29] He arrived in Birmingham on Sunday 5 April, and then spent a very frustrating few weeks while the authorities at King Edward's School decided when his employment should start. He divided his time between visiting the Grant family in Harrow, and Anthony in London. On 29 April Tom was at Oxford and took his degree, 'which was needed for holding the appointment'. His outstanding bills must have been paid (probably by his mother) or the degree would not have been granted. He returned to Birmingham that night and was told that 'they would not come to an election till midsummer', and so on 8 May Tom left London for Dover. He was on his way to join his mother in Paris, where she had gone with the family to write the travel book commissioned by Bentley. Hervieu had once again joined them, to draw the illustrations. Tom left Calais at 6 p.m. on Friday night 8 May 1835, and reached Paris at 3 a.m. Sunday morning.

At ten the next morning I went to No. 6 Rue de Provence, where I found my parents and my sisters at breakfast. The object of this Paris journey was twofold – the writing of a book in accordance with an agreement which my mother had entered into with Mr Richard Bentley, the father of the publisher, and the consultation of a physician to whom she had been especially recommended respecting my father's health, which was rapidly and too evidently declining. They had been in Paris some time already . . . I was told by my mother that the physician, who had seen my father several times, had made no pleasant report of his condition. . . . This, my first visit to Paris, lasted one month only, from the 9th of May to the 9th of June.[30]

Rue de Provence, where Fanny was living, is just north of the *Opéra*, then almost on the northern boundary of the city, and on the corner of Rue du Fauberg-Montmartre which was one of the areas most frequented by the artistic and literary circles. The narrow street has now fallen into shabby disrepair, but enough of the old houses remain, to give a flavour of the past. Fanny wrote *Paris and the Parisians* in the form of letters to the reader, describing her daily activities and the places and people she met. In the preface she admitted that she, 'learnt much of which I was – in common I suspect with many others – very profoundly ignorant. I found good where I looked for mischief – strength where I anticipated weakness – and the watchful wisdom of cautious legislators, most usefully at work for the welfare of their country, instead of the crude vagaries of a revolutionary government.'[31]

The first letter is dated 11 April 1835:

My Dear Friend,

In visiting Paris it certainly was my intention to describe in print what I saw and heard there; and to do this as faithfully as possible, I propose to continue my old habit of noting in my journal all things, great and small, in which I took an interest. But the task frightens me. . . . The very most I can hope to do will be but to skim lightly over the surface of things.

She wrote of the French Theatre, and of a visit to the Louvre. She was disappointed to find the Château de Versailles, 'that marvellous *chef-d'oeuvre* of the splendid taste and unbounded extravagance of Louis le Grand, is shut up, and has been so for the last eighteen months.' It was being prepared as a national museum by King Louis Philippe, 'the Citizen king'. She wondered, 'that Napoleon did not take a fancy to its vastness; but I believe he had no great taste in the upholstery line, and preferred converting his millions into the sinews of war'. She discussed modern writers, and was assured by one gentleman, that 'Victor Hugo is NOT a popular French writer'. However, Fanny believed that Georges Sand had, 'great, perhaps unequalled powers of writing . . . but she is and has been tossed about in that whirlpool of unsettled principles, deformed taste and exaggerated feeling, in which the distempered spirits of the day delight to bathe and disport themselves, and she has been stained and bruised therein.' However, 'would she but make one effort to free herself from this slough, she might yet become one of the brightest ornaments of the age.'[32] Fanny described Paris social life, and met Madame Récamier once again. 'She is, in truth, the very model of all grace. In person, manner, movement, dress, voice, and language, she seems universally allowed to be quite perfect. . . . Now that she has past the age when beauty is at its height, she is perhaps to be wondered at still more; for I really doubt if she ever excited more admiration than she does at present.'[33] Fanny was invited to Madame Récamier's salon in the Abbaye-aux-Bois, where she had the pleasure of being introduced to M. Chateaubriand, 'and had afterward the pleasure of repeatedly meeting him'. One day they saw King Louis Philippe walking in the Tuileries Gardens, and Hervieu sketched him.

Fanny was offended by the lack of sanitation in Paris: 'It really appears to me, that almost the only thing in the world which other men do, but which Frenchmen cannot, is the making of sewers and drains.' But she revelled in the social scene. 'French talk is very much like champagne. The exhilaration it produces is instantaneous: the spirits mount, and something like wit is often struck out even from dull natures by merely coming in contact with what is so brilliant.' She wrote seventy-two of these letters, filled with gossip and chat of the Paris and politics of 1835, and was delighted to be reunited with Mrs Garnett and Harriet, and her other old acquaintances from her previous visit in 1827. The Trollopes returned to Bruges in early June. When the reviews came out for *Paris and the Parisians* in 1836, they were generally favourable. The *New Monthly Magazine* declared: 'Flippant though she be, she is shrewd and observant; her perceptions are singularly quick, and all she writes is amusing, partly because of the originality of her own ideas, and partly because she has a curious way of illustrating the ideas of others . . . it will help to spend an unoccupied hour cheerfully at this season, for the merits and demerits of Parisian Society must always afford a topic for discussion in our more quiet salons.'

Tom stayed in Bruges until the beginning of October. He was beguiled by the lifestyle: 'It was a queer and not very edifying society, exceedingly strange, and somewhat bewildering to a lad fresh from Oxford who was making his first acquaintance with Continental ways and manners. All the married couples seemed to be continually dancing the figure of "*chassée croisez*," and I, who had no wife of my own, and was not yet old enough to know better, thought it extremely amusing.'[34] Fanny was more realistic about living in Bruges: 'Where everyone knows his place, and keeps it, there can be no danger of jostling. It is the eternal effort of every set amongst us to elbow themselves into the places next above them, which occasions that sort of self-protecting attitude so extremely distasteful to people of all classes on the Continent.'[35]

Between June and December 1835, with *Paris and the Parisians* finished, Fanny began to work on *Jonathan Jefferson Whitlaw*, a harrowing picture of the evils of slavery. It was published in the following spring of 1836, and was a precursor to Harriet Beecher Stowe's *Uncle Tom's Cabin* written fifteen years later in 1852. There were connections. Harriet Beecher Stowe moved to Cincinnati in 1832 when Fanny Trollope's *Domestic Manners of the Americans* was first printed, and so was very aware of Fanny Trollope's notoriety in that city. By the time *Jonathan Jefferson Whitlaw* was published, Fanny was one of the most popular English authors in America, and it seems likely, in view of the many plot similarities, that *Uncle Tom's Cabin* was strongly influenced by Fanny's earlier book. Much later, in 1860, Harriet Beecher Stowe stayed with the family at the Villino Trollope in Florence.

Tom made a brief return to Birmingham on 3 October, to check on the progress of his appointment. 'At Birmingham I found that the Governors of King Edward's School were still shilly-shallying.' He returned to Belgium, and made his slow way back to the Château d'Hondt, which he reached on 15 October, 'to find my father very much worse than when I had left him. He was in bed, and was attended by the Dr Herbout of whom I have before spoken. But he was too evidently drawing towards his end; and after much suffering breathed his last in the afternoon of 23 of October 1835.'[36] Thomas Anthony turned his face to the wall and died, at 3.30 in the afternoon of that bleak October day. Fanny was by his side.

Tom continued in his memoirs:

On the 25th I followed his body to the grave, close to that of my brother Henry, in the cemetery outside the Catherine Gate of the town. The duty was a very specially sad one. He was, and had been, I take it for many years a very unhappy man. All had gone wrong with him; misfortunes fell on him, one on the back of the other. Yet I do not think that these misfortunes were the real and efficient causes of his unhappiness. He was in many respects a singular man. My father's mind was, I think, to a singular degree under the dominion of his body. . . . But it is difficult for one who has never had a similar experience to conceive the degree in which this irritability made the misery of all who were called upon habitually to come into contact with it. I do not think that it would be an exaggeration to say that for many years no person came into my father's presence who did not forthwith desire to escape from it. . . . Happiness, mirth, contentment, pleasant conversation, seemed to fly before him as if a malevolent spirit emanated from him . . . and he was a man who would fain have been loved, and who knew that he was not loved, but who knew neither how to manifest his desire for affection nor how to conciliate it.

What so grievously changed him? . . . I believe that he was destroyed mind and body by calomel, habitually used during long years. Throughout life he was a laborious and industrious man. I have seen few things of the kind with more of pathos in it than his persevering attempt to render his labour of some value by compiling a dictionary of ecclesiastical terms. . . . And truly, as I have said, it was a pathetic thing to see him in his room at Château d'Hondt, ill, suffering, striving with the absolutely miserable, ridiculously insufficient means he had been able with much difficulty to collect, to carry on his work. . . . He was dying – he must, I think, have known that he was; he had not got beyond D in his dictionary; all the alphabet was before him, but he would not give up; he would labour to the last. My mother was labouring hard, and her labour was earning all that supplied very abundantly the needs of the whole family. And I cannot help thinking that a painful but not ignoble feeling urged my poor father to live at least equally laborious days, even though his labour was profitless. Poor father![37]

Fanny, always loyal to Thomas Anthony, took over the entire financial support of the family once she became aware of the state of his business affairs. The only glimpses we have of what must have been an almost intolerable situation come again from her novels. One such clue was the opening paragraph of *Love and Jealousy*:

Without meaning to be in the slightest degree uncivil to the lords of the creation, I certainly think that the demise of a husband may occasionally be felt rather a relief than as an affliction by his widow. Neither is it absolutely unnatural or impossible, that the death of a wife may, in like manner, produce less of sorrow than of thankfulness. But it is rarely that the condition of a widower can be so obviously improved as that of a widow by such an event.[38]

Later she wrote an entire novel about a man who made his young wife's life a living hell, because of his one fault, his unreasonable temper: 'and this was enough, and ever will be found so, to blight and wither all the gifts of nature and of fortune. . . . None can doubt it who have ever watched the influence of an ill-tempered husband upon every hour of his wife's existence.'[39]

Anthony, in his autobiography, wrote of his father:

I sometimes look back, meditating for hours together, on his adverse fate. He was a man, finely educated, of great parts, with immense capacity for work, physically strong very much beyond the average of men, addicted to no vices, carried off by no pleasures, affectionate by nature, most anxious for the welfare of his children, born to fair fortunes, – who, when he started in the world, may be said to have had everything at his feet. But everything went wrong with him. The touch of his hand seemed to create failure. He embarked on one hopeless enterprise after another, spending on each all the money he could at the time command. But the worse curse to him of all was a temper so irritable that even those he loved the best could not endure it. We were all estranged from him, and yet I believe that he would have given his hearts blood for any of us. His life as I knew it was one long tragedy.[40]

Shortly after Thomas Anthony's death, Fanny wrote a desperate letter to John Murray to ask for the advance of a little money on the sale of the second edition of the Belgium book. She explained that she did not wish to be troublesome, but was really in distress for the paying of some urgent claims. Unable to get a satisfactory answer, she went to England in November to try and sort out some of her business affairs, taking with her Emily, who was far from well. Fanny intended to settle the family into a new home, and then to take Emily to Rome for the winter in the hope that the climate would benefit the child. Dr Harrison examined Emily and advised that she required the greatest care, and would be better to remain in England until the spring. Fanny wrote to Tom, who had remained at the Château d'Hondt with Cecilia to supervise the packing up of their possessions.

> After this opinion, I can, of course, have no farther thoughts of Italy for the present. I have therefore determined on immediately looking out for a house near London. I much wish I could come to help you in getting through all the business you will have to perform previous to bidding a final adieu to Belgium, but this is quite impossible. She has by no means recovered the cold and fatigue of her journey hither. . . . She is very weak, and eats hardly anything. I am *miserably* anxious, but struggle to keep up my spirits, as I must set to work again directly.

Fanny was torn between her conflicting responsibilities and she wrote a few days later, 'My fears are all directed to one point, – the health of my dear Emily. If she is very ill, I much misdoubt my power of writing. Yet in any case I shall remember, dear Tom, that you have claims on me as well as my dear girl in her sick chamber; and I will earnestly try to do my duty to both.'[41]

Fanny eventually found a house in Monken Hadley, just north of London, but could not get possession of it until January. Until then she must stay in London, and she found lodgings in Northumberland Street near Anthony. Emily's condition deteriorated and Fanny wrote to Tom on 30 November, 'I am very greatly alarmed about my Emily. She has lost strength rapidly, she eats nothing, her cough is decidedly worse than it has ever been. *My anxiety is dreadful,* – and the more so because I dare not show it. But this is a theme I must not dwell on – for all our sakes.'[42]

Tom remained in Bruges to terminate the lease and sort out the furniture. Cecilia, who now must be kept away from Emily, spent the winter with Lady Milman at Pinner. Fanny, alone with her maid Mrs Cox, stayed in Northumberland Street to watch over the dying Emily.

CHAPTER EIGHT

'As dauntless as an Alexander'

Hadley. January 1836–Autumn 1838

After Christmas, in early 1836, Fanny and Emily moved into the sanctuary of their new house at Monken Hadley, a little village north of London. The house, Grandon, was recorded in 1832 as having been taken for £90 per annum for a period of seven years, and Fanny took over the last three years of this lease from a Mrs Bouchier; they were listed as joint tenants in the church rates of 1836. Frederick Cass, in his history of Monken Hadley, written in 1880, described the location: 'Mrs Trollope, the novelist, occupied about this time the residence on Hadley Green contiguous to the almshouses on the south.'[1]

The Wilbraham Almshouses squat solidly beside the London Road. They were built of local flint, with cobbled walls and they stand in a matronly row watching over the village green. A number of Georgian houses cluster around the green; the area has changed little since 1836, and the attractive eighteenth-century house leased by Fanny stands beside the Almshouses – the old red bricks glow in the afternoon sun. Inside are low beams, spacious rooms and uneven floors. The long front room, looking out over the duckpond and the goose common, was then two; the room at the far end, with wooden shuttered windows, was a study, and it was there that Fanny settled down to write some of her best books. The drawing room is large and comfortable, with an elegant bow window looking out over the well-kept garden at the back where roses still grow, and at the other end there was once a conservatory. It was to this peaceful haven that Fanny brought her beloved youngest child to die. Anthony now became his mother's main support. The village was served by coaches which left the Old Bell at Holborn twice daily; it was easy for Anthony to travel to and from his work in London. Meanwhile, in Bruges, Tom packed their possessions and concluded affairs at Château d'Hondt.

Emily faded fast. On 12 February Anthony told Tom:

It is all over! Poor Emily breathed her last this morning. She died without any pain, and without a struggle. Her little strength had been gradually declining, and her breath left her without the slightest convulsion, or making any change in her features or face. Were it not for the ashy colour, I should think she was sleeping. I never saw anything more beautifully placid and composed. . . . It is much better that it is now, than that her life should have been prolonged only to undergo the agonies which Henry suffered. Cecilia was at Pinner when it happened, and she has not heard of it yet. I shall go for her tomorrow. You went to the same house to fetch her when Henry died.[2]

Tom, in his memoirs, remembered his sister Emily as:

. . . full of fun and high spirits. There is a picture of her exactly as I remember her. She is represented with flowing flaxen curls and wide china-blue eyes, sitting, with a brown Holland pinafore on, before a writing desk and blowing a prismatically coloured soap-bubble. . . . Her youngest child had ever been to my mother as the apple of her eye, and her loss was for the passing day a crushing blow. But, as usual with her, her mind refused to remain crushed. . . . She had the innate faculty and tendency to throw sorrow off when the cause of it had passed.[3]

Or at least she did not allow that sorrow to be witnessed by her sons. As she wrote in *Fashionable Life*: 'The affecting of a light-hearted gay tone of feeling when the spirits are oppressed by heavy anxiety, is no easy task.'[4]

In the space of fourteen turbulent months, Fanny had lost two of her children to consumption, and her husband to what the *Dictionary of National Biography* described as 'premature decay, partly induced by an injudicious course of medicine'. Cecilia, too, was thought to be 'delicate'.

Today, with our better knowledge of the causes of tuberculosis, it is interesting to speculate whether the infection – which eventually caused the deaths of Henry, Emily and Cecilia – originated from the incessant, offensive spitting of the Americans, found so repugnant by Fanny.

The vicar of Monken Hadley was the Reverend R.W. Thackeray, who held the living left to him by his father in 1831. Anthony attended Emily's funeral; funerals were exclusively for men, and he later used the memory in *The Bertrams*, part of which he set in Hadley. Mr Bertram's house is almost certainly based on his mother's rented house, where he spent so much time. Fanny herself constantly used places and people she knew in her novels. She confessed to this in the opening paragraph of *Gertrude*. 'It is much safer, for many reasons, to give fictitious names to the various scenes in which the circumstances occurred, than to challenge the criticism which might discover either too much, or too little of truth in the details, were the real names to be given.'[5]

She, too, probably used Hadley as the village of Deepbrook in her anti poor-law novel, *Jessie Phillips*:

The parish church should, in every village, be as near to the centre of it as possible, – and so it was at Deepbrook. The few straggling buildings, which seemed as if they had run away from the quiet village green, at one corner of which the holy building stood, to the highroad leading to London, in order to be near the gay world, were the only dwellings in the parish that were not within a mile of its church. . . . The centrical little church had very close to it a centrical parsonage . . . and thus though close to the church on one side, to the goose common of the village, where there were no less than three very busy shops, on another, and flanked by one neighbour's grounds here, and by those of another there, the dwelling . . . was exactly what that of our English country clergymen ought to be – tranquil, gentleman-like, and comfortable.[6]

Emily's grave can be seen in the churchyard of St Mary the Virgin, with a stone at the head and the foot. It is set at the back of the church with the headstone close to the flinty church wall, yellow roses bloom alongside, and a bramble climbs around the grave. They say the sweetest blackberries grow there. The path through the churchyard leads out over Hadley Common, and it is easy to imagine Fanny and the children striding down the bridle paths to where the woods take over from the rough grass.

Fanny, with three adult children to support, began to pick up the pieces. Anthony, in London, was earning a small salary of about £90 a year which slowly rose to £140. It was barely sufficient for his needs, but with Fanny's help he could get by. As he wrote in his autobiography. 'During the whole of this time I was hopelessly in debt. There were two intervals, amounting together to nearly two years, in which I lived with my mother, and therefore lived in comfort, – but even then I was overwhelmed with debt. She paid much for me, – paid all that I asked her to pay, and all that she could find out that I owed. But who in such a condition ever tells all and makes a clean breast of it?'[7]

Tom was waiting for his appointment to start at King Edward's School, Birmingham, and he and Cecilia lived at Hadley. Anthony was at home certainly for part of that time.

Thomas Anthony, though a lawyer, had died without making a will. When the furniture and belongings were sent back to England they were seized, and granted to George Barnes, 'a creditor', by the Prerogative Court of Canterbury. George Barne (probably the same), who later assumed the family name Trollope, was a cousin of Thomas Anthony and the godfather of Arthur William the Trollope's third son. No doubt the goods found their way back to their rightful home. However, in the meantime there was an urgent need to raise some ready money, and Fanny, increasingly practical as she became more experienced, made an unusual agreement with Richard Bentley, her publisher:

27th, April 1836. Hadley.

Memorandum of an agreement entered into this day between Mrs Trollope of Hadley on the one part and Richard Bentley of New Burlington on the other part.

The said Mrs Trollope hereby undertakes to write and the said Richard Bentley to publish the undermentioned four works upon the terms hereinafter stated. viz.

First a novel founded on American Manners to be entitled *Jonathan Jefferson Whitlaw* and to form three volumes pst 8vo of similar extent to *Tremordyn Cliff.*

Secondly another work of fiction under the title of *The Unco' Good* (or by whatever name it may hereafter be called) and to form three volumes post 8vo of like extent.

Thirdly a work describing Mrs Trollope's travels in Austria and more particularly her residence in Vienna to be treated in a similar manner to her recent Book called *Paris and the Parisians* and to form two volumes 8vo equal in extent to that work.

Fourthly A similar account of her Travels and Residence in various parts of Italy to form also two volumes 8vo of like extent.

The said Mrs Trollope agrees to dispose of, and the said Richard Bentley agrees to purchase the entire copyright of each and every of the four above named works for the following consideration viz:–

1. Jonathan Jefferson Whitlaw 300 pounds Nine months from delivery.

2nd. The Unco' Good 400 pounds Nine months from delivery.

3rd. Travels in Austria for 500 pounds
    200 at 3 months, 200 at 6 months,
    100 at 9 months

4. Travels in Italy 550 pounds nine months from the date of delivery of entire copy.

There was also a further agreement in consideration of the above, 'that all the contingent right and interest . . . in a work called *Paris and the Parisians* is given up by her in favour of the said Richard Bentley and the entire copyright of such work now becomes his full property accordingly.

Lastly the said Mrs Trollope hereby agrees to furnish, whenever called upon to do so a regular assignment of either or all of the four above mentioned works and also of *Paris and the Parisians* at the cost of the said Richard Bentley.

Also preserved in the British Library is a strange little piece of paper entitled:

Memorandum of an agreement made *27 April 1836* Mrs Trollope of Hadley.

a work to be called *The Temporal History of the Popes* to form *4 volumes* 8vo containing at least *450 pages* of *36 lines each volume.*

However, she must have thought better of this idea because written across it in pencil is, 'cancelled by mutual consent May 1858. Cancelled by Mrs Trollope returning her agreement.'[8] One wonders who was to write the papal history.

The first of the promised books, begun in Bruges, was now completed. *Jonathan Jefferson Whitlaw* was published by Bentley in 1836 and went into a second edition in the same year. By the terms of the agreement, Fanny had to wait nine months for the first, and only, payment, and so she began work on the next novel immediately, *The Unco' Good,* which was published as *The Vicar of Wrexhill.*

Now with the trauma of Bruges behind her, and the promise of a more financially secure future, Fanny began to enjoy life. As Tom said of his mother:

> . . . her new home became a centre of social enjoyment and attraction for all, especially the young, who were admitted to it. . . . Our society consisted mainly of friends staying in the house, or of flying visitors from London. As usual too, my mother soon gathered around her a knot of nice girls, who made the house bright. For herself she seemed always ready to take part in all the fun and amusement that was going; and was the first to plan dances, and charades, and picnics, and theatricals on a small and unpretending scale. But five o'clock of every morning saw her at her desk; and the production of the series of novels, which was not brought to a conclusion till it had reached the hundred and fifteenth volume, though it was not begun till she was past fifty, never ceased.[9]

Fanny, in her novel *Love and Jealousy,* voices the same sentiments. 'The scheme on which all her thoughts had fixed themselves ever since the full consciousness of her liberty had succeeded to the agitation of her unexpected widowhood, was the collecting round her a circle of amiable, intellectual, and accomplished people, of whom she might become the centre and the idol.'[10]

Fanny decided once more to travel, as she was so often to do when she had survived a crisis. America, Brussels, Western Germany, and Paris, had all provided material for travel books in the past. Now, armed with a commission from Bentley, her destination was to be Vienna.

The party consisted of Fanny, Tom, who would act as courier, his Oxford friend, Mr Burberry, Hervieu, to draw the illustrations, Cecilia, and Fanny's maid, Mrs Cox. Fanny required a male escort and Tom, who was unemployed, was the obvious choice. Anthony, the only member of the family earning money, apart from his mother, was therefore not to be of the party. One can sympathize with his feeling of exclusion. The group assembled at Anthony's lodgings in London on the evening of 21 July 1836, and caught the night mail-coach to Dover, crossed the Channel, and then on to Paris where they collected Cecilia, who had been staying with the Garnetts. They stayed for a few days in Paris to see old friends, and then set off via the Tyrol and Salzburg to Munich and Ratisbon. From Ratisbon to Vienna they planned to journey down the Danube by cargo barge.

They stopped to view every sight which would add interest to the book, including one journey into the heart of a salt mine near Hallein in the depths of the Durremberg Mountains. Fanny described the experience for her readers. Putting on white linen jackets and trousers over their dresses they 'entered the mountain by a low narrow door, each armed with a candle'. They descended narrow timbered galleries, 'but every here and there the naked rock appeared sparkling with crystals of salt', and travelled downwards for 'above a mile' until they reached the mouth of an abyss:

It was, in truth, neither more nor less than a black yawning hole; and, as we stood trembling on the edge of it, we were told that we were to seat ourselves one at a time on an inclined plane, the first few feet of which were made dimly visible by the candle of one of the guides, and so slide into the impenetrable darkness of the gulf below. For a moment I felt that the thing was impossible, and said so.

However, the old miner, who was their guide, assured Fanny she would be safe if she trusted herself to him. Bravely she seated herself behind him, 'and shot down the distance, which was 126 ft, with a velocity that almost took away my breath. The black darkness before us, the flashing and imperfect light that the guide's candle threw around us as we flew downwards, and the dizzy swiftness of the motion, were altogether quite enough to fill the fancy. . . . This sort of downward flying was repeated four times.' They then arrived at an unforgettable scene:

an immensely large natural cavern, the middle of which is occupied by a lake as black as night, was made visible by a multitude of flambeaux arranged around the water's edge, the whole scene producing an effect terrific and solemn beyond that of any combination of objects I ever looked upon . . . a bark became dimly visible. We were given to understand that this spectre boat was destined to bear us across the black waters. . . . Slowly and silently we were wafted over the water. . . . Shortly after the voyage was accomplished, we came to the last and deepest of the gulfs by which the mountain is perforated; and slid down a distance of between 500 and 600 ft, with a velocity which I think was increased by the guide's improved opinion of our courage, and a wish that, before we quitted his subterranean habitation, we should be permitted to know at what rate mortals might safely approach the earth's centre.

Fanny described the nature of the transporting device.

Two round and highly polished pieces of timber, about a foot apart, go from the top to the bottom of these descents; along one of these passes a rope as thick as a man's wrist, and the person about to take flight, being seated on these cylindrical timbers, passes the right leg under the rope, which presses the limb with sufficient tightness to check the too violent rapidity of the movement. The right hand may also grasp this rope to assist in regulating the progress, while the left holds the candle.

For the last part of the journey the party were asked to sit astride a long narrow plank, 'and in this manner, almost as it seemed on the balance, with our feet carefully drawn in under us, we were drawn with great velocity down a steep descent on an iron railway by two men. The slightest movement, such as the extending a hand or foot a few inches, must have been followed by the inevitable fracture of the limb.' The whole excursion occupied three and a half hours, and the intrepid Fanny added a warning: 'Only those who are conscious of bearing a stout heart within them, should venture to follow me throught the bowels of the Durremberg.'[11]

It was, in truth, a daring adventure for a lady of fifty-seven who suffered from vertigo, but as Fanny wrote in *Hargrave*: 'When a woman of strong feeling is placed in a situation sufficiently exciting to make her thoroughly and entirely forget the weakness of her frame and the habitual cowardice of her nature, she becomes as dauntless as an Alexander.'[12]

The party travelled on via Salzburg to Munich where Fanny dismissed the new palace in one sentence. 'There are but few palaces of which very much can be said to good purpose, and this is not one of them.'

She warned her readers to take their own sheets: 'for the habit of using well-aired linen appears to be as little known or valued in German inns, as it could be in the realms of his majesty the water-king. . . . When you set forth to follow my steps, do not omit this precaution.'

In Ratisbon they explored the dungeons. The next day they were to embark on the Danube for the voyage to Vienna. Fanny confessed to her readers: 'I can hardly tell you whether I dread it, or wish for it most, for we have been down to the river's edge to see the boat, and it certainly does not look very promising of comfort; but there is nothing better to be had.' The boat, which was intended primarily for cargo, was no more than a raft-like structure of unpainted deal boards. On this was a cabin taking up almost all the deck space, which was full of cargo, with a small covered portion set aside for passengers in case of rain, containing plank benches with a rough dresser between them for a table. The only way down to this cabin was via a plank, 'with sticks nailed across it to sustain the toes of the crawler who would wish to avoid jumping down seven or eight feet'. The sloping roof on top of this ark was where the passengers were expected to sit, on a bench about 6 ft long, with their legs dangling over the river. Fanny was apprehensive:

> There is not the slightest protection whatever at the edge of this abruptly sloping roof, which forms the only deck; and nothing but the rough unslippery surface of the deal planks of which it is formed . . . can prevent those who stand or walk upon it from gently sliding down into the stream. . . . I presume we must by some means or other be conveyed to the before-mentioned bench on the roof, and there be stowed as safely as the nature of the position will admit. Well! . . . We have DETERMINED, one and all of us, to navigate the Danube between Ratisbon and Vienna . . . [13]

One can see where the phrase, 'a very Trollope' originated, which was used by the publisher, John Murray, to describe an enterprising tourist.

Luckily for the less stalwart members of the party, Tom, in his capacity of courier, managed to bribe the captain to allow them to have a plank fixed at the extreme bow of the boat, where they could have a space of some 9 or 10 square feet for their sole use. 'Our fruit, cold meat, wine, bread, and so forth, are stowed near us; desks and drawing-books can all find a place; and, in short, if the sun will but continue to shine as it does now, we shall consider ourselves the best accommodated travellers by land or by water.'[14] Unfortunately the next day it rained, and they were all forced to shelter, 'in the little deal box, and alas! not our suffering selves alone, but three or four incessant smokers with us! . . . and we with no more power to help ourselves than a parcel of poultry packed alive in a basket.'[15]

Eventually the clouds cleared and at nightfall they disembarked at Pleintling and sought beds for the night. The only accommodation to be had was in a dismal looking old house, where they were shown into a strange wild-looking chamber where there were six beds and such furniture, 'as might have been bought at sale by auction at the dismantling of a baronial castle in the fourteenth century'. The sour old fellow who was their host made a visit to inform them 'that, as they had only taken four of the six beds . . . he should bring in two men to occupy the remainder'. This caused the spare beds to be speedily removed to another room by the men of the party! The next morning when they were about to embark the host appeared again, and demanded double the reckoning agreed on the night before; which demand was refused. However, 'a multitude of men suddenly appeared on the water's edge, evidently prepared for some act of violence,' and surrounded the travellers. Fanny, fearing that they would all be murdered 'vehemently urged' the captain to go on shore and pay whatever sum might be demanded. This done, they were allowed to leave, but the incident was reported to the police at the next stopping place.[16] On 16 September 1836 the Trollope party arrived at their final destination, Vienna.

Following Waterloo in 1815, the Congress of Vienna had been held in the Imperial Palace to decide how to carve up Europe and restore the royal rulers to power. The leaders, Prince Metternich of Austria, Lord Castlereagh of Great Britain, William von Humbolt of Prussia and Czar Alexander I of Russia, plotted to control the Congress and the final compromise altered the borders of countries with little regard for the citizens, or their allegiances. The prizes of war were dealt out among the victors. In time this would have far-reaching consequences in Europe, leading to much unrest in the mid-nineteenth century and beyond, as the occupied states struggled to free themselves from foreign domination.

The Trollopes managed to find temporary lodgings for a month, and set off to explore the city. Fanny was surprised to find that a city which had received such international prominence as Vienna, was so small. 'The walls of Vienna can be walked round by a party of ladies, chattering all the time, within the hour; or, in plainer English, the circuit is about three miles.'[17]

They spent a romantic day exploring Durenstein, more than a day's journey from Vienna, and scrambled up a steep mountainside to explore the ruins of the castle where Richard the Lionheart had been imprisoned, and from which he had been rescued by his faithful minstrel, Blondel. It was a steep and dangerous climb. 'There are corners to be passed in ascending, which become more terrible a hundred fold on coming back, from whence the eye looks sheer down . . . how many feet I know not, but enough to turn my head, without a bush or a crag to save one from vertigo.' Fanny always suffered from vertigo, but seldom allowed it to stop her exploring. As she said, 'so few people take the trouble of penetrating to the distant and difficult spots best calculated to arouse the feelings.'[18]

Back in Vienna again, the family had to find more permanent lodgings, which proved no easy task. As Tom remembered, 'nobody who was anybody would have dreamed of living on the outside of the sacred barrier of the wall any more than a member of the fashionable world in London would dream of living to the eastward of Temple Bar . . . even in the case of foreigners like ourselves, it was deemed . . . necessary, or at least expedient, that we should find lodgings *in the city*, despite the exceeding difficulty and the high price involved in procuring them.'[19] Eventually, with the help of a friend, they found a furnished apartment in the Hohen Markt. 'These lodgings, which we consider ouselves as so happy to have found, consist of seven tolerably-sized rooms, with a small kitchen, for which we have paid £100 for the term, ending the 7th May.' Fanny was not impressed by the furniture and recommended, 'that for a family wishing to make Vienna their home for the winter, it would be a much better plan to take unfurnished lodgings, and hire furniture according to their wants and wishes.'[20]

We know in exactly which part of the Hohen Markt Fanny lived from the view, sketched by Hervieu, 'as taken from the door of the house in which I live'. Amazingly, the outlook remains unaltered, although parked cars have now replaced the far more colourful market stalls. On 30 October 1836 Fanny noted that 'a violent change has come over this mutable world of ours since my last letter'. It had begun to snow.

They went to the theatre and the opera and saw the Emperor and Empress. Fanny wrote that 'the people of Vienna are undergoing one of those fits of fashion to which all societies are occasionally subject . . . Vienna is in truth just now suffering severely from an access [sic] of waltzes, and rococo Handel, Mozart, Haydn, and the like, are banished from "ears polite", while Strauss and Lanner rule the hour.'[21]

'The celebrated Mrs Trollope', was the guest of honour at many parties during the winter of 1836/7, and enjoyed herself immensely. Tom noted:

The division of the society into classes, still more marked in Vienna than, probably, in any other city of Europe, at that time almost amounted to a division into castes. . . . The society of Vienna at that day – *society par excellence* – was a very small one . . . I forget entirely what were the introductions which placed my mother and her party at once in the very core of this small and exclusive society. But we did find ourselves so placed, and that at once . . . whatever was the 'Open Sesame' my mother possessed, the fact was that all doors were open to her with the most open-handed hospitality.[22]

Together with Tom and Cecilia, Fanny was invited to dinner with Sir Frederick Lamb, the British Ambassador, where she was to meet Prince and Princess Metternich. 'I am delighted at this: of all the distinguished men in Europe, Prince Metternich is the one I feel the greatest curiosity to become acquainted with.' Prince Metternich escorted Fanny into dinner, and they conversed in French. She found 'his person and manners eminently dignified,' and admired his air of 'calm philosophical tranquillity'. A few days later, the Trollope party were invited to dine at Prince Metternich's Palace, where Fanny met the Princess for the first time. She was very taken with the Princess. 'There is a variety, a mobility of countenance in her, that attracts the attention with a charm which it is difficult to describe; and moreover, she is perfectly free from affectation and the apparent consciousness of beauty than . . . I ever saw so pretty a woman. . . . It is, in truth, a face and a manner that one should never be weary of watching.'[23]

Tom was also smitten. 'She was one of the most beautiful women I ever looked on. She was rather small, but most delicately and perfectly formed in person, and the extreme beauty of her face was but a part, and not the most peerless part, of the charm of it. . . . Every feature of her face was instinct with meaning and intelligence.'[24]

While enjoying the social life, Fanny was disappointed by the 'remarkable absence of all literary discussion . . . in the salons of Vienna. . . . I discover that they read a great deal, and in several languages; but it certainly appears to be considered as *mauvais ton* to let this fact transpire in company.'[25] Tom agreed. 'In fact, the *grand monde* of that day in Vienna was frivolous, unintellectual, and, I am afraid I must say, uneducated to a remarkable degree.'

On 30 November 1836 Fanny and her family attended the installation of eleven Knights of the Golden Fleece at the Imperial Palace, and described the pomp and circumstance of the ceremony and the colourful scene. 'No robes of modern days can compare with the gold and crimson waves that floated round these noble knights. . . . It is, I should conceive, impossible that any ceremony of the kind could be more dignified, more magnificent, more stately, in all its features, than this installation.'[26]

In complete contrast, the next day, on 1 December, they visited the subterranean catacombs of St Stephen's. If Fanny had realized what she was about to view, 'we might have escaped gazing upon the most horrible scene that could be exhibited to mortal eyes.' They walked into the catacombs past neatly coffined bodies in vaults on either side of the passage, but then, they reached a large square vault:

> . . . in which our conductor paused; and, holding low the light he carried, showed us, stretched in horrible disorder on the ground, – which was rugged and uneven with huge masses of obscene decay, – a multitude of wholly naked and uncoffined bodies, in every attitude that accident could produce. . . . Had I been left in clearer possession of my judgement, I should surely have insisted upon turning back again, and regaining with all the strength left me the blessed sight of day and human life; but I felt sick, horror-struck, and utterly bewildered, and followed the party . . . without uttering a word.

They continued through vault after vault past heaps of carcasses and open coffins, until eventually they reached 'the blessed light of day'. As Fanny remarked, the contrast between 'this horrible museum of death' and the stately pomp of the previous day, was 'an awful practical sermon upon the evanescent nature of human greatness and of mortal splendour. . . . I returned from it, perhaps, more shocked than edified, and by no means feel disposed to recommend the lesson to any of my fellow-creatures.'[27]

Tom received the long-awaited summons to commence teaching at King

Edward's School in Birmingham. He was to start at the beginning of 1837, and so left Vienna in December. As Christmas approached, 'a more than usual degree of animation' began to pervade the town. Fanny saw her first Christmas tree, a custom not generally known in England until it was introduced by Prince Albert. She explained to her readers. 'The tree is called, "the tree of the little Jesus"; and on its branches are suspended all sorts of pretty toys, bijous, and bon-bons, to be distributed among those who are present at the *fête*.' Fanny and family were invited to dine at Prince Metternich's Palace to see the illumination of *the tree*, and watch the presents being given to the children, and, finally, the sugar-plums distributed. Presents were also given to all the guests.

In January 1837 the Carnival was in full swing, in every sense, as Fanny explained:

> The whole population seems as much actuated by one common and universal feeling, as if an irresistible spell had fallen on the empire, enforcing them all to waltz. . . . I have sometimes looked around with anxiety to see in what condition the tables and chairs might be; and have occasionally felt considerable alarm lest my own venerable feet should be seized upon by the same mysterious influence, and run away with me.[28]

Fanny noted the strict line of demarcation between the aristocracy and the merchants, who are always referred to as bankers. 'Where kindness has been shown on all sides, it is ungracious to say that one is either better or worse than another.' One group, whose rank and fortune placed them in the highest class of society, were a clique who called themselves '*la crème*', and a few spirits with even more exclusive pretensions, 'take up the strain at least an octave higher, and say "*Nous sommes la crème de la crème.*"' Fanny told the story of one gentleman who was permitted to call himself '*la crème*' and who was seen to be talking to a beautiful unmarried girl of high Austrian blood, but who was not of '*la crème*'. When he had finished his conversation with the beauty he was surrounded by three middle-aged, married, would-be dancing ladies, who were '*crème de la crème*', and who asked him if he had asked the Countess to dance.

'"Yes, I have!" was the bold reply.

'"You positively must not dance with her!" cried the three creamy ones in a breath . . . "at least, if you do, you will cease to be one of us."

'What would six months at Spilsberg [the jail] be, compared to this threatened banishment?' The young man hastily made his apologies to the girl.[29]

The cost of living in Vienna was high and Fanny was again running short of money; she wrote to John Murray to ask if there was anything left from the sale of the Belgium book. It seems there was not.

The original plan had been to go on to Italy from Vienna, to gather material for an Italian travel book, but after the gaiety of life in Vienna, Fanny decided to postpone the trip and return to Hadley. She wrote to Julia, 'Our reason for not going on to Italy was the appointment of Tom at Birmingham. It would have been impossible for Cecilia and I to have gone without him.' Fanny refuted the story that Cecilia, who was not strong, had found the rigours of the trip too taxing. 'Cecilia is very well and who ever told you that she suffered from her Vienna dissipation was not correct.'[30]

On 4 May 1837 Fanny and her party reluctantly left Vienna. On the last night they dined with Princess Metternich, and the next morning set off for England via Rotterdam and the Hague. A month later, on 10 June, they were back in England, and Fanny was once again enjoying the roses in her Hadley garden. They returned home just before the death of William IV on 20 June 1837. The Victorian age was about to begin.

The promised books appeared at regular intervals. *The Vicar of Wrexhill*, begun in the spring of 1836, came out on 7 September 1837. *Vienna and the Austrians* was written during the stay in Vienna, and was in the hands of the publishers by 4 July, a month after their return. It was published in 1838. Concurrently, using her own observations and experiences, Fanny set to work to create a fictional account of Austria which she called *A Romance of Vienna*, sold to Bentley in December 1837, and published in 1838. The agreement with Bentley was being kept.

The Vicar of Wrexhill was a satirical attack on the Evangelical Church and its religious excesses, and contained the first, and most hard-hitting, of Fanny's numerous fictional religious dissertations. Fanny, the Reverend Milton's daughter, used both her father's opinions and her own enquiring mind, to satirize and discuss many religious beliefs with telling effect, an ability which Anthony inherited. The much-disliked Reverend J.W. Cunningham, from Harrow days, was thought to have been the model for the Reverend W.J. Cartwright in the novel; an accusation denied by Fanny. However, T.H.S. Escott had heard that 'The more carefully wrought accounts of mental distress, aggravated by Calvinistic Treatment, were a transcript of the ordeal through which her friend Henrietta Skerrett had passed. Subsequently she had misgivings lest her caricature might have gone too far.' In the novel, the vicar insinuated himself, by means of unctuous prayers and passionate prayer meetings, into the hearts of the wealthy widows and young girls of the village of Wrexhill. Using Evangelicalism as a disguise for his own ambitions, he married the wealthy, but naive, widow of one of his parishioners, and all but seduced her daughter.

'How sweetly does youth, when blessed with such a cheek and eye as yours, Miss Fanny, accord with the fresh morning of such a day as this! I feel', he added taking her hand and looking in her blushing face, 'that

my soul never offers adoration more worthy of my Maker than when inspired by intercourse with such a being as you!'
'Oh! Mr Cartwright!', cried Fanny.[31]

The rich widow was persuaded 'in the name of the Lord', to change her will in favour of the vicar; and her children were forbidden to visit. In the end, by some clever twists and turns, and the disclosure that he had fathered the bastard child of one of his parishioners, the vicar was exposed and defeated.

When the novel was released in 1837, the reviewers were both attracted and repulsed, and somewhat shocked. There were explicit scenes of the vicar caressing and praying in the garden with young girls, even kissing them! *The Athenaeum* warned possible readers:

Handsome, silkily-spoken . . . with his black eyes and caressing hands, which make such sad havoc among the bevy of admiring village ladies. He glides on his way, like a serpent – glossy, silent, and poisonous – throwing out hints here, innuendoes there; blighting with the language of brotherly love, and under the mask of Scriptural sanctity, creeping steadily upwards towards wealth and power. His is a fearful character; and some of his later doings are too dark and terrible to have been written down by a woman, – aye, or a man either; but Mrs Trollope loves debateable ground.

William Thackeray, who wrote a review of the book for *Fraser's Magazine*, was scandalized, and condemned the book as, 'a display of licentiousness, overt and covert, such as no woman conceived before,' He advised her, 'Oh! . . . that ladies would make puddings and mend stockings! That they would not meddle with religion, except to pray to God, to live quietly among their families, and more lovingly among their neighbours!'

Elizabeth Barrett wrote to her friend Miss Mitford, 'What a lamentable book – & to be written by a woman – . . . And the manner in which scriptural perversions are put into the mouth of such who never *do* pervert Scripture, in this book is revolting in the extreme. . . . And I just remember that you call her "your accomplished friend!" – Ah! but she cant be a friend of yours in the real strict sense. Mrs Trollope cant be Miss Mitfords friend!'[32]

When Anthony later portrayed a very similar character, the Reverend Obadiah Slope of Barchester, there were no such scandalized outpourings. However, the controversy added to the public's curiosity, and *The Vicar of Wrexhill* became one of Fanny's best-selling novels.

Tom had by now been at King Edward's School in Birmingham for nearly a year. 'The boys were all day boys, and our business was to teach them Latin and Greek during certain hours of every day.' He found that his eight years as a Winchester schoolboy 'had not constituted a favourable preparation for my present work'. The boys were unruly, and unwilling to learn, and Tom found himself caning them frequently, 'for the preservation of order and silence during the school hours. . . . It appeared to me that I was engaged in the perpetual, and somewhat hopeless task, of endeavouring to manufacture silk purses out of sows' ears. . . . I tried hard to do my duty; but I fear that I was by no means the right man in the right place.'[33] In late 1837 Tom wrote to his mother and told her of his dissatisfaction with his work.

Fanny's reply was swift.

I am fifty-eight years old, my dear Tom. And although, when I am well and in good spirits, I talk of what I may yet do, I cannot conceal from you or from myself, that my doings are nearly over. . . . Your friend has left you, and you are dull. But think you that my work is not dull too? Think you that at my age, when the strength fails and the spirits flag, I can go on for ever writing with pleasure? . . . You know what heavy, uphill work I have hitherto had; and may pretty well guess what the effect on me would be, of sanctioning your throwing up a certain maintenance, before I have cleared myself from the claims that still hang upon me. . . . But give me the great comfort of knowing that you have sufficient strength of mind and resolution, to stick to it for a little while, till we see our way clear before us. . . . I have not yet been able to resume my daily task. I have not yet recovered my strength after a severe cold. But if God gives me health, I do not mean to spare myself, be assured.[34]

This rare admonition drew a quick denial from Tom, and an apology from Fanny: 'I give you a thousand thanks, and I beg you to give me a thousand pardons.'

The Christmas of 1837 was a happy family gathering, with all the children present, together with many old friends. Hadley was bursting with Christmas cheer. Fanny told Tom, 'Don't think me wickedly extravagant for this. I have worked so hard, that I think I may try to give my children a merry Christmas with a safe conscience.' John Tilley, one of Anthony's friends from the Post Office Department, came to stay for Christmas, and a romance began between Cecilia and himself.

Christmas over, Fanny began to find the peace of Hadley rather dull. She considered the possibility of renting a house in London and subletting Hadley:

. . . a change which both Anthony's occupations and mine renders very desirable, albeit I love my pretty cottage very much, and we have fallen into one or two cordial village intimacies that I shall regret to lose. – But in truth four hours out of every day is too much for Anthony to pass in, or on, a coach, which is what he now does – and moreover I find the necessity of seeing London people, whether for business or pleasure, recurs too frequently for convenience of economy. – So I have given good Mr Hosney notice that I shall leave his house in June. . . . I hope to be among clever literary people.[35]

All the family were decimated by influenza in the spring of 1838. Cecilia after two days' illness, fainted when she stood up, and Anthony was so weakened that he did not have the strength to lift her onto the bed. Fanny's eyes became badly affected and she was unable to write for a month.

Fanny proposed two more novels to Bentley. 'Provided the kind public continues to abuse and read me, I shall write and *publish* two novels in each year – if I wish to do so.'

Fanny's next novel, *The Widow Barnaby*, published on 26 December 1838, was a new and rollicking adventure, and a departure from the travel books, the Gothic romance, the anti-slavery novel, and the anti-Evangelical warning. The widow was one of Fanny's most glorious creations, who barnstormed her way through three novels. 'Fair, fat and forty', the recently widowed Mrs Barnaby resolved to leave her home in Silverton, a village near Exeter, and seek her fortune in the fashionable resort of Clifton, which Fanny knew so well from her childhood. The widow planned her future:

Q. What is it I most wish for on earth?
A. A rich and fashionable husband.
Q. What is required to obtain this?
A. Beauty, fortune, talents, and a free entrance into good society.
Q. Do I possess any of these? . . . and which?
A. I possess beauty, fortune and talents.
Q. What is wanting?
A. A free entrance into good society.
   'TRUE!' she exclaimed aloud, 'It is that I want, and it is that I must procure.'

Once in Clifton, Mrs Barnaby set out to make her mark, and caught the eye of the fortune-hunting Major Allen. They began to stalk each other. 'It was impossible that anything could be more fascinating than the general appearance of Major Allen; and if, upon farther enquiry, it should prove that he was indeed, as he appeared to be, a man of fashion and fortune, the whole world could not offer her a lover she should so passionately desire to captivate.'[36]

Mrs Barnaby 'feathered, rouged, ringleted and desperately determined to share the honours of the hour', was accompanied to a ball by her young and beautiful niece Agnes, who provided the perfect contrast to her flamboyant vulgarity. The widow was in her element:

Her eyes did not only sparkle, they perfectly glared with triumph and delight. She shook her curls and her feathers with the vivacity of a Bacchante when tossing her cymbals in the air; and her joyous laugh and her conscious whisper, as each in turn attracted attention from all around, were exactly calculated to produce just such an effect as the luckless Agnes would have lived in silence for ever to avoid witnessing.[37]

Eventually the Major and the widow discovered they had been deceiving each other, and in a wonderful scene of parry and thrust, extricated themselves without losing face or fortune. The widow, 'that painted and plumaged giantess', then resolved to try her luck at another fashionable resort, Cheltenham. She entered the Assembly Rooms in full dress. 'She no longer thought it necessary to restrain her fancy in the choice of colours; and, excepting occasionally on a provincial stage, it would be difficult to find a costume more brilliant in its various hues than that of our widow. . . . Agnes came after her, like a tranquil moonlit night following the meretricious glare of noisy fireworks.'[38]

The widow captured the amused attention of a gentleman at some distance, and, 'flattered, fluttered, and delighted beyond measure', Mrs Barnaby enquired of her neighbour:

> 'Can you tell me, sir, who that tall, stout gentleman is in the green frock-coat, with the lace and tassel? . . . That one who is looking this way with an eye-glass?'
>
> 'That is Lord Mucklebury, Mrs Barnaby.'
>
> The sight of land after a long voyage is delightful . . . rest is delightful after labour, food after fasting; but it may be doubted if . . . these joys could bear comparison with the emotion that now swelled the bosom of Mrs Barnaby. This was the first time, to the best of her knowledge and belief, that she had ever been looked at by a lord at all . . . and what a look it was![39]

Eventually after many misadventures, Agnes finds true love, and the widow marries a young and charming reformed gambler, whom she befriends, while they are both imprisoned for debt in the Fleet prison. The unlikely pair feel it might be wise to leave the country for a spell, and the handsome husband, who had 'exchanged the race-course, the billiard-table, and the dice-box, for the course of an extemporary preacher', was elected to the office of missionary from the independent congregation of Anti-work Christians of London, to the independent congregation of Anti-work Christians of Sydney. Australia was to be blessed by the presence of the Widow Barnaby.

In the second of the Mrs Barnaby books, published in 1840, *The Widow*

Married, she returned from Australia to London with a daughter, Patty. Following the death of her preacher husband she had married Major Allen, who had been transported to Australia after a clash with the law. On their return to England, the wily pair plotted, schemed and caused immense embarrassment to her niece Agnes, and her aristocratic relations.

Mrs Barnaby was to meet Lord Mucklebury once more. 'Her great object was to look nearly as possible like what she had been some eighteen years before, when his Lordship had made her poor heart leap like a porpoise after a storm.' She was confident of her unfading ringlets and her unfading rouge, and even her unfading bright eyes, 'But she could not, poor lady! conceal from herself the disagreeable fact that of late years she had become what friends call *en bon point*, and unfriends, corpulent.'[40] She therefore carefully designed a dress for herself.

'The general outline,' thought she, 'must be indistinct'. . . . Inspired by this idea, the skilful lady set to work, and . . . she contrived to fabricate a dress, the capes, sleeves, flounces, and furbelows of which seemed to wander, and fall, and undulate, and rise again, till, according to her ingenious intention, it would have been difficult for the most accurate eye to detect the points where the lady ended, and her dress began.[41]

Mrs Barnaby and her daughter managed to wheedle an invitation to be presented to the young Queen Victoria, and appeared in the most sensationally vulgar court dresses. 'What with feathers, veil floating mantle of stiffened muslin, and her own august expansiveness, it struck Mrs Stephenson that she had never seen anything so large in her life before.'[42] After the presentation, Mrs Barnaby, 'began backing out of the room, bending deeply forward at every step, like the head of a ship in a *too* fair wind, and reciting, "GOOD morning! GOOD morning! GOOD morning!" till she reached the door.'[43] By the end of the book, Major Allen was discovered cheating at cards, and once again a quick exit had to be arranged, this time to America.

The third, and last, Barnaby book, *The Barnabys in America*, did not appear until 1843. In it, Mrs Barnaby followed Fanny's own route through North America, and Fanny put a 'Barnaby' twist to her own experiences. We have Mrs Barnaby's view of the North Americans, their attitudes to the English, to slaves, and even to authors. One of Mrs Barnaby's hostesses declared:

. . . you know only too well . . . how shamefully the United States have been abused, vilified, and be-littled by all the travellers who have ever set foot in them for the purpose of writing books about us. . . . I'll give any one leave to judge what it must be to the feelings of a free people, who know themselves to be the finest nation in the world, to have one atrocious, unprincipled monster after another, come and write volumes upon volumes, in order to persuade the rest of the world that we are lots behind-hand with everybody, instead of being, as we really are, first and foremost of the whole world.[44]

Fanny allowed her creation to seize the moment. Mrs Barnaby promised that, as a famous author travelling incognito, she would endeavour to produce a book for her hostess, that would be considered fit to be read by Americans. The book she wrote was called, *Justice Done at Last* or, *The Travels of Mrs Major Allen Barnaby*. Fanny, in the character of Mrs Barnaby, and with her tongue firmly in her cheek, wrote:

> My principal object is to wipe away from the minds of my readers every trace of all they have read or heard upon that subject before [America]. Nobody properly qualified to write upon this wonderful country could behold a single town, a single street, a single house, a single individual of it, for just one single half-hour, without feeling all over to his very heart convinced, that not all the countries of the old world put together are worthy to compare . . . with the free-born, the free-bred, the immortal, and the hundred thousand times more glorious country, generally called that of the 'Stars and Stripes'. . . . It is just the biggest and the best, and that is saying everything in two words. . . . I do believe most truly that the reason why so much, as I am told, has been said about the backwardness in elegance of this most great and glorious country is, that all the people who have come here before are of an inferior class, and not used so much to the very first circles, as I confess I have been.[45]

Fanny, having thus parodied her own achievements, toured her creation through North America, with devastating results for the Americans. She obviously enjoyed the company of her heroine immensely for she wrote: 'I scruple not to confess that with all her faults, and she has *some*, I love her dearly: I owe her many mirthful moments, and the deeper pleasure still of believing that she has brought mirthful moments to others also.' The public agreed, and even the critics found her vulgarities, and blatant social climbing 'charming'. *The Times* wrote: 'The Barnaby is such a heroine as never before has figured in a romance. Her vulgarity is sublime. Imaginary personage though she be, everybody who has read her memoirs must have a real interest in her. . . . Such a jovial, handsome, hideous, ogling, bustling monster of a woman as maid, wife, and widow, was never, as we can recollect, before brought upon the scene.' *New Monthly Magazine* agreed: 'Mrs Trollope played the literary chaperon to a lady of great character and definite idiosyncrasy – one who stands out as a distinct and living form among the accepted celebrities of the English novel. And this is the Widow Barnaby.'

In spite of the constant output of novels, life was still uncertain for Fanny. About this time she wrote to Tom of her financial straits: 'I work, and work, and work. And if God spares my life and health, I hope that the time will come when I may call myself out of debt, and may calculate on *spending* the money I have earned, instead of fretting that it does not cover all my liabilities.'[46]

In March 1838 Fanny met Charles Dickens for the first time in London. She wrote to Tom, who was two years older than Dickens: 'I had a good deal of talk with him. He is extremely lively and intelligent, has the appearance of being *very* young, and although called excessively shy, seemed not at all averse from conversation.'[47]

In the summer of 1838 Cecilia and John Tilley announced their engagement, much to Fanny's joy, and this made her move to London even more necessary. Anthony seemed settled at the General Post Office for, as Tom wrote of him: 'work to him was a necessity and a satisfaction'. For Tom this was not so. In June, just before Fanny moved, he returned to Hadley for a talk with his mother. A major change was proposed, after 'much consultation and very many walks together round the little quiet garden at Hadley, it was decided between us that I should send in my resignation of the Birmingham mastership, defer all alternative steps in the direction of any other life career, and devote myself, for the present at least, to becoming her companion and squire.'[48] Fanny had no wish to live alone, and with Anthony working, and Cecilia about to be married, this seemed an ideal solution. Tom had not given up his own ambition to write, and thought he would be better able to do so if he were not tied to Birmingham. In June Fanny found a London house at 20 York Street, Portman Square, but did not move in straight away. She had once again been ill, and together with Tom and Cecilia, went for a holiday for a few weeks to Dover, where they stayed in lodgings. The Reverend Mr Maule, the rector of St Mary's, Dover, had married one of Fanny's Bristol cousins, and they spent several very pleasant evenings at his house.

On returning to Hadley, they packed their belongings once more and removed themselves to the bustle of London. Before Christmas 1838, they were installed at York Street, Portman Square, and busy making preparations for Cecilia's wedding. Fanny, now fifty-nine, was once again in her element.

CHAPTER NINE

'So much read, so much admired, and so much abused'

20 York Street, London. Winter 1838–July 1840

Once settled in London, Fanny quickly plunged into the social round, entertaining her old friends as before. Anna Drury, the teenage granddaughter of the William Drury who had employed Anthony for a brief time in Brussels, went to stay at Portman Square. She remembered Fanny with great affection:

> I have heard my dear Aunt speak of her remarkable gift of reading aloud. Of this I know nothing; but her talk was simply delightful in those days when I was able to hear it. . . . I spent two days with her, of which I principally recollect an unlimited allowance of books by day, and, as I shared her room, a most delightful talk at night until one next morning! I was young enough then to think a night's rest of no consequence, in comparison with such a treat; but as she was full of work by day, it was different for her! And she said afterwards that it must not be repeated. I remember some of the things she said; but chiefly her kind indulgence in listening to my youthful aspirations and plans for possible stories, and the good practical advice which she gave me from her own experience. It has always seemed to me that those who only knew her through her novels, did not half know her ability. To do that, it was needful to listen to her conversation. . . . I was present when Rogers the poet met her at luncheon. . . . This was the only time I ever saw Mr Rogers, then an old man with a pallid face that looked like wax. She sate next him at table; and presently he turned to her and observed, 'They told me Mrs Trollope was to be here. She has written a very great deal of rubbish, hasn't she?' 'Well,' she immediately replied, 'she has made it answer!'. . . . Mr Rogers was so annoyed when he found what he had done, that he very soon took his departure.[1]

Once established at York Street, Fanny threw herself enthusiastically into preparations for Cecilia's wedding. John Tilley had been promoted to Post Office Surveyor for the Northern District of England, at a starting salary of

£300 per annum, and when married, the Tilleys would live at Penrith, on the edge of the Lake District in Cumbria. London became a bustle of shopping expeditions and parties.

The wedding took place in London on 11 February 1839 at St Mary's Church, Bryanston Square. Cecilia's bridesmaids were Mary and Kate Grant, friends from the early days at Harrow. After the departure of the bride and bridegroom, Fanny, Tom, and Anthony drove with the two bridesmaids down to Hayes, where the Grants were now living, and they all stayed the night. The following day, on 12 February, Fanny took her first train journey, and returned to London on the Great Western Railway. It had been fourteen years since the first railway was opened in 1825 between Stockton and Darlington.

Fanny had work to do. Before Cecilia's marriage, she had been asked by Lord Ashley, who later became the Earl of Shaftesbury, to write a book exposing the appalling conditions under which young children were forced to work in the textile factories in northern England. So Fanny, armed with letters of introduction from Lord Ashley, accompanied by Tom and with Hervieu to draw the illustrations, travelled by mail train to Lancashire on 20 February. There she would visit the textile mills in Macclesfield and Manchester and obtain some accurate background information. She stayed in Lancashire for a month and uncovered some horrifying facts. As Tom wrote in his memoirs:

> It is useless here and now to say anything of the horrors of uncivilized savagery and hopeless abject misery which we witnessed. They are painted in my mother's book, and should any reader ever refer to those pages for a picture of the state of things among the factory hands at that time, he may take with him my testimony to the fact that there was no exaggeration in the outlines of the picture given.[2]

The Life and Adventures of Michael Armstrong, the Factory Boy, is a powerful book which first appeared in February 1839, in one shilling monthly instalments. Few women writers had their work published in this way, but it was to ensure that the book would reach the maximum number of readers. Dickens' *Oliver Twist* had appeared in this form in the previous year, and, in the same manner that Dickens had exposed the grim corruption of children in London, Fanny Trollope exposed the exploitation and slavery of the factory children in the cotton mills of the north.

The *New Monthly Magazine* declared:

> It is a great mistake, and a still greater injustice, to suppose that Mrs Trollope offers *The Factory Boy* as anything like a pendant to the admirable works of Mr Dickens, which have appeared under a similar form. The

great and leading characteristic of those works, is humour – broad even to caricature. . . . But *The Factory Boy* has a deeper design, and aims at the accomplishment of that design by other, and still more rare and estimable means. It is evidently intended to be a deep, moral satire, having a serious, and even a solemn purpose to accomplish – with truth alone as the means and medium of its accomplishment, and good alone as the ultimate end; every step of the path being made irresistibly attractive by the inexhaustible amusement that is scattered over it.[3]

Fanny researched her project thoroughly. She attended meetings in the chapels and listened to the preaching of the reformers. She also visited the slums to see the degradation and filth of the wretched workers. She described the situation in stark detail:

It was the most deplorable hole in the parish – a narrow, deep rutted parish road . . . led from the turnpike down a steep hill to the town of Ashleigh. Exactly at the bottom of the hill, just at the point where every summer storm and winter torrent deposited their gatherings, there to remain and be absorbed as they might, began a long, closely packed double row of miserable dwellings, crowded to excess by the population drawn together by the neighbouring factories. . . . The very vilest rags were hanging before most of the doors as demonstration that washing of garments was occasionally resorted to within. Crawling infants, half-starved cats, mangy curs, and fowls that looked as if each particular feather had been used as a scavenger's broom, shared the dust and the sunshine between them, while an odour, which seemed compounded of a multitude of villainous smells, all reeking together into one, floated over them.[4]

Fanny and her party managed to visit the cotton mills by pretending to be idle travellers, 'anxious to see all objects of curiosity, particularly the factories, which were, as they observed, so famous throughout all the world'.

In the story, Michael Armstrong, a nine-year-old factory boy, was adopted by the mill owner, Sir Mathew Dowling, in a sentimental gesture to impress a lady, after Michael had rescued her from the menaces of a very ancient cow. Sir Mathew publicly announced his action throughout the district, to divert attention from the deplorable conditions in the mill. He was a boorish sadist, who quickly tired of the pretence, and then decided to get rid of the boy by apprenticing him to a remote mill run as a slave camp, and employing unwanted pauper children who were, literally, worked to death. One of Hervieu's stark illustrations showed the starving boys scrambling to steal pig swill from a trough. A Miss Brotherton, one of Fanny Trollope's independent heroines, heard of Michael's disappearance and set off, unsuccessfully, to find him. Eventually Michael, after ten years of hard labour and many trials, escaped from his overseers and was reunited with his crippled brother and Miss Brotherton.

Fanny used the reactions of her heroine, Miss Brotherton, to paint the scene in the mills.

> The hot and tainted atmosphere seemed to weigh upon her spirits, as well as upon her lungs . . . as she watched the children who dragged their attenuated limbs along. . . . Two hundred thousand little creatures, for whose freedom from toil during their tender years the awful voice of nature has gone forth . . . taken and lodged amidst stench and stunning, terrifying tumult, – driven to and fro, till their little limbs bend under them – hour after hour, day after day – the repose of a moment to be purchased only by yielding their tender bodies to the fist, the heel, or the strap of the overlooker![5]

Through the telling of Michael's own experiences, and the search by Miss Brotherton, Fanny was able to paint a graphic and shocking picture of life in the textile factories and the mill villages. Her purpose was to awaken the national conscience. However, contemporary society found the facts hard to accept. They wanted to believe that this story was an exaggeration; that parents were only exploiting their children by sending them to work in the mills; children were only beaten because they were lazy; and that Christian teaching would help them to accept the hardships. Fanny exposed and destroyed the myth of those popular justifications. She wrote:

> You – I – every acquaintance I have in the world, may aid and assist in putting an end to this most atrocious factory system, WHICH OUGHT TO WEIGH HEAVIER UPON EVERY CHRISTIAN ENGLISH HEART THAN EVER THE SLAVE-TRADE DID. If the whole British Empire . . . did but know what we are about here . . . the horrors . . . would cease before another year was come and gone.

Once again the majority of critics were enraged. They liked their women writers to be feminine and gentle. Jane Austen and Mary Russell Mitford, both of whom wrote of village life, were lauded as good examples. Mrs Trollope was an agitator; coarse, vulgar, unfeminine, and, potentially dangerous.

The Athenaeum accused her of 'scattering firebrands among the people' and asked her to remember 'that the most probable immediate effect of her pennings and pencillings will be the burning of factories'.

The *New Monthly Magazine*, however, saw the work differently:

> This striking and forcible tale improves on the reader at every step.

Nothing can be more fearfully, yet touchingly true, than some of the descriptions. . . . Those will grievously mistake the design of this work who look to it for nothing beyond the mere amusement of an idle hour. It seeks at once to impress a deep moral lesson, and to work a great social change, and we are greatly mistaken if it do not ultimately effect its purpose.[6]

The 'social change' did eventually come eight years later, in 1847, when the Factory Act was passed forbidding the employment of any child under eight in the textile mills.

Before returning to London, Fanny and Tom went north to the Lake District. They stopped for just long enough to take a sail on Lake Windermere with Captain Hamilton, the friend and author who had observed the family at Niagara Falls. During the expedition they very nearly capsized and drowned, an episode which Fanny used in *The Laurringtons*, a novel written later and set in the Lake District. They also visited William Wordsworth who talked almost exclusively to Fanny, and only about himself, or so Tom reported, who was not overly impressed by the poet. 'He sat continuously looking down with a green shade over his eyes even though it was twilight; and his mode of speech and delivery suggested to me the epithet "maundering" though I was ashamed of myself for the thought with reference to such a man.'[7] They also visited Cecilia and John Tilley who were now living nearby, at Penrith.

Once back in London, Tom set off for Brittany to collect material to write his first book, while Fanny, worn out by her strenuous months of constant activity, collapsed into bed with a severe inflammation of the trachea. She was now sixty.

The year before, in August 1838, Tom had become intrigued by the new science of magnetism, and had accompanied a family friend, Henrietta Skerrett, to a seance. He had been fairly sceptical about the results, but had, nevertheless, continued with his interest. Two days after Cecilia's wedding, Tom had taken his mother to meet a well-known mesmerist, Dr Elliotson. Tom was impressed. 'He was a gentleman, a highly educated and accomplished man, and so genuinely in earnest on this subject of "animal magnetism", as it was the fashion then to call it, that he was ready to spend and be spent in his efforts to establish the truthfulness and therapeutic usefulness of its pretensions.' They watched Dr Elliotson magnetize, or mesmerize, two children, who then performed a series of tasks as requested and, moreover, the little girl, although in a trance, was able to state exactly what every other member of her family was doing and where they were. 'My mother and myself came home fully persuaded that, let the explanatory theory of the matter be what it might, there had been no taint of imposture in what we had witnessed.'[8] Séances were to remain a continuing fascination for both Fanny and Tom.

Fanny, who was severely ill, was being attended, successfully, by this same Dr Elliotson. By 6 July she was well enough to write to Tom, 'Truly, and sincerely, and on the faith of an honest mother, my dearest Tom, I am, save a cough, quite well again. I owe much to Dr Elliotson.'[9] Fanny's involvement with Dr Elliotson had been noted by her friends, and Miss Mitford wrote to Elizabeth Barrett:

I have had two or three interesting visits lately dearest. One . . . from a Dr Carter, a friend of Dr Elliotson, and a believer in, if not a practicer of, animal magnetism. I wish you had seen Dr Carter, you would have been pleased with him. He told me what I did not before know, that Mrs Trollope is a thorough-going mesmerite, constantly at Dr Elliotson's, and believing through thick and thin.[10]

Throughout all this time the books continued to appear. *Michael Armstrong* came out in one shilling monthly numbers between March 1839 and May 1840, and was printed by Colburn as a book in 1840.

The Widow Married was serialized in the *New Monthly Magazine*, between May 1839 and June 1840. It was then printed as a book, again by Colburn.

One Fault, however, was printed by Bentley in 1840. It was written for the most part while she was staying with Cecilia in Penrith in 1839, and finished when she returned to London.

The *New Monthly Magazine* in a 'Memoir of Mrs Trollope' written in March 1839, discussed the nature of her success:

That Mrs Trollope has from the first commencement of her career up to the present time, been uniformly and eminently successful as an author, no one can gainsay or doubt. But on the other hand it is equally clear that scarcely any of her works – the charming *Widow Barnaby*, perhaps excepted – have escaped the vehement and angry censure of some portion or other of the press. Certainly no other author of the present day has been at once so much read, so much admired, and so much abused. Now how is this to be accounted for? Does it not arise from the bold, and uncompromising expression of her own honestly formed convictions and opinions, on every subject whatever they may be, on the one hand; and from the intrinsic talent, and charming style of her works on the other? We can trace the circumstance to no other cause.[11]

In *One Fault*, her latest story, Fanny once again departed from the expected romantic novel, and gave expression to her 'honestly formed opinions'. She wrote of a marriage which failed because of the husband's one fault, an ungovernable and jealous temper. It was unusual to write of marriage at all; most romances were about courtship and ended when the lady's fair hand was won. This, however, was a story which started with a marriage, and then followed the painful subjugation of the young wife to her husband's jealous manipulations. 'And why was this marriage so fatally unhappy? Why was all joy for ever a stranger to her heart? Why was peace unknown to her? *Solely because her husband was an ill-tempered man.*' Fanny, with many years of living with a husband with just such a 'fault', ended the story with a dire warning: 'TO ALL MOTHERS AND ALL DAUGHTERS, WITH MOST KIND WISHES FOR SUCCESS IN ALL THEIR PROJECTS; TOGETHER WITH A FRIENDLY REQUEST THAT THEY WILL BEAR IN MIND ONE IMPORTANT FACT; NAMELY, THAT ALL ILL-TEMPERED MEN WHO MAY MAKE LARGE SETTLEMENTS, DO NOT DIE AT THE AGE OF TWENTY-SIX YEARS.'[12]

In this book Fanny also introduced the wonderful Misses Lucy and Christina Clark, based on her Exeter cousins, Mary and Fanny Bent. The elder, Miss Lucy, indulged in endless 'carpet-work', or embroidery, and Miss Christina, a bluestocking with decided and unorthodox ideas, expounded to all and sundry on the powers of the female mind. 'May we not hope to see the time when the equality which nature has established between the male and female intellect shall have fair play permitted to its exhibition; and that the senate, the pulpit, and the bar may all profit by the acknowledged brilliance of female eloquence?'

A fierce advocate for the rights of women, Miss Christina talked of 'the flagrant injustice of suffering millions of highly enlightened beings, who live and die as much devoid of all political rights as the beasts which perish'. She went on to tell her brother-in-law, the vicar, that he should employ women as curates in his church, that women should have the right of election, and the right of being elected, and also:

... were there as much sagacity among men as among sparrows, society would not long remain ignorant of a truth equally notorious and important; namely, that to single women, those who hold themselves apart from the meaner offices of their sex, to such it especially belongs to keep a look out upon what the world is doing. There is a stirring spirit within us that leads us, as by inspiration, to the task, and were we listened to as we ought to be, many of the worst political blunders that still continue to exist would be speedily removed. ... My purpose is to show, that neither by her formation, nor her capacities, is she unequal to the duties of a Member of Parliament – I shall have previously proved her rights as a citizen – and I cannot but flatter myself that the often recognized, and, indeed universally acknowledged fact of our great superiority in facility of utterance, will go far towards convincing the world that nature did not intend to exclude us from an assembly in which the art of talking is so decidedly the principle requisite.[13]

This had been the siren call of Frances Wright ten years before, when Fanny had so eagerly accompanied her to America. Fanny had not forgotten, and she now, through the pages of her novels, began to fight for the right of women to control their own destinies. These novels were written for a society in which women had no rights at all, and they were stirring words indeed.

The critics, however, ignored Miss Christina completely, and were uncertain about the theme of ill-temper. *The Literary Gazette* complained: 'To have three long volumes devoted to the development of one ingredient, and confined to the effects of the conduct of a husband upon a wife . . . is too much.' To have a whole book chronicle the development of a husband's obsessive personality was also decidedly unusual. The next time this was attempted was in the character of Louis Trevelyan in Anthony Trollope's book *He Knew He Was Right*, written in 1869.

Tom returned to London on 23 July 1839, and on the 26th started with his mother for Penrith to stay with Cecilia and John Tilley. The Tilleys' house was just to the north of Penrith, and Fanny described the scene to Julia. 'Nothing can be prettier than her residence. Her windows look out upon the pretty Lake mountains, which though on no very large scale, are beautiful in no ordinary degree, from the boldness of outline and the great variety of picturesque combinations they display.'[14] Fanny and Tom stayed at Penrith for the whole of August, and enjoyed the walks and drives in the area. They were entertained by Sir George and Lady Musgrave of Edenhall; Sir George was said to be the best landlord in the county, and, as Tom said, 'the most hospitable man in the world'. He was also the inheritor of the 'Luck of Edenhall', an ancient glass goblet which had engraved upon it:

> *When this cup shall break or fall,*
> *Farewell the luck of Edenhall.*

At the end of August Fanny returned to London to work on the completion of three books: *Michael Armstrong*, *The Widow Married*, and *One Fault*. Tom was busy completing his manuscript on his travels in Brittany.

Fanny's output was prodigious. In nine years she had produced sixteen novels and travel books in forty-two volumes. Multi-volume novels were demanded by the circulating libraries such as Mudie's, established in 1842, who charged by the number of volumes borrowed, rather than the whole book. Fanny was immensely popular with her readers, who waited eagerly for the 'next Mrs Trollope novel', and one contemporary critic remarked caustically:

. . . again and again are novel-readers on the wrong scent, and have quite lost the trail, when asking one another, 'Have you read Mrs Trollope's last?' finding that what they supposed her most recent venture has been superseded by two or three others. Depend upon it her literary executors will be entrusted with a few bales of 'copy', containing work for generations of compositors and readers yet unborn, so that novels of the approved Trollope fabric may, by a judiciously frugal rate of publication (say two or three per annum) be made to last some half-way into the next century.[15]

On 4 December 1839 Fanny escaped from the English weather, and met Tom in Paris, where they were to spend the winter. As Frances Eleanor said, 'She was again in the midst of the most brilliant society – fashionable and literary; and the only drawback to her enjoyment was that the incessant invitations consumed nearly all the time she wished to dedicate to her work.'[16]

As Fanny wrote to Julia:

. . . what a winter of incessant dissipation has this been dear Julia! Once entered into it I found it perfectly impossible to stop. . . . I might truly say that I have never had a single hour disengaged after my first week here. I look back on it all as if I had been in a mill whirling round and round with increasing velocity – and truly sometimes I have felt somewhat giddy. . . . I brought a work here, of which I had sketched the plan, intending to complete it in three months, and to this I have not added a single line. . . . So much for the *profitable* result of being *fêtée!*[17]

She attended the fashionable soirées of Miss Clarke, (later Madame Mohl), visited the house of Princess Belgiojoso and that of Madame Récamier, and met once again General Pepe of the old Harrow days. She also met Rosina, Lady Bulwer, a poor, sad, garrulous creature who had been badly ill-treated by her husband, who had forcibly separated her from her two children, as was his legal right. Fanny wrote to Cecilia, 'I believe her character to be perfectly irreproachable. But she is not so quiet as I would wish her to be, in her grief; and were it not that the enforced absence of her children excuses any violence of sorrow, I should say she compromised her dignity by her lamentations.'[18]

There were other distractions; Queen Victoria married Prince Albert on 10 February 1840, and Fanny was a guest of Lord Granville at the brilliant Embassy ball held in honour of the event. She was worried about finding enough time to complete her book and wrote to Tom in April 1840: 'I do not believe that the whole earth has any spot where it would be more difficult for me to write, as in Paris. Kindness, in consideration of my solitude, neutralizes all my good resolutions.'[19] She told him of another memorable meeting: 'The greatest exploit I have to tell you of, is having been presented at the Tuileries by Lady Catherine Bernard. My reception was a most gracious one; King, Queen, Duchess de Nemours, Princess Clementine and Madame Adelaide, all spoke in a flattering manner of their having long known me by my books, etc. . . . The King asked me, with a look of something like fun, if I should like to go back to America. *I longed to return the question to him!*[20] Louis Philippe had been exiled in America when Fanny was there in 1828.

Somehow, during all this activity in Paris, Fanny managed to write her next novel, *The Ward*, which was ready in August 1840 and appeared in 1841. Once again she broke new ground, this time introducing as the main character a young girl, Sophia Martin, who was unscrupulous, clever, and ambitious. Wheedling her way into the affections of a rich old man, by a pretence of meek admiration, she became his heiress, but on his death revealed her true character by spurning the relations who had been her guardians, and setting herself up in state in her new home, Thorpe Combe. Still a ward until her majority, she treated her kindly relations as servants. In the end the true heir returned, and penniless, she had to flee. The reviewers gave it grudging approval. *John Bull* thought Fanny had added 'a new creation to the stock of the novelist, and a new study to the student of human nature'.

During the early months of 1840 Anthony stayed with his mother in Paris and joined in the festivities. 'It is a promise of long standing to Anthony,' Fanny wrote to Julia, 'whose official duties prevent his sharing the travelling delights of his errant family, and who will on this occasion will [*sic*] be permitted to be with us for a few weeks – a couple of months we hope – which will give him, perhaps the only opportunity he may have of seeing *la belle ville*.'[21] Fanny reported that he was 'going to many good parties', but one wonders how much he enjoyed the visit. Excluded from the family wanderings for so long because of 'official duties', this was his first visit to the Continent since the miserable days at Bruges. On his own admission he was a hobbledehoy, his French was poor and he was always in trouble. Being swept into the social maelstrom of Fanny's Paris would only have emphasized his lack of sophistication and the contrast with his London life. It is probable that during this visit he voiced his hopes that he might join the ranks of Trollope authors; an idea from which Fanny tried to dissuade him. When Anthony returned to England in March, Fanny wrote to him:

You left school sooner than you ought to have done, or than we once expected there would be any need for you to do. Make good the dropped stitches of your education before you take upon yourself to teach or amuse others in print. Remember the time for reading is now. Reading you must have, not so much because of what it will tell you as because it will teach you how to observe, and supply you with mental pegs on which to hang what you pick up about traits and motives of your fellow creatures. . . . We Trollopes are far too much given to pen and ink as it is, without your turning scribbler when you might do something better. Harrow and Winchester will stand you in good stead at the Post office; make St Martins-le-Grand the instrument that will open the oyster of the world. Imitate my particular industry as much as you like, only do not let the publishers break your heart by treating its products as their playthings.[22]

Excellent advice, and similar to the counsel she had given Tom seven years before; but for Anthony, who was searching desperately for a way of escape from his humdrum post office job, it must have seemed as though she had no faith in his abilities. Tom had been able to leave his job at King Edward's School, why must he stay on at the hated post office? In his autobiography he wrote:

Could there be any escape from such dirt? I would ask myself; and I always answered that there was no escape. The mode of my life was itself wretched. I hated the office. I hated my work. More than all I hated my idleness. I had often told myself since I left school that the only career in life within my reach was that of an author, and the only mode of authorship open to me that of a writer of novels. . . . But the months and years ran on, and no attempt was made. And yet no day was passed without thoughts of attempting it, and a mental acknowledgement of the disgrace of postponing it. What reader will not understand the agony of remorse produced by such a condition of mind?[23]

He became inexplicably ill. Fanny returned to England at the beginning of June; she had planned to spend only three days in London, and then head north to Penrith for the christening of her first grandchild, Frances Trollope Tilley. However, worried by the severity of Anthony's symptoms, she abandoned her plans and stayed in London to nurse him. York Street had been given up before she had left for Paris, and so she took temporary lodgings at No. 3 Wyndham Street to care for her son.

The illness, a deep depression, which was probably exacerbated by the apparent pointless drudgery of his life, took the form of asthma with severe weakness and wasting. The doctors who were consulted could find neither reason nor cure. Even Dr Elliotson, in whom she had so much faith, was unable to suggest a solution.

Dr Elliotson had in the past used two sisters, the Okey girls, as mesmeric subjects, who, because of repeated experiments had become very dependent on the doctor. Fanny was very concerned for their future, and felt that Elliotson had a duty to provide for them. If they declared that they 'saw Jack' at a person's side, it meant that the person would die. Anthony had made their acquaintance before he became ill, and now they said that they 'saw Jack . . . but only up to the knee'. This was hopefully taken to mean that he would get better. Fanny described Anthony's condition to her friend Rosina Bulwer:

He is frightfully reduced in size and strength; sure am I that could you see him, you would not find even a distant resemblance to the being who, exactly three months ago, left us in all the pride of youth, health, and strength. Day by day I lose hope, and so, I am quite sure, do his physicians; we have had three consultations, but nothing prescribed relieves him, nor has any light been thrown on the nature of his complaint.[24]

Once again Fanny was nursing a dangerously ill son, and again she had to continue with her writing. In this instance, realizing that Anthony's illness was compounded by his sense of failure, and understanding the driving force of his aspirations, she wrote two books as a guide and a bitingly satirical warning of both the pleasures and pitfalls for authors in the London literary set.

The first, *Charles Chesterfield: or the Adventures of a Youth of Genius*, was a glorious swipe at reviewers, combined with some very sound advice to the would-be novice writer of the dangers of the London publishing world. The second, *The Blue Belles of England*, was a wicked exposé of the lionizing clique of London's intellectual society, the bluestockings of her youth. The books appeared simultaneously in monthly parts in the *New Monthly Magazine* and the *Metropolitan Magazine* between July 1840 and December 1841.

Charles Chesterfield, the eponymous hero, was a naive country boy, and 'when it was too late to help it, the whole family began to discover that poor Charles was a great deal too learned to be useful. . . . It was the world, it was London, for which he panted. Fame, renown, applause – applause, renown, and fame.'[25]

Charles inherited £4,000, and set out to become a writer in London. 'The larger portion of the time was spent in a sort of inward ecstasy, during which *nothing* could have had power to compete with the wildly ambitious hopes which filled his soul.'[26] He was introduced into the literary set by his mentor, Sir George, who had designs on Charles' money, and he met the famous Marchmont, the reviewer for *The Regenerator*, 'one of the omnipotent WE, a member of the secret tribunal, in whose frown there was death, and whose smile brought food, lodging, hackney-coaches, and satin-gowns.'[27] As Charles' literary hostess told him, 'the penalty of not standing well with Mr Marchmont is utter destruction, believe me, to all literary hopes – except in some very out-of-the-way cases indeed, where nothing good or bad seems to make any difference. But speaking in general, nobody can have any hope of getting on if Marchmont is against him.'[28] Marchmont allowed Charles to do some work for him (without payment), and explained the system:

> 'What a greenhorn you still are, Chesterfield. . . . Do you really, truly, and bona fide believe that the almighty confraternity of WE read the books that they review ?'
>
> 'You don't mean to tell me,' cried Charles, 'that this omnipotent business of reviewing . . . you don't mean to tell me that it is all humbug and that books are admired or condemned solely by chance without having been ever read by the reviewer at all?'
>
> 'By Chance? – Oh, no! my dear fellow, not by chance, most certainly. God forbid that I should belong to so extremely childish and unprincipled a community . . . our principles are immutable, our judgements ever clear: all we require to know is the name of the author in all cases where the name is known, or the principles in which he writes where it is not. This is sailing by a compass that cannot fail us, my dear Chesterfield'.[29]

Fanny knew all too well the power of reviewers, and Marchmont is so minutely drawn, his appearance, his conceit, his posing, and even his lodgings, it seems probable that he was very familiar to her.

Mrs Sherbourne, the lady novelist, was another almost recognizable character; indeed, as Fanny confessed, 'Those who are familiar with the authorial world of London, must know, or have known, more than one person in many points exceedingly like Mrs Sherbourne. She was, beyond all doubt, past her first youth, but she was in the fullest meridian of her second.'[30] Fanny described her as very tiny, and she punctuated her conversations with French and Italian, and welcomed 'without reserve all those who could assist her in her pursuits, either by criticism or patronage'.

'The morning dress of Mrs Sherbourne never varied, at least as to its style. Summer and winter she was always *décolletée*, and summer and winter she was always enveloped, more or less, in a black cashmere shawl.' She had large eyes, a pug nose, a wide mouth with beautiful teeth, and 'an ever-ready and pretty dimple'. Her mind 'was of a flimsy, loose, and unstable quality'.[31]

> For the success of her works, on which she almost entirely depended for her existence, she trusted to what she called the intensity of her own feelings. Nor did she trust in vain. No circulating library from the Orkneys to Land's End, dared to confess they had not got Mrs Sherbourne's last work: and *The Condemned One, The Entranced One, The Corrupted One, The Infernal One, The Empyrean One* and *The Disgusting One,*

and all in succession conveyed her intensity into every village of the empire, and brought in return wherewithal to 'live and love, to dress and dream . . . very much to her satisfaction.'[32]

When she was running short of money, Mrs Sherbourne negotiated with Marchmont to sell her risqué memoirs. She then promised that she would kill herself by a certain date, providing thereby excellent publicity when they were published posthumously.

'Few of your profession, or mine either, Mr Marchmont,' she resumed with a melancholy smile, 'are ignorant of the fact that biting personal anecdotes are the most marketable of all literary commodities; and when they are skilfully given . . . the demand is, I believe, as certain as that for green peas during the last days of May.'

'You are quite right, Mrs Sherbourne.' [replied Marchmont] 'It is the only literary speculation I know of that is absolutely without risk. Scorn and scoffing on certain subjects will sometimes run, but occasionally there is a check to this. Impassioned writing also, when it is thrown off in a style sufficiently unrestrained, will often prove extremely saleable. But this altogether depends upon the critical notices. If nobody can be found sufficiently obliging to sing out that such a work is too improper to read, the chances are greatly in favour of its proving a dead loss. But sharp personalities will cut their own way to notice pretty generally without fail, and are, as you justly observe, by far the best business we have.'[33]

The warning against a literary life was explicit, and Charles Chesterfield, having nearly lost both his heart and his fortune, decided that London was not for him, and returned, very much wiser, to his loving family.

Marchmont, according to a letter from Elizabeth Barrett to Mary Russell Mitford, was modelled on Forster, 'Between Mrs Trollope and her "grateful though obliged friend" Lady Bulwer, poor Mr Foster[sic] is done no gentle death!' John Forster, the son of a Newcastle butcher, moved to London in 1828 and devoted himself to literary pursuits. In 1840, aged twenty-eight, he was the Literary and Dramatic critic for *The Examiner*, and 'the influence of his powerful individuality soon made itself strongly felt'. He became a prominent figure in distinguished literary circles.[34] Mrs Sherborne was thought to have been based on Mrs Jameson, a prolific author and traveller, who had kept a journal in which was a fictitious account of her own death. It was published anonymously under the title of *A Lady's Diary*, and the publisher promised her a guitar out of the profits – if any. Elizabeth Barrett was intrigued. 'Mrs Jameson . . . Mrs Sherbourne!!! Why I must remain very sorry! But Mrs Sherbourne! My dearest friend, Mrs Sherbourne, Mrs

Sherbourne! She is everything of a devil but it is sublime! I can scarcely catch and carry the idea of such a thing! . . . Have you read *The Blue Belles*? Do – it is very clever – and besides I want you to send me the little key which belongs to the personalities.'[35]

The Blue Belles of England, written concurrently, was a witty exposé of London society. '*The Blue Belles of Mayfair* is the proper title for this satire of the lionizing coteries in the fashionable world' wrote *The Spectator*. 'The vanity of the worshippers who offer the incense of their adulation to the idol of the hour, and the sickly cant that passes with them for oracular profundity, are cleverly ridiculed; and if flippancy and caricature are allowable at all, it is doubtless in dealing with such flimsy inanities as the pet poetasters and lady lion-hunters.'

As Fanny had written in *The Blue Belles*:

If people would but *leave themselves* alone, society, instead of being the wearisome series of pale withered mimicries which we find it, would offer a racy variety in thought, feeling, and expression, that would make this world infinitely more amusing and agreeable than it is at the present. But as long as nine-tenths of the race are straining all their faculties to get themselves mistaken for belonging to the other tenth, it is quite impossible that they should be otherwise than dull.

Again, in *Blue Belles*, Fanny takes a young naive heroine from the country, introduces her to London society, and records her impressions. *Blue Belles* follows her through the salons of Fanny's own circle, the poets, writers, the patrons, and, the young ladies. This time there was no doubt that the characters were drawn from life, though disguised just enough to make the discovery of the originals challenging. In her own copy she had pencilled some of the names in the margins, and seems to have told at least one of her friends, as revealed in the letter which Elizabeth Barrett wrote to Mary Russell Mitford on 11 January 1842:

Thank you dearest friend for the Key.
I used it with the eagerness of Bluebeard's wife – & am satisfied, thank you, to the uttermost of the curiosity of my malice — or of the malice of my curiosity — whichever it should be philosophically. I had guessed a good many of the names – but from the want of personal knowledge was quite at a loss for many – for instance I stared myself blind at Lady Dort, Lady Stephens, Bradley! I did not guess *Contrarius*, either the least – & mistook Rolfe for Roscoe instead of Mathias! . . . You cannot think how your letter has amused me. . . . Mrs Trollope's book *is* clever, do you not admit?
And Bradley is Edwin Landseer! Well![36]

Lady Dort was, in Fanny's book, an influential hostess who collected celebrities, and was said to have been based on Mrs Skinner of Portland Place, one of Fanny's former neighbours, Fanny described her as:

. . . tall and thin to a degree which may probably be considered as the extremest excess to which attenuation can go, consistently with the powers and operations of life. But far from considering this lamentable leanness as a personal deformity, she assisted the anatomical exhibition of her unfleshed skeleton by every means in her power . . . she was splendidly habited in a robe of violet coloured satin, which had every appearance of having been glued in little mathematically-cut portions to her person . . . her waist was immeasurably long, and might easily have been spanned by the claw of an ostrich, while her flat bust was as immeasurably wide, looking like an antique slab of yellow marble, placed edgeways, the well articulated shoulder representing a sort of volute termination to it.[37]

Contrarius was a portrait of Samuel Rogers, the gentleman who at an earlier dinner party had referred to Fanny's writings as 'rubbish'.

That diminutive form appears to be the earthly habitation of two perfectly distinct spirits. Contrarius is wise and weak, generous and little-minded; his very soul appears graceful and refined – his imaginings beautiful, his aspirations pure. Yet will he condescend to be pitiful and spiteful, and for the sake of giving utterance to a pointed word, or stinging jest, render himself more notorious for his ill words than his good deeds. [Thus Fanny had the last word.]

As for Bradley/Landseer:

Bradley the inspired! Who has not heard of Bradley? He has a patent privilege . . . of falling in love with every face he paints, and every face he paints smiles on him in return with safe impunity; for what all do, none need fear to do. . . . Had it not been for a sort of faded look that fatally contradicted the supposition, Mr Bradley might have been taken for a lad of sixteen; and but for that same faded look, he would have been a pretty lad too.[38]

Other members of the contemporary London scene who may have served for models were Joanna Baillie, Harriet Martineau, Letitia Elizabeth Landon, Lady Hessey, Mrs Opie, and even Elizabeth Barrett herself.

Fanny knew that fame had a price:

'We literary people,' as the Blue Belles invariably call themselves. London

Blue Belles! Poor young man! [the poet] He has suffered martyrdom at their hands! After his first volume of poems came out, and was favourably reviewed, he received, they say, three hundred and seventy-six invitations to dinner within a month. . . . That was but the opening of the campaign. One hundred and twenty, as I am told, sent their albums, green, red, yellow and blue, beseeching that he would write a few original lines in his own delicious vein of poesy therein. Seventy modestly entreated that he would only vouchsafe to inscribe his name at full length on a scrap of paper. It is positively asserted, that one hundred and three requested, each of them, a small lock of his hair; and fifty-two of them sent him poetry of their own composing . . . I grieve to say it, but the drawing room incubus, which settles so heavily on the breast of England's poets (rhyming or not rhyming), is feminine.[39]

Fanny gives a wonderful, if sardonic, picture of the soirées of the beginning of Queen Victoria's reign. The book is peppered with cameo pen portraits of the celebrities of her time, now so hard to identify. 'Mr Mortimer, the male coquette, and his confidential friend, Mrs Gardener-Stewart, who laps the sybarite in a sensual elysium, are painted with the minute details of miniature portraits', wrote *The Spectator*. Mrs Gardener-Stewart, who drapes herself amid flowers 'upon her soft silken sofa', and ensnares young men, became a model for Anthony's later portrait of Senora Madeline Neroni.

These two books were Fanny's answer to Anthony's desperate cry for help. For two months he had his mother's undivided attention and care; for the first time he was able to watch minutely how she set about her work, how she divided her day, and how the characters in her novels were mainly created from her contemporaries. Cared for by his mother, and doubtless amused by her wicked caricatures of their friends, Anthony slowly began to get better, and by the end of July he was well enough for Fanny to leave him and make the postponed visit to the Tilleys at Penrith. She set off by train to see her first granddaughter.

16. Marchmont, the reviewer for The Regenerator.
Marchmont takes a composing draught. 'He was a reviewer; one of the omnipotent WE, a member of the secret tribunal, in whose frown there was death, and whose smile brought food, lodging, hackney-coaches and satin gowns.'
(From Charles Chesterfield, *illustration by* 'Phiz')

17. Mrs Sherbourne, the author.
'For the success of her works, on which she almost entirely depended for her existence, she trusted to what she called the intensity of her own feelings. Nor did she trust in vain. No circulating library from the Orkneys to the Land's End, dared to confess that they had not got Mrs Sherbourne's last work.' (From Charles Chesterfield, *illustration by* 'Phiz')

18. *Fanny Trollope, an etching by an unknown artist completed in about 1840. (National Portrait Gallery)*

19. *Carlton Hill.*
The house built at Penrith in 1842 by Fanny Trollope where she lived for less than a year. It was subsequently lived in by her daughter and son-in-law, Cecilia and John Tilley, and their five children. (Author photo)

20. *Rose Heseltine.*
This sketch of Rose as a young girl is entitled The Fortune Teller. *It shows Rose and her sister Isabella, and was drawn by her oldest sister Ellen, an artist who migrated to Australia with her husband. (Hugh Trollope)*

21. *Theodosia Garrow at Torquay. (Hugh Trollope)*

22. *Thomas Adolphus in Florence as a young man. (Hugh Trollope)*

23. Villa Trollope, 1909.
*'The Villa Trollope has long been a favourite
haunt of well-known English and American
writers and those of the artistic world generally.'*

24. The drawing-room.
*'There is a large drawing-room with stage, leading onto open and covered terraces overlooking the
garden.' (Brochure for Villa Trollope 1909, after it had been converted to an English guest-house. In
the possession of the author.)*

25. The garden.
'The beautiful garden was planted with olio fraganza, magnolia, orange, lemon, loquist and other rare and choice trees by Mr Thomas Adolphus Trollope.'

26. The staircase.
'There are spacious and lofty bedrooms all having a pleasant outlook.' . . . Mr Thomas Hardy, the novelist, wrote Tess of the D'Urbervilles (1891) in Room 60. George Eliot, novelist, wrote part, if not the whole of Romola in Room 36.

27. Anthony Trollope posing with a hat.

28. Frederick James Trollope, Anthony's son, aged sixteen. It is interesting to note the likeness between seventeen-year-old Anthony (No. 10) and this photograph of his son Fred, aged sixteen. (Hugh Trollope)

29.   *Fanny, Tom, Theo and Bice, taken* c. *1860 posed on the terrace of the Villa Trollope.*

30. *Fanny Trollope aged eighty. (Hugh Trollope)*

31. *The English Cemetery, Florence.*
This is a wild neglected place, where some of the
most loved writers of the nineteenth century lie
in anonymous graves. (Author photo)

CHAPTER TEN

'Freely, honestly, and boldly expressed'

Penrith. July 1840–September 1843

The last 50 miles of the northward journey was completed by coach, for the rail track had not yet been extended as far as Penrith. The rapid spread of the railway system was beginning to revolutionize travel, and Fanny considered the global future in the prophetic introduction to *Town and Country*:

Steam! steam! steam! Steam has so changed the face of the country, from John o'Groat's house to the Land's End, that few persons of the present day who are still basking on the sunny side of fifty, either have, or can have, any accurate idea of what England was, during the early part of the present century. . . . Opinions may differ as to the comparative value of what has been lost and what has been gained by this great change, but it can scarcely be doubted that accuracy of detail is to be counted among the losses, though if tediousness has gone with it, the sprightly new world around us will probably account the loss a gain. That we, in some degree, lengthen our lives by thus shortening our distances, is quite certain, and this, where life is usefully employed, is great gain; and it is a great gain, also, if we can so manage as to acquire many ideas in the same space of time which it formerly took us to acquire a few; but who ever saw a medal that was equally admirable on both sides? It is impossible to move onward so rapidly as we are doing now without overlooking many interesting objects by the road-side. And then this steam, which brings all the world together so easily, knocks off as many corners of character as of road, and thereby makes one people so very like another people . . . that our old comedians . . . would be terribly at a loss for a type whereby to sketch a striking character. . . . Nevertheless, it seems to me that those who have lived long enough to remember what the manners of the middle classes were in the more remote counties, before the invention of steam-boats and railroads had caused them to be jumbled all together, till every trace of rural freshness was rubbed off, might fix upon less interesting periods for the employment of a gossiping pen.[1]

Now that Anthony was recovering, Fanny was happy to leave London behind her. She wanted to be closer to Cecilia and her first grandchild, young Frances Trollope Tilley. Tom planned to spend the summer of 1840 walking in Picardy and then to winter in Paris, where Fanny hoped to join him and take the much-postponed visit to Italy.

It was a time of assessment. Fanny was sixty-one, with no permanent home, and still with debts to be paid. Where, and with whom, was she going to live?

Tom would go wherever she went; Anthony was living in London; and Cecilia, happily married with one child and already expecting another, was settled in Penrith. The Tilleys were always welcoming, and Fanny, worried about Cecilia's delicate health, decided that she would make Penrith her home. She started looking for somewhere to live.

There was a house belonging to the elderly Mr de Whelpdale, which she was interested in buying, but the sale fell through. Fanny, unable to find anything else she liked, decided to build and bought some land at the top of a hill overlooking the ruins of Brougham Castle and the confluence of the Eden and Lowther rivers. She planned to build a house on the highest elevation, looking out over the misty Lake District views. The location lies just south-east of Penrith, and was then not far from Edenhall, the home of Sir George and Lady Musgrave, and near to Lowther Castle where Lord Lonsdale had his seat. In the autumn, Anthony, now recovered, came up from London to join them for a flying visit.

Once again Fanny decided to postpone her visit to Italy until the spring of 1841, and gave as a reason the disturbing reports of mob violence in Paris, and the outbreak of Anglophobia which was said to be raging in Europe. The other more pressing reason was that she needed to earn more money to build the new house at Penrith, which was to be called Carlton Hill.

Soon she met some of her neighbours and was invited by Lord Lonsdale to spend the night at Lowther, which she enjoyed. 'I spent as agreeable an evening and morning as I can remember. The old man is *delightful*, and so is his daughter Lady Frederick Bentinck.'[2] It was to Lord Londsdale that Fanny wrote when she was petitioning for a pension in the autumn of 1841. Her application was forwarded to Sir Robert Peel, with a recommendation by Lord Lonsdale; but the request was regretfully refused. Peel wrote that Lord Melbourne had granted, 'every shilling of the small pittance allowed for pensions (£1,200 per annum in the whole to meet any claim of literary merit, scientific discovery or public service), and has left nothing whatever available for the ensuing year.'[3] Fanny, as always, would have to rely on her own industry and she set to work once more.

She wrote to Tom: 'I get up at half-past four every morning, and get nearly the whole of my day's task accomplished before breakfast.'[4]

She was finishing *The Ward of Thorpe Combe*, for Bentley, and *The Blue Belles of England*, which was being published by Messrs. Saunders and Otley in serial format. Colburn had published *Charles Chesterfield* in the same form, and had agreed to take a further novel from her to be called *Hargrave, or a Man of Fashion*. When Colburn, who Lady Bulwer once described as 'an embodied shiver', discovered that Fanny had given the manuscript of *The Blue Belles* to a rival publisher he was highly incensed, and refused to honour his agreement to buy and publish *Hargrave*. He threatened to fight the case if she insisted on her rights, and, worse still, to publish all the particulars of her business transactions with him. Fanny had always, until then, had a good relationship with her various publishers, and she took it very much to heart. She was so deeply upset that she wanted to withdraw the novel and release Colburn from his contract; anything to avoid a public squabble; but when she wrote to Tom and her brother Henry suggesting this, they took counsel with the family lawyer, John Young, and she was advised that Colburn had no case. Fanny wrote: 'Of one thing I feel quite sure:– namely, that John Young will not advise a suit through which he cannot see his way. And therefore if he advises legal proceedings, and you agree with him, I submit.'[5]

The threat of a law suit was enough, Colburn paid the agreed amount of £625, and the novel was eventually published in 1843. After the affair was all over Fanny wrote to Tom: 'I am almost ashamed to own the utter discouragement and depression into which I had fallen. It has been totally out of my power to write regularly, since the blow fell upon me. But now I shall start with fresh vigour.'[6]

The money was already bespoken. The agreement to buy the land for Carlton Hill had been signed, with instalments to be paid at stipulated times, and her books were the only means of doing this.

Hargrave was a venture into the world of the crime writer, another new field, especially for a woman. Hargrave, a vain Englishman with expensive tastes, lived in Paris with his daughter and stepdaughter. He fell deeply into debt, the only solution for which appeared to be a wealthy marriage for his beautiful daughter. He gave a sumptuous ball to advertise his daughter's charms which he paid for with borrowed money, but forced to repay his creditors when the expected proposal did not eventuate, he resorted to robbery and eventually kidnapping. There was suspicion the kidnap victim might have been murdered, as her jewellery settings, minus the stones, were found buried in Hargrave's garden with blood on them. The Paris police were brought in and Hargrave fled to Germany in disguise, followed by his daughters who were disgraced by their father's scandal. They all lived in seclusion in a ruined castle outside a little village near Strasbourg (which Fanny had described in her Belgian travel book). In the end all was resolved, the daughters found true love, and Hargrave, embracing the Catholic religion, was eliminated by the Secret Tribunal.

Fanny used as her setting places she knew well; the Paris society in which she had recently spent a winter, and the wild country around Strasbourg, which she had explored for her Belgium and Western Germany travel book in 1833.

The requirements of the three-volume novel could, as *New Monthly Magazine* explained, lead to problems such as, 'an injurious clogging of the main action by superfluous incidental minutiae, these are faults almost inherent in the required form of the modern English novel, which by reason of the Procrustes' bed on which it places the writer (exactly neither more nor less than three volumes) often forbids that unity and concentration of interest which are so important to the perfection of a narrative.'[7]

Hargrave, which was a gripping murder mystery for the first two volumes, suffers from just such an over-extended ending. The critics, however, enjoyed it. *The Athenaeum* declared that readers, 'will find it difficult to lay it aside, when once they have taken it in hand'.

The *New Monthly Magazine* was full of praise.

Certain it is that Mrs Trollope has, on the present occasion, chosen a subject, and adopted a style of treating it, that, while they show her talents in an entirely new light, make a more distinct and direct appeal to mere popular favour than is to be found in any one of her previous works. . . . *Hargrave* is entirely different in its general character and construction from any of Mrs Trollope's previous works . . . where else in fictitious narrative, to find so intensely interesting a tissue of events, so skilfully concentrated together, so exactly fitted for the purposes for which they are brought before us, and so ingeniously developed . . . is more than we know.[7]

Even Elizabeth Barrett wrote to Miss Mitford, 'I have been reading to my amusement, Mrs Trollope's *Hargrave*. She has great skill in the construction of a story & shows it here; altho' I do not think that otherwise & generally, the work is of her cleverest. It is in the Widow Barnabys & such large deer, that she glorifies herself.'[8]

On 2 April 1841, when affairs on the Continent had become more peaceful, Fanny left Penrith for Italy and travelled via Austria to Bavaria, where she met Tom. There they stayed for a while with Fanny's old friend the Baroness de Zandt (formerly Lady Dyer), and then set off for the long-promised journey south which was to produce *Visit to Italy*. They arrived in Italy on 13 April 1841 and stayed until February 1842, visiting Rome, Florence, Venice, Pisa, Naples and Bologna, among many other stops. In Florence they called on the American sculptor Horatio Greenhough, who 'found her (quite contrary to our expectations) a very sensible well-bred old woman, rather "brusque", but decidedly a good specimen of her age and occupations.'

Fanny's book of her travels, written to fulfil her contract to Bentley, is more commonplace than most of her work. She writes interestingly enough of the places and people she saw and met, but it lacks the originality of her other travel books. It was published in 1842. One of the highlights was an account of an unusual performance in Florence by the famous Madame Sacqui, the tight-rope walker, who Fanny found to her dismay was the very Madame Sacqui she remembered from her childhood, now aged seventy. 'The exhibition was a very terrible one. Strength and activity . . . displayed by a wrinkled crone who looked as if she had reached the very last stage of human existence. It really was *tremendously horrible!*' She was even more horrified to find her 'decked out with all the meretricious decorations of an opera girl of eighteen'. After the performance on the stage, 'She set off, with an enormously heavy-looking flag in each hand, to walk to the very highest part of the large Theatre, over the heads of the people in the pit!' Fanny, expecting some dreadful catastrophe, noted the 'extraordinary stillness through the house', and when Madame Sacqui, on her return, 'stopped midway and waved her flags aloft, there was a burst, and a scream, that she, I suppose took for applause, which was almost deafening, and then we got up, and made our escape, rather ashamed perhaps of having been among the crowd who had looked upon such an unseemly spectacle.'[9]

Fanny wished to be back at Penrith in early 1842 to be with Cecilia for the birth of her third child, and the only way they could return was through the snow-bound Mount Cenis. They took the mail-post carriage from Turin as far as the road permitted and then had to transfer to a sledge. 'The miserable box was half full of snow, and therefore, though lined throughout with woollen serge, we were but little better off than if we had been packed in a wheelbarrow . . . our only chance of not having to sit for many hours in water arose from the hope that we might be sitting on ice instead!' The party was accompanied by a troop of mountaineers with huge wooden spades in order to dig them out if necessary. It was a frightening and dangerous journey. Afterwards Fanny wrote: 'I have more than once been, or fancied myself, in danger, when there was just sufficient excitement from it to make it a matter of doubt afterwards whether the sensation had been made up with more of pleasure or of pain. But not so of this midnight passage of Mount Cenis.'[10]

Once safely through, the party spent a few days in Paris to recuperate, and then returned, thankfully, to Penrith. Fanny arrived back in March 1842, in time for the birth of her third granddaughter, and stayed with Cecilia until Carlton Hill was ready.

Anthony, while his mother and brother were away in Italy, had at last found a way of escaping from his stifling London job. He accepted an appointment in Ireland, as a Surveyor's Clerk. He admitted, 'I was at that time in dire trouble, having debts on my head and quarrels with our Secretary-Colonel, and a full conviction that my life was taking me downwards to the lowest pits. . . . This was the first good fortune of my life.'[11] It was to be the beginning for him of a new and much happier existence.

After finishing the *Visit to Italy* and getting it to the publisher, Fanny set to work on *The Barnabys in America*, which was to be published in twelve monthly parts in the *New Monthly Magazine* by Colburn. In this last tale of her favourite heroine, The Widow Barnaby comes back in full splendour and carves a path of confidence trickery through North America following the route taken by Fanny in 1828.

Fanny was disappointed with the terms Colburn offered her, but she felt obliged to accept them as she needed the money to complete the building of Carlton Hill. She asked Tom to be careful in his spending for her, explaining, 'If you were sixty-two years old, and had to get up at four o'clock every morning to work for it, you would not wonder at my saying this!'[12]

On 23 July 1842 Fanny and Tom spent the first night in the newly completed Carlton Hill. It was the first time since the building of Julians in Harrow in 1818 that Fanny had lived in her own house. Julians, too, had been built to her own design, and the grounds landscaped to her specifications. In each case the costs exceeded the estimates. In each case the stay was very short.

Carlton Hill is an imposing house in a beautiful setting high on a hill. The driveway, crowded by massive yew trees and huge banks of rhododendrons planted by Tom, winds up the hill from the road below. As Tom wrote later: 'I put in some hundreds of trees and shrubs with my own hands, which prospered marvellously, and have become, I have been told, most luxuriant shrubberies.'[13]

At the top of the rise the drive opens on to a gravel sweep, with a wall separating it from the garden. The house is large, two storeys high, with bow windows and a conservatory looking out over the large terraced garden falling down to the valley and the red crumbling ruins of Brougham Castle. At the bottom of the garden is a spring-fed lake, surrounded by shrubs. Originally known as St Michael's Well, it had been diverted by Fanny in order to build the entrance drive, much to the dismay of Sir George Musgrave, who said that they had moved a holy well and as a consequence would never establish themselves in that place. It is very isolated even now. It must have been even more so then. Nothing is to be heard but the bleating of sheep and the swish of persistent rain.

During the summer Anthony came over from Ireland to stay at Carlton Hill. He and Tom tramped for miles over the fells, and when Anthony returned to Ireland, Tom went with him. Fanny was left alone in the great house. There were pleasant neighbours, and the Tilleys lived at Fell Side about half a mile away, but it was worlds away from the gaiety of London, Paris, and Italy. As Frances Eleanor explained: 'the pleasant persons were widely scattered over a considerable tract of country. The plums in the social pudding were too few and far between both in space and time; and, to state the case, not completely, but compendiously, she found the life dull.'[14] It was also very expensive.

Soon after Tom returned from Ireland, their dearly loved cousin Fanny Bent came to stay. She was a welcome visitor. The two Fannys must have talked over the problems of isolation, and considered possible solutions. As winter drew in and the weather became more severe, it became difficult to get out of the house. Tom and Fanny T. discussed the possibility of going to Moselle in France the following year to escape the severity of the winters in Cumbria, and before Christmas had begun to make travel plans.

Instead, surprisingly, Carlton Hill was abandoned in the spring of 1843. The decision to settle in the Lake District had been a terrible mistake, and Fanny went south to stay with friends. She had lived in her new house for less than a year. Tom wrote: 'The assignment of the severity of the climate as the cause is an admirable euphemism. The truth is that we found our neighbours too dull and stupid.'[15]

While Fanny had been enduring the rigours of a Cumbrian winter, she had been working on another reform book, to be called *Jessie Phillips: A Tale of the Present Day*. In order to reach the maximum number of people, as in the case of *Michael Armstrong*, it was published in eleven monthly parts in the *New Monthly Magazine*. The first chapter appeared on 31 December 1842, and the parts ran until November 1843. The novel is a stark picture of the results of the injustices of the new Poor Law of 1834.

The old Speenhamland Poor Law was drawn up in 1813, when, instead of fixing upon a living wage in relation to the price of bread as was advocated, the commissioners decided to supplement wages out of the parish rates. This was done to a scale. The breadwinner should earn 3s a week, every other member of his family 1s 6d. Any shortfall came from the rates. There was now no motive for the employer to pay a living wage, and as prices and rents rose, wages fell to below subsistence rate. The self-respect of the labourer was destroyed as he saw himself becoming a pauper for life. In 1834 the new Poor Law was passed in an attempt to rectify the degrading situation, and restore some self-respect to the rural poor. The new law was to be administered by centralized Commissioners appointed by London. Payment of 'outdoor relief' was instantly abolished in an attempt to force a wage rise, and anyone who needed help had to attend the Union Workhouse, and put their case before the local board of guardians. The instant loss of relief drove mothers and children into the fields in the 'gang' system, under terrible conditions. The poor were once again exploited. Those who were sick or unable to work could only obtain relief within the Union workhouse, and only the most needy cases were admitted. *Jessie Phillips* was written to expose some of the worst inconsistencies.

Dr Maxwell, one of the board of guardians, argued with a fellow board member, Mr Lewis:

'I shall be very grateful if you will show me how the admission of eight human beings into the poor-house, to be wholly and entirely provided for at the expense of the parish, and that for a period unlimited, can be a less burden upon us than giving the aid of a few shillings a week, for a short time, in compliance with the wishes of our chairman.'

'The LAW, sir, – the LAW,' cried Mr Lewis, eagerly, 'It is the law, sir.'[16]

Conditions were appalling; the aim being to make life for the paupers inside the workhouse far worse than outside. Not only were the sexes segregated, but family members were separated and not allowed to communicate. Food was meagre, work was forbidden to all except those who worked in the institution. The elderly and sick were confined in a small uncomfortable room. As Fanny described it:

Its one window looked out upon a small interior court, the principal, and, indeed, nearly the only object in which was a pump, with a cistern under it, where all the inmates of the establishment, old and young, male and female, performed their ablutions. Round the walls of this small chamber, and firmly fixed to them, were wooden benches, as narrow as it was well possible for an adult human being to sit upon.'[17]

Jessie Phillips was a young and beautiful village girl, loved by all, who got into trouble when she caught the eye of the squire's arrogant and spoilt son, Frederick. She was seduced by him, believing his promises of marriage. Her mother died, Jessie found she was pregnant, and when she asked Frederick to honour his promise, he denied responsibility and offered her £10 to disappear. With nowhere to go, and ostracized by the local families who had once employed her, she was forced to apply for parish relief. She was taken in to the Union workhouse. Upon admission her clothes were taken away, and workhouse garments handed out, 'which were ill suited for comfort, either in heat or cold.' When Jessie was admitted she had her long hair shorn.

It was the degradation which she shared in common with the felon inmates of a gaol which caused her spirits to sink, and almost die within her. An involuntary, but irrepressible sentiment of indignation swelled her heart as she thought how many miserable human beings were exposed to this degradation, who were guiltless of any crime, save poverty. . . . Dismal and dreary, Oh! frightfully dismal and dreary was the daily routine of that last refuge of helplessness and want.[18]

One of the other inmates advised Jessie to confront Frederick and ask for enough money to bring up the child. The only way she could get out of the workhouse was to disguise herself as Silly Sally, a simpleton, who was allowed to come and go as she wished. Jessie went to the village lawyer for advice, but learnt from him that under the new Poor Law she had no rights of demand from the father of the child. The Paternity Act had been repealed. This explanation, 'opened to her a perfectly new view of the case. It was not only then to punish the offending woman, but to spare the pocket of the fondly protected man, that this new regulation was established.' As Fanny commented:

The severest penalty that had ever been exacted by the law, so unhappily repealed, was to oblige a man to make that woman his wife whom he had made the mother of his child. . . . But how did the law stand now? The frail creature who had no defence against her own love, and that of its dear object strong enough to combat the hope that she should become his wife, is doomed, when that hope . . . fails her, to become answerable in the eye of the law for all the consequences of the mutual sin! . . . Let us look at the wisdom, justice, and humanity of the choice which has selected the woman as the sacrifice. . . . Alas, poor wretch! she is the victim of her lover . . . a victim of the short-sighted policy of her own country, which, while hoping (vainly) to save a few yearly shillings from the poor-rates, had decreed that a weak woman (that is to say a weak *poor* woman) who has committed this sin shall atone for it by being trampled in the dust, imprisoned in a workhouse with her wretched offspring till driven from it to seek food for both by labour. . . . Now our precious gentlefolks have been clever enough to find out that by leaving one to suffer for both, and letting t'other go free, they have made the girl's share too bad to bear, and so they shall get quit of the paying, either by the poor wretch killing herself, or her child, or both.[19]

Jessie, shocked by the callousness of the lawyer, went into labour on her way back to the workhouse and crawled into a cowshed to give birth. A kindly yeoman took her to his cottage but knew nothing of the baby. The evil Frederick, who had been watching, entered the shed, and finding the baby, kicked it to death and hid the body. When the body was discovered it was Jessie, of course, who was accused of murder, and later died in prison.

Fanny, by following the fortunes of various village families, both cottagers and gentry, was able to put the arguments against the new law strongly, and from various points of view. It is a powerful book, and, more importantly, the first book to challenge the bastardy clause of the new Poor Law, which was generally considered unjust.

In 1839 the *New Monthly Magazine* had written about Fanny:

There may be many persons more competent to form an opinion on many subjects than Mrs Trollope. Her views may be distorted by prejudice – (as whose are not?) – or she may form a judgement too hastily; but we confess that we set a very high value on Mrs Trollope's opinion for this reason: that we are sure that be the subject what it may – and displeasing whom it may – that opinion will be freely, honestly, and boldly expressed. That is, it is true, a course, which must and will make enemies (or opponents rather); but we would hold up the example of Mrs Trollope to all writers, as a proof that in authorship as well as in all other crafts, honesty is the best policy.[20]

However, *John Bull* was shocked: 'Mrs Trollope has sinned grievously against good taste and decorum. The particular clause of the Act which she has selected for reprobation is the *bastardy clause* – not perhaps the very best subject for a female pen.'

It is interesting to note that in 1844, the year after the book first appeared, the House of Commons passed 'The Little Poor Law', returning to unwed mothers the rights which had been taken away from them. The bastardy clause was amended.

When Fanny left Penrith in April 1843, she went to stay in Clifton with the Misses Gabell, her friends from childhood. While there she heard of the plight of Mary Russell Mitford, who was beset by financial problems. Crippled by arthritis, and responsible for her father's gambling debts, she tried to support them both with her writing. Miss Mitford too, had applied for a pension and been refused. In the spring of 1843 her numerous friends raised £1,300 by public subscription. Among the subscribers were the Queen Dowager, young Queen Victoria, bishops, archbishops, dukes, and many friends and fellow writers. Mrs Trollope gave £5 which was a generous gift for someone who was herself in straitened circumstances. Miss Mitford was delighted and she wrote to a friend, Miss Harrison: 'This is very gratifying; so are the names of those from who I have received money.' She wrote to another friend on 15 March 1843: 'I have been very poorly, but am getting better and reckon much upon my journey to Bath and into Devonshire. Did I tell you that I hope to meet Mrs Trollope there, and that I have promised (DV) [*Deo volente*] in some future year to visit her in Paris. One can hardly fancy a more agreeable introduction to the things and people best worth seeing in Paris, than Mrs Trollope.' Miss Mitford did meet Fanny in Bath and 'was charmed with the old city'.[21]

Tom remained at Penrith to sell the house, and to organize the packing of the furniture, books and plate for storage. On 11 May Tom went to London to do some business with the publishers for his mother. He probably saw Nelson's Column, newly erected in Trafalgar Square. On 1 June 1843 he joined his mother at Fanny Bent's house in Exeter. A week later, Wednesday 7 June was recorded as the momentous day when Fanny and Tom decided to make their home abroad for at least a year: 'Dresden was talked of. Rome was considered. Paris was thought of. Venice was discussed. Finally Florence came on the *tapis*. We had liked it much, and had formed some much-valued friendships there. It was supposed to be economical as a place to live in, which was one main point. . . . And eventually Florence was fixed on.'[22] Fanny, now sixty-four, wanted to live somewhere warm, and among lively and intelligent company. Italy was to become her home for the rest of her life.

The remainder of that summer was spent mainly in Devonshire staying with Fanny Bent, or travelling with her to visit Mary Clyde, Fanny T.'s sister, whose elderly husband, the Admiral, was an invalid.

Fanny started another book, based on her experiences of the social life at Carlton Hill. It was about a family who thought themselves better in every way than their neighbours. It is called, *The Laurringtons, or Superior People* and it is a wonderfully wicked caricature of all her neighbours. One can understand why she left Penrith. At the end of the book she writes a tantalizing disclaimer: 'If some among my Laurringtons are not recognized among some of my readers as portraits, it will not be because the sketches are not after nature, but because I wished not, for many reasons, to make any of them too strikingly like to the originals.'[23]

The main characters were, naturally, the family of the Laurringtons. William, the eldest, was ponderously vast, and the general expression of his countenance was 'placid and self pleased'. The eldest girl, Mary, aged twenty-nine, 'was greatly soothed by the perpetually recurring conviction that in talent, beauty, birth, and position, she was incomparably superior to any individual of her acquaintance.' The original of the third Laurrington, Miss Aramita, was well known to Fanny. She was:

> . . . decidedly, and in one comprehensive phrase, a woman of genius . . . she was more pre-eminently musical than any other young lady had been, or, in fact, was ever likely to be. As she really played with a great deal of what is called 'execution' . . . it might puzzle many to discover the reason why people lived in greater dread of her piano than of any other in the whole neighbourhood. The fact is, that though there were dozens of young ladies who played infinitely worse, there was not one who had the strength to play anything like so long. . . . It was like someone reading a poem in a language he did not understand.[24]

Miss Cornelia Laurrington's position 'in her distinguished family was that of beauty *par excellence*', and there was also a younger sister, Cecilia, who was beautiful and good, and who was fortunate enough to be brought up in London by her Aunt Watts, away from the pretensions of Laurrington Lodge. Mary declared patronizingly, 'no one who bears the name of Laurrington can ever be considered in civilized society as being on a level with any one bearing that of Watts.'

The book discloses how the insufferable Laurringtons eventually meet their match. There is a revealing description of a party given by a neighbour, Lady Willbury. There was to be dancing with breakfast afterwards, 'as it is customary to call the excellent dinner provided on such occasions', which was to be followed by charades. The setting was the garden at Bury Hall, and all the guests were to come in rustic dress. The descriptions of the guests are truly Trollopian: 'Miss Celestina March curvetted on beside the tranquil Charlotte Verepoint, very like a great unbroken Flanders colt, beside a dainty-paced little Arabian. . . . Her robe was of very thin orange-coloured silk, which, being quite new, and very fully flounced, stuck out in all directions to such an extent that she seemed almost to fill the room.' The Laurringtons behaved in their usual pompous and insensitive ways. The appalling Frederick eventually succumbed to the charms of the fortune-hunting Miss Masterman, who, after they were married, ruled him, and the rest of the family, with a rod of iron. She treated her husband with observed contempt. 'The gentlemen to a man declared that she was captivating, and the ladies, almost as harmoniously, that she was intolerable.'

Once again, the descriptions of people and houses are tantalizingly real, and scenes, such as that of a boating accident, reflect known events from Fanny's own experiences. There is a strong feeling of truth underlying the satire. 'The Domestic Manners of Penrith' maybe? The book was published by Longmans in 1844.

In that same year Colburn published *Young Love*, written by Fanny at the same time. Once again it has a feeling of being set among her erstwhile friends, although she vowed:

. . . our nameless county was neither Westmorland nor Cumberland. . . . For reasons which have been sufficiently explained I have declined naming the county in which the scenes which I am about to portray occurred, I shall not be equally scrupulous respecting the people who took part in them, but take the liberty of describing the most prominent among them with equal freedom and sincerity. That they shall all be real human beings, who are existing, or who have existed, I faithfully promise; but I faithfully promise likewise, that I will so manage matters as to leave no clue whatever to the recognition of the originals.[25]

This time we have a spoilt young man, Alfred Dermont, aged twenty, seduced by a fortune-hunting older woman, Miss Amelia Thorwold, aged twenty-nine. Amelia was a very fascinating creation. She set her cap at Alfred because in a few months she 'will be between thirty and forty, deeply in debt without a shilling in the world'. It was desirable that she marry someone as soon as possible, and she told her chaperone Mrs Knight, 'it is quite within the reach of probability that I shall be arrested if I do not.' Amelia was bored by Alfred and asked Mrs Knight to 'tell me if you think that women actually die of fatigue when boys make love to them?' She managed to avoid a declaration from him, and instead eloped with an old flame, Lord William Hammond, 'The darling of Almack's, the pride of the park, the glory of the drawing room, the pet of the boudoir, and the sovereign of the opera.' After a few weeks dalliance, he abandoned Amelia, and she vowed to return and capture young Alfred. In this she almost succeeded, but at the last moment she was revealed in her true colours and had to flee in order to avoid arrest. It is a good story.

New Monthly Magazine positively praised it.

Her Widow Barnabys, her Mrs Robertses, and the rest, are capital game to fly at, and the slaughter that Mrs Trollope makes among them is admirable sport, not to mention its excellent result of clearing the land of nuisances that no less tender handling can be expected to abate. But it is not for this that Mrs Trollope has received, and cultivated to their highest pitch, faculties never before possessed and cultivated in an equal degree by any woman. . . . They are, we repeat, superior to anything of a similar kind that the writer has previously done, and prove her to be as much without a female rival in the delineation of passion and pathos as she is in breadth of humour and force of comic painting.'[26]

On 2 September 1843 Fanny and Tom set off in a new direction. Florence was the destination. It was in that same September that Anthony, now happily living in Ireland, began his first novel, *The Macdermots of Ballycloran*. It was not to be published until 1847, but for him too, it was an important step towards a new and rewarding life.

CHAPTER ELEVEN

'Ever eager for fresh materials to work upon'

Florence. September 1843–September 1847

When Fanny and Tom arrived in Florence they were welcomed by Rosina, Lady Bulwer, as guests at the Palazzo Passerini. Here they would stay until they found their own apartment. Lady Bulwer was a very volatile person; Tom described her as, 'brilliant, witty, generous, kind, joyous, good-natured, and very handsome. But she was totally governed by impulse and unreasoning prejudice . . . totally devoid of prudence or judgement.' The less pleasant aspects were, 'more perceptible on close intimacy'.[1]

On one occasion, when Lady Bulwer was unwell, she declared she could not afford to call in a doctor, 'But she had hardly got the words out of her mouth when the servant entered the room saying that the silversmith was at the door asking that an account which he laid on the table might be paid. The account . . . was for a pair of small silver spurs and an ornamented silver collar which she had ordered a week or two previously for the *ceremonial knighting of her little dog Taffy.*'[2] Fanny and Tom became irritated by the inconsistencies.

Lady Bulwer was, however, a devoted friend to both Tom and his mother, and eulogized Fanny for her 'straightforward, unflinching, courageous integrity'.

Eventually the Trollopes found an apartment for themselves in the Casa Berti. The house was next door to the east end of the church of Santa Croce, and the rooms looked out onto a large garden. Within a few weeks of settling in, the new home became the centre 'of attraction and pleasant intercourse', where Fanny held weekly Friday receptions, which were always crowded. The British minister in Florence was Lord Holland, and he and his beautiful wife were the hub of the large expatriate English community that had settled there; the Italians thought of them as 'the gold-bringing foreigners from that distant and barbarous western isle'. The social life was lively. There were balls, dinners, whist parties, and musical evenings that Fanny joined into with zest, often staying in the crowded salons until three and four o'clock in the morning. There were also walking and driving expeditions to the beautiful Tuscan hills. It was for this lifestyle that she had left the isolation of Penrith. During all this time Fanny continued writing.

Charles Dickens had been invited to make a triumphal tour of America following, in the main, Fanny's route down the Mississippi. He had written his *American Notes* (1842) and the American section of *Martin Chuzzlewit* (1843) on his return. The latter was published in twenty parts between July 1843 and July 1844. The two books show many similarities to Fanny's *Domestic Manners of the Americans* (1832), and even more to her novel *The Refugee* (1833). Elizabeth Barrett was not impressed by Dickens' behaviour and wrote to Miss Mitford on 28 May 1843: 'To think of a man . . . a man with a heart . . . going to a great nation to *be crowned* – for they did no less than crown him . . . and then to come home & hiss at them with all the venom in his body! – The last number of Chuzzlewit, & one former number, are worse than malignant – & Mrs Trollope is charity herself compared to the Boz of them!'[3]

Fanny had written to Dickens to congratulate him on his *American Notes*, and received a reply on 16 December 1842: 'I am convinced that there is no writer who has so well and so accurately (I need not add so entertainingly) described it, [America] in many of its aspects, as you have done; and this renders your praise the more valuable to me.'[4]

On 1 January 1844 Fanny was presented to the Tuscan Grand Duke and Duchess at the Pitti Palace in Florence. Two nights later she developed an alarming chill and was delirious for twenty-four hours. She was 'bled, blistered, and mustard-plastered' for the next five days, and grew steadily worse. Her practitioner was the leading doctor in Florence and was described by Tom as: 'a very good fellow, and an admirable whist player; and I do not think that the members of our little colony drew a sufficiently sharp line of division between his social and his professional qualifications.'[5] Tom thought she was going to die. Lord Holland visited the house to enquire after Fanny's health and was so alarmed that he insisted on a second opinion. He sent his own medical attendant who ordered port wine, bark, and nourishment, and nothing more. As a result Fanny rapidly recovered her health, but lost one of her favourite whist players.

Tom wrote an enlightening description of some of the balls held at the Pitti Palace:

The guests used to behave abominably. The English would seize the plates of bonbons and empty the contents bodily into their coat pockets. The ladies would do the same with their pocket handkerchiefs. But the Duke's liege subjects carried on their depredations on a far bolder scale. I have seen large portions of fish, sauce and all, packed up in a newspaper and deposited in a pocket. I have seen fowls and ham share the same fate without any newspaper at all.[6]

He reported, however, that he had never seen any large bottles of wine being carried off and thought that the servants must have had orders to prevent it. There were numerous English in Florence at that time, and an increasing number of Americans.

In the spring of that same year, Fanny and Tom first heard of Anthony's engagement to Miss Rose Heseltine, and in May, they left Florence for England to visit the Tilleys at Penrith. It had always been Fanny's plan to winter in Florence and visit the family in England in the spring.

The Tilleys had moved into Carlton Hill, though it is not certain if they had bought the house from Fanny or were paying rent. Cecilia now had three little girls and was pregnant again. She was not well and Fanny was concerned about her. 'She cannot walk without suffering so much from fatigue that I content myself with taking her to a beach near the sea, and sitting there till I think she has inhaled a sufficient quantity of *iodine*.'[7]

It was during this visit that Anthony married Rose Heseltine on 11 June 1844, in Rose's home town of Rotherham. Rose, born in 1820, was the third youngest of four daughters of Edward Heseltine, a bank manager of Rotherham in Yorkshire. She and Anthony had met while she was on holiday with her family in Ireland. Only Rose's family attended the wedding, but Rose met Anthony's family during the honeymoon in the Lake District. Rose seems to have enjoyed meeting her famous mother-in-law for she wrote:

Nothing could have been kinder or more affectionate than the way she received me – kind, good, and loving, then and ever afterwards. No one who saw her at this date could suppose she was in her sixty-fourth year, so full was she of energy. There was no one more eager to suggest, and carry on the suggestions, as to mountain excursions, picnics, and so forth. And she was always the life and soul of the party with her cheerful conversation and her wit. She rose very early and made her own tea, the fire having been prepared overnight – (on one occasion I remember her bringing me a cup of tea to my room, because she thought I had caught cold during a wet walk in the mountains) – then sat at her writing-table until the allotted task of so many pages was completed; and was usually on the lawn before the family breakfast-bell rang, having filled her basket with cuttings from the rose-bushes for the table and drawing room decorations.[8]

Fanny liked her new daughter-in-law, and was sorry when the honeymoon was over and Anthony and Rose returned to Ireland. In the middle of July 1844 Fanny and Tom left Penrith and went to Ovington, near Winchester, where they stayed with Baroness von Zandt (formerly Lady Dyer), her very old and dear friend, who was now widowed for the second time. They stayed in England until 1 September when Fanny returned to Florence and the Casa Berti.

Cecilia's fourth child and first son, Arthur William, was born in December of that year. Fanny, who was becoming increasingly anxious about Cecilia's health, was delighted that all was well. She wrote to John Tilley from Florence: 'Other folks can cry for joy, my dearest John, besides the grave Ann. And my breakfast was made most delicious this morning by a mixture of this species of salt water with my tea. Whatever else distance may lessen, it does not lessen anxiety. And did you know what multitudes of gloomy dreads and fears have been haunting me, you would guess *a little* what sort of welcome your letter received.'[9]

In that winter of 1844 the rains were torrential in Florence and the Arno flooded, causing immense damage to the city. There were grave fears for the Ponte Vecchio as the onlookers watched the floodwaters rise to within a foot of the keystone of the highest arch. 'At last came a cry from those who were watching it close at hand' when they saw that the flood had reached its peak. When Tom tried to return to Casa Berti in the Via dei Malcontenti, he found the road 5 ft under water; the only way he could get back was by boat, and then to clamber up a ladder from the boat and in through a window. It was several days before the floods receded enough to use the roads again.

While Fanny and Tom were in Florence they were visited by Charles Dickens and his wife. It was the first time Tom had met Dickens, who was two years his junior, and at first sight he was disappointed: 'What we saw was a dandified, pretty-boy-looking sort of figure; singularly young-looking, I thought, with a slight flavour of the whipper-snapper genus of humanity. . . . In later life he lost this D'Orsay look completely, and was bronzed and reddened by wind and weather like a seaman.' He went on to say that Dickens', 'wonderful eyes which saw so much and so keenly, were appreciably, though to a very slight degree, near-sighted eyes'.[10] Later, Tom and Dickens became firm friends, and Tom was a frequent contributor to Dickens' *Household Words*.

Fanny meanwhile was writing *The Robertses on Their Travels*. This was based on her own observations of the uncouth behaviour of the English abroad.

In recently looking over a miscellaneous collection of old travelling notes, made at various times, and in various lands, I found such constantly repeated expressions of regret and vexation at the effect produced on the minds of all foreigners by the strange, and often offensive, manners of many among the multitudes of English travellers who thronged their cities . . . and which tended to account for and justify the universal sentence of condemnation which has been passed upon English manners by every nation on the Continent. . . . Sometimes I have been tempted to believe that it arises from the unwonted lightness of spirit, produced by the change of climate. . . . The animal spirits rise. The customary restraints imposed by the manners and habits of home, and the check produced by the presence of familiar eyes being withdrawn, the gay travellers become fantastic first, and then impertinent, and like children invited out without their governess, appear in the eyes of those they visit to have much worse manners than they ever exhibit at home.[11]

The tale was of the Roberts family on their first visit abroad. Mr Roberts, a banker, had retired, and was reluctantly persuaded to take his overbearing wife and three revolting children on a visit to France and Germany. Mrs Roberts, 'had heard people talk familiarly of "Lords, Dukes, and noble Princes", as among their daily associates during their continental excursions; she had heard, too, from the same persons, that sixpences would go as far as a shilling. On these two statements had all her hopes and all her projects been founded.'[12] She looked down on all foreigners. 'It is the duty of an Englishwoman . . . to teach all foreigners that we are the first people of the earth in all ways. And that is what I *will* teach them.' The family began their journey in Paris, ran up huge bills for carriage hire, dresses and hats, and as a result had to leave rather suddenly.

The Robertses fell into most of the pitfalls experienced by ignorant and self-opinionated travellers, and eventually returned to England wiser and considerably poorer. The book was a witty, cautionary tale for travellers, of whom the majority at that time were English. Frances Eleanor wrote: 'They, and their solid, neat-looking portmanteaus, clean-shaven faces, and well-filled purses, were periodically expected over large tracts of Europe, as the farmer expects the harvest, or the fisherman herring and mackerel.'[13]

The book was printed by Colburn in 1846. The critics and the public enjoyed the satire, and claimed to recognize many of the characters.

Fanny and Tom spent the winter at Casa Berti. But then their landlord required the house for his invalid mother-in-law and they found themselves new lodgings at Casa Olivieri in the Via del Giglio. The move was sudden and inconvenient, but they could hardly refuse. Tom stayed in Florence for most of the summer of 1845 to complete the move, while Fanny returned to England in April. This time she went by boat from Leghorn to Marseilles. She spent a day or two in Paris visiting friends on the way to England, and in London she called on Colburn to discuss terms and contracts for future publications. Two novels were agreed upon, *The Attractive Man* and *Father Eustace*. Fanny also agreed to write a two-volume book of travelling sketches to follow the success of *The Robertses*. It was entitled *Travels and Travellers: A Series of Sketches*, and is a mishmash of anecdotes, stories and travellers' tales, but sadly makes rather uninspired reading. After London Fanny visited friends in Clifton for a week, and so to her final destination, Carlton Hill.

The next book, *The Attractive Man*, was a tale of confidence trickery and deception, and described what happened in a peaceful country village when an imposter charmed his way into the community. Theodore Vidal was the 'attractive man' and his aim was to marry for money. In this he was abetted by Lucy Dalton, a penniless servant's daughter, who had been living as the favoured companion of the squire's only daughter, Mary. It was this heiress, Mary, who Theodore intended to marry. Lucy Dalton was a truly evil heroine, who would stop at nothing to achieve wealth and independence. When her plans were discovered by her mother who threatened to disclose them to the squire, Lucy gave her three bottles of gin, knowing that she would become violently drunk. When this happened, Lucy called in the apothecary, and declaring her mother to be mad, had her committed to the Asylum where she would be safely locked away.

Later in the book, in another scene, a husband endeavoured to have his wife declared insane so that he might inherit her fortune. M. Marathone, a Frenchman of twenty-five, married a wealthy old lady of seventy hoping that she would die and leave him all her money. In order to make others believe that she was demented he revealed to her some experimental research he was engaged in. She, in turn, told her nephew, who began to suspect 'that if his handsome uncle was not mad himself, he had been deliberately endeavouring to bring his wife into that condition.'[14] The aunt recounted to the nephew that her husband had conducted experiments during which he made dead beasts come to life again, and he could go into his laboratory and make little living creatures of some sort or other. (Mary Shelley's *Frankenstein* had been published in 1818.) That however was not the worst of it. God had not created man.

'By means of electricity there began to be lots of little fishes . . . they were very shabby scrubby little fishes at first, but then every fish had a child that was a great deal better looking and cleverer than itself . . . when the fishes married, they had rats for children, and when the rats married, they had birds, or else the birds came first, and they were confined with rats, and then the rats had cats, I believe, and the cats had dogs, and the dogs monkeys, and the monkeys men and women. . . . Is it not enough to make one shudder?'

[At this point old Madame Marathone's nephew reassured her.] 'I suspect, my dear aunt . . . that you must have misinterpreted what these scientific gentlemen say. Depend upon it you did not understand them rightly. No person could be found seriously to utter such blasphemous nonsense as you have now spoken to me.'[15]

This must have seemed a very bizarre story to Fanny's readers. Charles Darwin's *On the Origin of Species by Natural Selection* was not published until 1859, fourteen years later.

The *New Monthly Magazine* enjoyed Fanny's new book when it was printed in 1845.

There is some admirable by-play . . . in the character of a philosophic aunt who gives a most strange but very true and acute 'travestie' of what the theories of the author of 'The Natural History of Creation' would be, if carried to their extreme by an uneducated person. . . . The same perfect ease and freedom of style, the same quick and humorous perception of character comes out more harmoniously and more pleasingly from the absence of the grotesque and *The Attractive Man* must take a high stand among its author's productions.

The *Literary Gazette* did not agree:

The Attractive Man is not an attractive novel. On the contrary it is repulsive. . . . It is positively disagreeable, and almost disgusting, to read three volumes in which the development of emotions and passions in the breasts of women affords nothing more refreshing to human nature than such weaknesses, follies, vices, and crimes. Heaven forbid that we should not consider the whole to be a false and malicious libel!

In July 1845 Anthony and Rose visited Carlton Hill, and so, later, did Fanny's brother Henry Milton. Anthony had with him the manuscript of his first novel, *The Macdermots of Ballycloran*, which he gave to his mother asking her to try and place it with a publisher in London. He was the last member of the family to take up writing and was understandably defensive about how the rest of the family would react:

There were three or four in the field before me, and it seemed to be almost absurd that another should wish to add himself to the number. My father had written much – those long ecclesiastical descriptions – quite unsuccessfully. My mother had become one of the popular authors of the day. My brother had commenced, and had been fairly well paid for his work. My sister, Mrs Tilley, had also written a novel which was at that time in manuscript – which was published afterwards without her name, and was called Chollerton. I could perceive that this attempt of mine was felt to be an unfortunate aggravation of the disease.[16]

Anthony asked Fanny not to read the book, and said, rather unjustly, 'I knew that she did not give me credit for the sort of cleverness necessary for such a work.' Anthony, in his insecurity, was no doubt thinking of her earlier letter of advice which he remembered as criticism rather than encouragement.

Fanny made every effort to help both Anthony and Cecilia find publishers. Cecilia's book was placed with John Ollivier, and Thomas Newby was persuaded to take Anthony's manuscript. When Newby eventually published it, the agreement was that Anthony would receive half the profits after expenses had been deducted. No money was ever forthcoming, and Newby, an unscrupulous opportunist, published the book under the single name 'Trollope' which must have been galling for Anthony.

There were now four small Tilleys, Frances, Anna, Cecilia, and Arthur, who were a great joy to Fanny, but also a distraction. She wrote to Tom:

> I trust if my health continues as good as it is at present (enabling me to get up at four o'clock every morning) I shall be able to accomplish my task. But you must allow that it is less easy to do this in a house surrounded by company, than it would be without it. . . . If I do get through the novel – 340 pages each volume *by agreement* – by the end of August, I shall consider it a great *tour de force*. But as to doing it in *less* time, I certainly do not mean even to attempt it.[17]

The book was finished on time, however, and in September she met Tom as arranged, at the estate of Seehof near Bamberg in Bavaria where the Baroness von Zandt now lived. They stayed there for two weeks, and Fanny, worried about the health of her friend the Baroness, advised her to dispose of the castle and return to England to live.

At the end of September 1845 Fanny and Tom were back in Florence settling into their new quarters in the Via del Giglio. Their apartment was on the ground floor, and though less agreeable than Casa Berti, it had the great advantage of a flower garden and a greenhouse. In the winter of 1845/6 Fanny was the centre of a whirl of engagements. Frances Eleanor wrote in her biography: 'Mrs Trollope entertained a great deal, and received at her dinner-parties and soirées, emphatically the best society that Florence had to boast. . . . Scarcely any one of mark visited Florence in those days, without finding his way to her salon.' She tried to explain why this was so. 'She was not wealthy; and though she was a successful writer of books, she did not hold a pre-eminent position in literature. But she had admirably good sense, much genuine humour, great knowledge of the world, a quick appreciation of other's gifts, and, above all, a character of the most flawless sincerity, and a warmly affectionate heart.'[18]

Fanny wrote an account of one of the many balls she attended:

> Lord Holland's *bal costume* was the first at which the court was present, – and one thousand one hundred and twenty-five persons besides! I went as a Quakeress; and Lady Holland admired the dress so much, that she sent to borrow it the next morning, and had one made like it for Prince Demidoff's! I had, moreover, the honour of receiving a message from court, requesting that I would come there in the same dress. There's glory for you![19]

One of the things Fanny enjoyed most was organizing her friends into theatrical performances, always one of her favourite pastimes. Her productions had ranged from the early days of charades at Harrow, the creation of Dante's Inferno in the bleak days at Cincinnati, the theatricals at Hadley and Penrith, and now to an amateur performance of Locke's operatic Macbeth which was to be performed in her drawing room in Florence. *Galignani's Messenger* reported:

An English lady of distinguished merit, Mrs Trollope, has had the idea of getting up in her house a performance of the choruses of the witches in Macbeth, composed half a century after the time of Shakespeare, by Locke, a musician celebrated in England. She had a little stage fitted up in her drawing room, and every care was taken to perform those traditional scenes with the greatest accuracy in regard to costume and everything else. A numerous party of English ladies and gentlemen sang the choruses, and acquitted themselves very well.[20]

Quite a number of the English community joined in the theatricals. There was an Arthur Vansittart who engaged the Cocomero Theatre for private performances and 'defrayed the whole of the expense out of his own pocket'. Tom remembered him as 'an exceptionally tall man, a thread-paper of a man, and a very bad actor. He was exceedingly noisy and pushed vivacity to its extreme limits.' Another was Edward Hobhouse, who was 'far and away the cleverest and best-educated man of the little set'. One of the plays performed was Sheridan's *The Rivals* in which Tom took the part of Sir Anthony Absolute, and Fanny 'brought the house down' nightly, as Mrs Malaprop.[21] There are descriptions in many of Fanny's books of charades and *tableaux vivant* recounted in loving detail. In *Charles Chesterfield*, for instance, Fanny describes a scene when the authoress, Mrs Sherbourne, attended the first rehearsal of the play she had written:

By the time they were seated, they found Mrs Winterblossom and Mr Periwinkle going at full gallop through the first scene.
    'What are they about?' demanded the irritated Mrs Sherbourne, 'Do they call this rehearsing? . . . Gracious heaven! May I not hear that speech? May I not be permitted to give an opinion on the meaning given by the performer to the equivocal words before it? This is too, too hard!' and the poor woman actually forgetting beauty and everything belonging to it, burst into tears.[22]

Fanny had an acute ear for speech patterns and accents, and in her novels much of the dialogue is written almost as a script. There were many performances to attend in Florence, and at one court concert she noted that the Bonaparte Princess Demidoff had a seat of honour in the front row next to the duchess: 'And what do you think was the principal piece performed? A sort of music in action called the Battle of Waterloo! Soldiers heard marching, and distant drums and trumpets placed in all the rooms of the palace so as to give it quite the effect of reality. I sat immediately behind the Princess, and it was very evident that she did not like it *at all.*'[23]

Anthony and Rose's first child, Henry Merivale, was born in Ireland on 13 March 1846, but Fanny was not yet to meet him. That year, instead of returning to England, the Trollopes decided to escape the heat of Florence by going to the Tyrol, Bohemia and Silesia. They were accompanied by a friend, Lady Normanby, her daughter, and Luigi, the Trollopes' Italian servant. Tom was beginning to suffer from rheumatism, and Lady Normanby from dyspepsia, so it was decided they should try the famous cold-water treatment at Gräfenberg. This small village was situated at the top of a hill and consisted only of a bathing establishment and a house for the patients. There was not a great deal of accommodation, and arriving in Gräfenberg on 13 July 1846, the party had to rent an unfurnished apartment in the nearby village of Freiwalden. The water cure was rigorous. The patient rose at 4 a.m., was wrapped in a wet sheet and rubbed briskly. Then they had to wind 3 yards of wet cloth around their waist, followed by a dry cloth of the same size over the top. The patient then had to walk and drink copious draughts of water. Food consisted of brown bread, fresh milk, butter and strawberries. There was a routine of being rolled in a wet sheet and covered with a blanket to encourage sweating, followed by a plunge into a cold bath and vigorous exercise. Fanny thought the sight of all these scantily clad people very funny, and said that they had 'the air of having escaped from their keepers'. However, in spite of the mirth, she was impressed with the establishment. 'The result of all I have seen and heard of Dr Preissnitz and his practice, has been to inspire me with sincere respect and admiration for him.'[24] It was not reported what effect the treatment had on Tom's rheumatism. After Gräfenberg the party went to Vienna for two nights, and so, slowly home to Florence, stopping on the way. By early November they were back in the Via del Giglio.

Earlier that year, at a dinner party in March, Fanny had met a young man, Frederick William Faber, who had been at Harrow at the same time as Anthony. While at Oxford he had become a disciple of Newman, and following his example, had been converted to Roman Catholicism. 'By far the most brilliant person with whom I have made acquaintance is Faber. He is, I think the most eloquent person I ever heard talk. I dined with him at Mr Sloane's last week, and on Thursday he dined here. On both occasions I sat next him, and have rarely listened with such *wonder*, and, I must confess, with such admiration to any one.'[25]

Fanny was now working on the last chapters of her next book, *Father*

Eustace, a Tale of the Jesuits, which was published by Colburn in 1847. *Father Eustace* exposed the power that the Jesuits had over their followers. This was a contentious issue in Rome at that time and the idea for the story may have come from her meeting with Faber.

Father Eustace was summoned by his superior in Rome, and sent on a mission to England. He was to regain, on behalf of the church, an estate which had belonged to the late Lord Randolph, a Catholic married to a Protestant. Lord Randolph lived in shame for having married a heretic, and had become 'a puling penitent for life'. On his death the estate passed to his daughter Juliana, a Protestant, but the Jesuits were convinced it should have been theirs by right.

Father Eustace, who was young and handsome, was to charm the daughter, convert her to Catholicism, encourage her to take the veil, and so to leave the estate to the church. 'So deeply rooted was that first lesson, which inculcated the necessity of crushing the individual will, however pure its dictates, in order to follow, with the INERTNESS OF A CORPSE (for such is the acknowledged and proclaimed law of the Jesuit creed), the command of his superior, that judgement was paralysed within him, and conscience slumbered.'[26] Father Eustace took the name of Edward Storment, and carried out his commands with great skill, until he made the fatal mistake of falling in love with his convert. She, too, fell in love, not knowing that he was a priest. The end was tragedy.

Catholics in England had been emancipated for eighteen years, since 1828, but were still viewed by many English with great distrust, fostered by years of discrimination. Both the Oxford Movement and Catholicism aroused fierce antagonism. One aspect of the book was to discuss the nature of Catholicism and set it in contrast to the beliefs of the Protestant clergyman and his parishioners.

The *New Monthly Magazine* was unsure of the book:

> It is impossible to peruse it and not feel that the care and power thrown into it attest that there has been much study and investigation employed, and that there must be some groundwork for the details. Mrs Trollope has, indeed, seldom been less herself – that is to say, lightly descriptive, biting, and epigrammatic – she is here neither frivolous nor humorous, she seems to have felt that she had a great and very serious subject in hand, and she labours . . . with an earnestness of purpose that is alone suited to the character and details of this sad but eventful history.

In April 1847 it was time to return to England to visit the Tilleys in Penrith. Cecilia was once again pregnant and her fifth child, Edith Diana, was born in May. Rose was pregnant with her second son, Frederick James Anthony, who was born later in the year on 27 September, and Fanny had not yet seen Henry Merivale, born the previous March. Fanny and Tom travelled via Genoa and the Riviera through the south of France and then Lyons to Paris. There they stayed for a few days before crossing from Boulogne to Folkestone. After two weeks in London to sort out some business matters they arrived in Penrith in mid-May. The stay was short, and no doubt very busy with four small children and a new baby in the house. Fanny was concerned at the number of children Cecilia had produced in such a short time, but loved them dearly. 'Very nice little creatures, and all well both in mind and body – this is some little consolation for their having come upon us so rapidly.' Cecilia was beginning to show signs of the dreaded consumption. She had become very religious and a passionate follower of the Oxford Movement, and following her conversion, dated her letters by red letter saints' days. Her book *Chollerton* was about a relationship which extolled good works and High Church practices, as a preferable state to marriage.

The Anglican Church was divided into three camps. The strictly puritanical Evangelical movement, the middle-of-the-road Established Church which was pleasure-loving and somewhat *laissez-faire*, and the Oxford Movement, whose members with their crucifixes, incense and candles wanted to take the church nearer to Rome. This latter became known as High Church, or the Puseyites, after one of the leaders the Reverend Edward Pusey. *The Spectator* of 1842 had made fun of the name, heading an article 'The Pewseyites':

It is now obvious to all the world, that the great mission of the Oxford Theologians is to put down the nuisance of the Pews. What created Pew could fail to be blown out of church by such a whirlwind of indignant eloquence? It is to be feared that Pews are doomed. . . . Pews are English; in Presbyterian Scotland they have only 'bottom-rooms'. There is something indelicate in the notion of substituting 'bottom-rooms' for pews: no stately dowager, no elegant young lady, could occupy the former.[27]

The high box pews of the Established Church tended to monopolize the centre of the church and were privately owned by local gentry, mainly concerned with displaying their status. Not only were the divisions in the Anglican Church an unending source for discussion and argument, but the Catholics and Protestants added fuel to the fire. It is not surprising that so many of both Fanny and Anthony's books used the differences of religion as a main theme. It was a common topic of conversation.

Fanny's next book, *The Three Cousins*, was a well put together tale of three very different ladies. Mrs Morrison, the 52-year-old wife of the Bishop of Solway, was a woman of enthusiasms, imagination, and an enquiring mind.

Mrs Cobhurst, a 34-year-old widow, had 'a very desperately firm purpose of becoming the sole heiress of all that the elderly Sir Joseph Lexington had to bequeath. . . . It mattered not whether he fell in love with her or adopted her.' Finally, Laura Lexington was the young, beautiful heroine, who had been abandoned by her father and brought up by her grandmother.

Mrs Morrison was a New Woman, whose beliefs and enthusiasms reflected those of Fanny and her circle:

Her mind, which was active to excess, and ever eager for fresh materials to work upon, became, to all intents and purposes, a spiritual knight-errant, roaming through the intellectual world in search of adventures. No new idea, however mistily caught sight of, or however distant from the ordinary ground upon which human reason employs itself, ever failed of fixing her attention, of rousing her faculties, and of calling forth all the energy of her spirit, in order to conquer, or be conquered by it.

The application of steam to ships was, perhaps, the first event of her life; for she was then quite young, which set her firmly, and for ever, on the hobby on which she galloped with admirable courage and perserverance to the end of her life. . . . Though a mere child at the time, she watched the struggle of gas, from almost its first twinkle to its present midnight splendour, with intense interest. Electricity, when its power was first practically displayed to her, produced an effect on her imagination which kept her awake all night. . . . Her first journey on a railroad produced a paroxysm of rapture, that exhaled itself in sketching a network of railroads over the earth and under the sea, by aid of which she expected to make a morning visit to a sister at Madras, and return to Europe in time to hear Grisi sing, somewhere or other, in the evening. As she firmly believed that the whole created world, moral and physical, was in a state of gradual development, she hailed everthing new, as a visible step onwards. For a short time she was strongly inclined to have faith in homeopathy, but at last came to the conclusion that Preisnitz was the only physician who really knew how to set the human frame to rights when it went wrong. As to her belief in all the mysterious powers of animal magnetism, it is difficult to state to what length it went, because imagination was so mixed up with conviction, that it is impossible to say where one ended and the other began. . . . Phrenology was another of the avant couriers of human knowledge which she had rushed forward to meet, with an eagerness that had put her, as it were, intellectually out of breath, rendering her much more unfit than she might otherwise have been to acquire the information which she so passionately desired to possess . . . every idea that was new had a wonderful attraction for her. The new idiom of Carlyle, the new colouring of Turner, the new preaching of Newman, the new tintamarra in music, the new system of conveying both light and manure in phials, etcetera, etcetera, etcetera, all excited an enthusiastic degree of interest in her mind.[28]

When she talked about a book of which she disapproved, Mrs Morrison declared to her cousin, Sir Joseph Lexington:

'It is what I call a very flabby book'.
'A *flabby book*, my dear lady? What on earth does that mean! I have heard of a flabby fish, but never in my life of a flabby book.'
There were moments when the eagerness of Mrs Morrison in conversation was so great, that she occasionally coined words to help herself along; and if not that, she used old words in new senses, in such a manner as to often startle and sometimes puzzle her hearers.[29]

Mrs Morrison's enthusiasms were tempered little by the fact that she was the wife of a bishop.

The novel also gave an interesting insight into the wiles and necessary ploys of the young widow Mrs Cobhurst, who, left with very little money, used her considerable charms to try and obtain a husband or benefactor.

She was not in the slightest danger of falling really in love, but she was in great danger of falling really into debt, unless she gave up her passion for display, or found some means or other of obtaining funds to support it.[30] . . . There be some ladies and pretty Mrs Cobhurst was one of them, who, without making any great movement, contrive to render themselves, particularly to gentlemen, the most conspicuous persons in company. They have a sort of gentle tame-pigeon-like way of fluttering their feathers, which seems invitingly to draw attention, without asking for it.[31]

Alas, Mrs Cobhurst overplays her hand, and at the end is left with nothing. 'As society is now constituted the happiness of English women seems to depend too much upon the *accident* of being married, or not married. It is rarely that a bought husband turns out worth having.'

In 1847 the only alternatives to re-marriage for a widow without funds, were obtaining a position as a governess or companion, or becoming the 'poor relation'. Fanny had, herself, experienced the situation and had resolved it by providing for her financial needs from the ceaseless production of books, and by employing Tom as her male companion and business manager. The work was demanding, but she kept her independence. Now she was beginning to pass the message on to her readers. She suggested in *The Old World and The New.* 'The wise of *both sexes* will become daily more inclined to hold themselves aloof from the life-enduring chain of matrimony, till the time shall arrive – and come it must –

when it shall be so equally borne between them, that its weight shall not be painfully felt by either.'[32]

Tom and Fanny stayed in London on their return journey to Italy and met the young author, Miss Elizabeth Lynn Linton, at dinner at Henry Milton's house. She was the daughter of a Keswick parson, and had just published a novel *Azeth the Egyptian*, which had in it a free-thinking element, 'which is very surprising in a country clergyman's young daughter, home-bred in a very remote locality'. Tom liked her, 'a very religious minded unbeliever!'. Miss Linton approved of Fanny, and wrote in her memoirs: 'She was in no way a poseuse, but just a vulgar, brisk and good natured-kind of well-bred hen wife, fond of a joke and not troubled with squeamishness.'

Fanny and Tom left London on 13 July with the intention of steaming up the River Rhine, and spending ten days at Baden-Baden, then travelling via Lake Como to Venice, where Tom was to meet some learned friends in Congress; and so back to Florence by the last week in September. They were accompanied by Lady Sevestre and Miss Hall, who were also returning to Florence. The party had reached Baden-Baden when all their plans were thrown into turmoil. On 2 August 1847 a letter arrived from John Tilley: Cecilia's health had rapidly deteriorated. The doctors had ordered her to spend two years in Italy, and providing she could find an escort, Cecilia would join her mother in the autumn. It was decided that Tom would return to England, collect Cecilia, and bring her back with him. The whole party travelled together to Switzerland where Tom departed, leaving the three ladies to explore Berne and Geneva. He made all haste back to England, but when he arrived at Ramsgate found a letter waiting for him from John Tilley to say that Cecilia was too ill to travel by land and so would take the boat from Southampton to Leghorn. The next day Tom retraced his steps back to Switzerland and met Fanny in Vevey, where he was in time to join their cousins, Colonel Charles Trollope and his wife. The party set off to attend the Scientific Congress which was being held in Venice. This was the seventh such congress, each one held in a different city, and each striving to outdo the others: '. . . in the magnificence and generosity of their reception of their "scientific" guests'. It was a time of political unrest in Europe, and as Tom said the meetings became, 'more and more mere social gatherings in outward appearance, and revolutionary propagandist assemblies in reality. . . . There were concerts and excursions and great daily dinners the gayest and most enjoyable imaginable, at which both sexes were considered to be equally scientific and equally welcome.'[33]

Tom had another reason to visit Venice. Theodosia Garrow was there with her parents, and Tom was in love. The Garrows had been introduced to the Trollopes in Florence in the previous year, and had attended one of Fanny's Friday receptions. There had been some gossip about Mr Garrow's Indian mother. Elizabeth Barrett, who had married Robert Browning in 1846 and now lived in Florence, passed it on to Miss Mitford: 'Mr Garrow was not Sir William Garrow's son in any sense – but he was his natural brother – Mr Garrow's father not having married the "dark ladie" – To the darkness, his own complexion is said to testify – but he is a sensible intelligent man & an active magistrate & useful citizen, sufficiently so to to [*sic*] put his pedigree out of people's heads!'[34]

Sir William Garrow was the third son of the Reverend David Garrow of Hadley, Middlesex, where it seems, after the death of his parents, Theo's father was brought up. The grave of the Reverend David Garrow is not far from that of Emily in Hadley churchyard. Mr Garrow, while still young, married a widow of over fifty with a son and daughter. After the marriage they had one daughter, Theodosia. There was more gossip about the true parentage of Theo, who was adored by her half-sister Harriet and much disliked by Mrs Garrow, who 'was a very fierce old lady, and did not, I fear, contribute to the happiness of any member of her family.' Theo was intelligent, and although not beautiful, had magnificent dark brown hair, and large, deep set, grey eyes. During the season at Florence she and Tom became close friends, and Tom visited the family at Lucerne in Switzerland, and again, in the romantic setting of Venice. 'The summer days were drawing in, but there was the moon, quite light enough on the lagoons; and we were a great deal happier than the day was long. . . . Ah, those were pleasant days! And while Italy, under the wing of science, was plotting her independence, I was busy forging the chains of that dependence which was to be a . . . source of happiness to me.'[35]

The Trollope party arrived back in Florence in the middle of September 1847, and on the last day of the month Fanny went to Leghorn to collect Cecilia who looked very pale and weak. She was by now suffering from advanced consumption, and, once again Fanny was to go through the pain of nursing another of her children. Fanny was now sixty-eight.

CHAPTER TWELVE

'I can bear anything better than uncertainty'

Changes. September 1847–November 1849

Fanny took Cecilia to Florence in the autumn of 1847, and put her under the care of a homoeopathic doctor. By the middle of October she seemed no better, and the doctor thought that the winter climate of Florence would be most unfavourable for her condition and that the greater warmth of Rome would be more conducive to her recovery. Tom's old headmaster from his teaching days at Birmingham, Dr Jeune, dined with the family during the month, and wrote: 'I expected to find Mrs Trollope epigramatic, – I found her clever, intelligent, and domestic.'[1]

Once again Fanny changed her plans in a desperate bid to help her daughter. A large sunny apartment was taken in a small palazzo in the Via delle Quattro Fontane in Rome. During Cecilia's few weeks in Florence she and Theo had become firm friends, and so it was arranged with the Garrows that Theo would go with them as a companion for Cecilia. Theo's parents had no idea of the growing relationship between Tom and their daughter, as Tom said, 'If they had had such, she would certainly never have been allowed to accept my mother's invitation.' Theo's adoring elder sister, Harriet Fisher, was much in favour of the liaison, and encouraged her parents to let Theo take 'advantage of such an opportunity of seeing Rome'.

Europe was in a state of unrest. The agreements and resolutions made at the 1815 Congress of Vienna were becoming unravelled as nationalists sought to regain control of their homelands. Italy was a collection of independent states. Austria ruled Lombardy and Venetia; Naples was a kingdom; Tuscany a dukedom under the Austrian, Ferdinand III; Rome one of the Church states under a despotic Pope; and among the liberals there was a movement afoot for unification.

Earlier in the year, Fanny had thought about relinquishing the lease on the Florence house and moving to Paris, which had the advantage of being nearer to England. But France was no safer; a letter from Madame de M. warned: 'Should the King die, or the harvest fail, or – in short, anything unexpected happen, I fear that things would go badly here. These people are so apt and ready to lay hold of every possible occasion to create a disturbance.'[2] According to Tom, Madame de M. was Judith de Montalk, a friend of Fanny's who lived in Paris; she was English by parentage, Italian by education and French by marriage. Rome was reported to be safer, and so it was there they went in search of a cure for Cecilia.

When Theodosia was a young girl living at her parents' home, The Braddons in Torquay, she had become a friend of Elizabeth Barrett, who was living then at Beacon Terrace in Torquay. They exchanged letters and Theo visited Elizabeth, ten years her senior, who was very delicate and confined to a day bed. When Elizabeth Barrett was twenty-seven she had suffered a burst blood vessel in her lungs, and two years later at Torquay witnessed the death of her favourite brother by drowning. She took to her bed and for a while her life was in danger. Elizabeth Barrett Browning was now married and living in Italy, and she and Theo remained friends throughout their lives. When Tom first met Theo, poetry and art were her interests and she had already published several poems. Later she became a fierce champion of Italian liberty and unity, and converted Tom to her way of thinking. Their love affair blossomed, and on 31 December 1847 they announced their engagement.

Fanny was delighted, and promised to give Theo a home as long as she should live – but where was that home to be? Tom wrote in his memoirs: 'We then had much discussion as to the next step to be taken. Our first notion was that I should go to Florence in the spring, and sell our things there. After-thought, however, led us to the conclusion that it would be more prudent to remain, at least until the end of our lease, at Florence.'[3]

There was, however, one major difficulty to overcome – Theo's father. He was a well-educated man, quick, intelligent and well mannered, but unmitigatedly selfish. Theodosia was his devoted companion, he enjoyed her society and was proud of her accomplishments. Mr Garrow could see no reason why he should allow her to marry and renounce her company; it would be too great a sacrifice to expect from him, and Tom was not a good catch. He had no independent means except from his writing, and little expectation of any inheritance from his mother. As Tom admitted, 'I on my side possessed nothing at all, save the prospect of a strictly bread-and-cheese competency at the death of my mother, and "the farm which I carried under my hat," as somebody calls it.'[4] Theo possessed just £1,000. Tom wrote to Garrow, and noted later in his diary: 'Much opposition, and very harsh letters in reply. Days of distress and anxiety. Garrow fixed to come here on Thursday. Our anxiety at agony point. He came, awfully savage. Terrible scenes !'[5]

Theo was deeply distressed; she loved her father dearly, had been ruled by him and was, in many ways, timid and self-distrustful. She found herself torn between two loyalties in what must have seemed an impossible situation. Fanny's good sense and tact saved the day, and she managed to persuade Mr Garrow to give his consent to the marriage, which was planned to take place the following March. In the meantime Mr Garrow took his daughter back to Florence. Tom, who could not bear to be parted from his Theo, followed them about two weeks later at the beginning of January, and made his peace. Fanny wrote to him on 26 January 1848: 'I congratulate you heartily on the restoration of Mr Garrow to health and spirits. This must greatly enhance dear Theo's happiness, and consequently yours also.'[6]

It was a difficult time for Fanny. Tom was her business manager and companion, and she knew that his marriage must inevitably alter this. Although the present proposal was to share a house and she loved Theo as a daughter, her situation must change. Cecilia had once written to her: 'I could not help thinking of the numberless times that I had known you seize, or *make*, opportunities of giving any one of us a pleasure, at no matter what sacrifice to yourself, – the alacrity, and ingenuity with which you would smooth away any difficulty, – dear, dearest mother !'[7]

The sacrifices were still being made.

Cecilia's health had at first seemed to improve in the new surroundings, but now a reaction had set in.

She was not allowed out of doors as the weather was so cold, and Fanny was 'hurrying on to get as many pages done as possible before the departure of Mr M who has promised to carry a packet for me.' The 'packet' was the manuscript of her next book, *The Young Countess, or Love and Jealousy*. It was set in the wilds of Austria, in an old castle which was remote, lonely, and in need of repair. It seems likely that the idea for the location had come from the Bavarian castle of her old friend Baroness von Zandt, visited by Tom and herself the previous year.

In the story, the Countess, young, handsome, and recently widowed, was lonely. 'She felt that there was one thing essentially necessary. . . . This one thing needful was a dear, faithful, intimate friend, of her own sex, before whom all ceremony might be banished, every thought revealed, and with whom every project might be discussed before it was brought forward to meet the light of day.'[8] She took as a companion, Caroline, a beautiful young girl from the village, and they became close friends. After the mandatory year of mourning had passed, the Countess visited the court at Vienna with the avowed intention of returning with a house party of friends; this she did, and the guests were described at length and in minute detail based on Fanny's Continental acquaintances.

Mademoiselle Chambrey was one of them, and it was the 'great object of Mademoiselle Chambrey's existence to suggest the idea of an ancient statue. . . . It was impossible to help lamenting, while looking at the faded and unmeaning little face beneath, that what looked like a very well-preserved antique in one direction, should look so sadly out of repair in another.'[9]

While in Vienna, the Countess had fallen desperately in love with young

Count Albert, and 'she deliberately gave herself over to the passion which had taken possession of her.' Unfortunately the Countess, having observed Alfred taking an interest in her young protégé, Caroline, became savagely jealous, and the innocent girl was converted into, 'a sort of perpetual blister upon the breast of her benefactress'. The strength of the story is in the description of the characters and their behaviour as house guests of the Countess. Throughout, the plot is carried forward by charades, masques, and picnics, giving full reign to Fanny's own powers of invention, and providing the reader with an insight into the society of her time. The end is predictable, if somewhat melodramatic. Caroline runs away and takes refuge in a nunnery. Alfred is incarcerated in a secret dungeon during one of the masques. The Countess, realizing what she has done, loses her reason, but in a moment of lucidity she confesses her crime to the local priest. The poor man is released, and all ends well.

The story has the Gothic feeling of one of Fanny's earlier books, *Tremordyn Cliff*, written when she was in a state of anxiety over the health of Henry and Emily. Fanny was now sixty-nine and being confined with the dying Cecilia in the apartment in Rome, must have triggered unhappy associations. One of her lifelong friends once said of her, 'She had more imagination than she could afford to display in her writings. What the public demanded, they received; but if she could have allowed herself more time, there was that within her that would have brought out lasting work.'[10]

Now the manuscript of *Love and Jealousy* was out of the way, Fanny set to work on her next book, but there was a lack of paper. She wrote to Tom on 10 February 1848: 'If I had only some suitable paper, I should forthwith go on with my new novel. But here the paper is a *bajocco* (a halfpenny) a sheet, and most abominably bad. Will you, therefore, bring me three of four quires of the best you can get in Florence? Let it be large post.'[11]

This next book, *Town and Country*, was set in Cornwall and London in the year 1811, when the Prince Regent was on the ascendant. The two protagonists were Harriet, the young ambitious daughter of a Cornish vicar and Mr Cuthbert, an elderly, rich, and very vain, friend of her father's, whom she agreed to marry for his position in life. Believing himself vastly superior to his young wife, he trained her in the ways of the world before introducing her to society. 'She had been converted, in the space of a few months, from the very brightest and happiest human butterfly that ever wantoned amidst the sunshine and flowers, into a still bright-coloured, but very hapless insect, caught and imprisoned for the sake of its unlucky beauty.'[12] His touch made her shudder, and 'she turned away from him as he attempted to kiss her, with irrepressible disgust.'[13]

Harriet was launched successfully into society and caught the roving eye of the Prince Regent. This vicar's daughter from a quiet background 'was much more likely to have suspected a new Gunpowder Plot, than to have conceived any fears that the aged Regent intended to make love to her, or that her aged husband was exceedingly well pleased that so it should be.'[14] Mr Cuthbert used his innocent wife as a decoy in order to obtain a peerage for himself, and finally, during a weekend as the guest of the Regent at Brighton, the longed-for reward was given. 'The deed was done; the act was consummated; HE WAS CREATED; and there he stood, as positively and irrevocably Lord Corwyn, as his friend George was Prince of Wales.'[15]

Harriet now realized how she had been used. 'Her worthless husband had now obtained that for which he had so basely laboured while betraying her to the contempt of all – even to that of her own father.'[16] The new Lord Corwyn, his purpose achieved and seeing that his wife despised him, decided to dispose of her. 'There were two ways – death or divorce,' but on reflection he decided to 'give up the divorce, and stick to the insanity.' Harriet's maid told her that Lord Corwyn had sent for a medical man, and warned her, 'Unless you listen to me now, you will die in darkness and in chains, though you are in your right senses.' The maid helped her to escape, and she returned to the vicarage, where, now knowing the truth, she was welcomed by her family. Eventually Lord Corwyn died from a heart attack, leaving Harriet a wealthy widow.

The particular interest of this book lies in the description of the village life of Fanny's own youth, the farmers, the vicar's family, and the snobbery of some of the gentry. It is also a wicked portrait of the Regent and his social circle, and gives a chilling picture of the absolute power that husbands had over their wives. It was written during the bleak winter in Rome, and published in late 1848. Elizabeth Grant, the author of *The Highland Lady*, had read both *Domestic Manners* and *Town and Country*, and was faintly scandalized by Fanny's attitude. She described her as: 'really a very underbred woman who makes people act in the most inconsistent manner, yet writes so cleverly that the reader is, in spite of feelings, interested in her characters.'

Lady Sevestre and Miss Hall, the two friends who had travelled with Fanny and Tom in Europe when they first heard of Cecilia's illness, now wrote and asked if Fanny could find them apartments in Rome. As there were no rooms to be had, Fanny proposed that they should stay with her, although the arrangement meant that she had to move into a smaller bedroom which was inconvenient. She also missed Tom.

I have no news to tell you, my dear Tom, except that I am well, and Cecilia much the same as when you left her. I hope to be able to resume our drives today, which I am confident will do her good. The intense dullness of Rome to me is greatly beyond my powers of description. I *cannot* walk alone. It is vain to attempt it by way of recreation, for it is only pain. I think Cecilia's gentle, even, nay often cheerful state of spirits, is quite wonderful. She is an admirable creature![17]

Paris was no longer an option as a place to live. After the uprising in 1848, King Louis Philippe, the citizen king, had taken refuge in England. Fanny received a letter from her friend Madame de M. describing some of the scenes:

They have stolen 125,000 francs from Jacqueminot at the Tuileries – and they talk of not having pillaged! . . . No imagination can come up to what I saw even in my retired street, where I spent the day between two barricades. Men with naked arms up to the shoulder, all dabbled with blood, wearing the caps, bonnets, etc., of the poor Princesses. Women . . . brandishing the blood-red flag of '93, shouting, *'Mort à Philippe!'* Remnants of the throne carried upon naked swords or pikes. The poor Queen's pet cat writhing in death agony on the point of a spear held by a *bonnet rouge.* . . . My best and dearest friends, who but last week were in the possession of rank, fortune, and position, have now lost all. . . . The poor Tuileries is being converted into an almshouse for decayed workmen. . . . My insignificance has made me acquainted with more than most people know. There are many lurking ambitions waiting to spring up especially among *Communists* . . . I must add, *stay away from Paris.*'[18]

Even Rome was in a state of unrest. Tom who returned for his mother in February, noted in his diary: 'Rome has been, and is, in a very excited state. An outbreak of the populace is feared from day to day. The promised constitution lingers.' Pope Pius IX, who was hated for his tyranny and association with the dreaded Jesuits, managed to escape in disguise to Gaeta, then under the protection of the Austrian Empire. The constitution was proclaimed in Rome on 15 March, and volunteers were called for to march to Lombardy to assist with the revolution to free the northern part of Italy from Austrian dominance.

In the middle of all this turmoil, Tom escorted Fanny, Lady Sevestre and Miss Hall back to Florence for his wedding. Cecilia, who was very ill, went by sea to Leghorn. On 3 April 1848 Tom Trollope, now thirty-eight, married Theodosia Garrow, at the British Legation in Florence. It seems to have been an informal occasion, as Tom recorded:

'I told my good friend Mr Plunkett . . . that I wanted to be married the next day.

"All right," said he, "Will ten o'clock do?"

"Could not be better."

"Very good. Tell Robbins (the then English clergyman) I'll be sure to be there."

So, at ten the next morning we looked in at the Palazzo Ximenes, and in about ten minutes the business was done.'[19]

Tom and Theo spent their honeymoon travelling around Tuscany. Their circle of friends was rather surprised at the match. Harriet Garnett wrote to her sister Julia:

> The marriage is a very good one for Tom, and I am pleased at the great pleasure it gives his mother. He will I am sure make an excellent husband, for he has been and is a most devoted son. He has been in the best society at Florence, and his manners are much improved, – still I wonder that so distinguished a girl as Theodosia Garrow, who is just twenty-nine, should have taken a fancy to him. I think the mother must be as great an attraction as the son, and to live with her may be a great inducement in the young lady's mind.[20]

Elizabeth Barrett Browning wrote to Miss Mitford on 28 May: 'Are you aware that Miss Garrow, praised by Landor, has married Mr Tom Trollope, praised, I believe, of horse-jockeys generally? He is said to be goodnatured – & they are to live with Mrs Trollope. . . . & Robert was sitting with Powers the sculptor [now working in Florence], when a tribute of wedding cake arrived for the latter. It strikes me as a strange marriage – only the natural marriages are the exception always perhaps.'[21] The reference to horse-jockeys reflected the feeling that Tom was not taken seriously as a writer.

Cecilia had been away from her husband and children now for eight months. The cure had not worked, she was growing weaker daily, and all she wanted was to go back to her family while she was still able to travel. Fanny wrote to Tom on his honeymoon: 'Her weakness is excessive. And it often seems to me impossible that she should endure the fatigue of the voyage. But she will not listen to the idea of postponement.'[22] Fanny went with her at the end of April to Pisa, where they met Tom and Theo; and on 3 May 1848 Cecilia set sail from Leghorn for England. Sir James Clark, Cecilia's English physician, examined her on her return and declared that the case was hopeless and that they should be prepared to hear the worst at any moment. However, as sometimes happens, Cecilia's illness went into remission, and she showed some improvement.

Political chaos continued throughout Europe, and many foreign residents left for home, including Lady Sevestre and Miss Hall. Not so the Trollopes, who decided to stay on in Florence and see what eventuated. In the heat of the Tuscan summer they escaped for a much needed holiday to the comparative safety of Switzerland, where they spent three peaceful weeks in Lucerne, and then went on to Berne, Thun, and Interlaken. News from Paris continued to be grim. Madame de M. wrote to Fanny: 'Not one of my friends has escaped unhurt; and all around me I hear nothing but lamentations and complaints. You would not know Paris. *The grass grows in the streets.* And they might make a tolerable crop of hay in the Place Vendôme.'[23]

By September the dire warnings of revolution in France and the threat of civil war in Italy became too much for Fanny. She asked Tom to return immediately from Switzerland to Florence and to sell all their property; and having done that to rejoin them in Vevey, where they would all spend the winter. Tom had only just arrived in Florence, and had begun to organize the sale, when she changed her mind, and wrote that she and Theo were coming back to join him. It was the 'not knowing' which caused her such anguish. As she wrote; 'You know I can bear anything better than uncertainty. The apprehension of misfortune has often agitated me even to agony; but when once the misfortune was there, I have not been cowardly.'[24] They stayed safely in Florence all through that winter, and continued to entertain; as Elizabeth Barrett Browning told Miss Mitford: 'I hear your friend Mrs Trollope holds royal "drawing-rooms" some once a week – for, remain in Florence quite enough English, in spite of our Italian patriots, to do the usual English work of routs & whist & double gossip.'[25]

It was in that year of revolutionary unrest that the Pre-Raphaelite Brotherhood was founded in London by a group of young artists. They decided to change the mannered formalism of contemporary art, and return to what they perceived as the innocence and purity of the early Italian painters. They wanted to escape from the constrictions imposed on them and draw their own perceptions of nature, using themes that had a moral value. One of them, Millais, later became a close friend of Anthony's, and illustrated many of his books.

One great sadness for Theo was the unexpected death from smallpox of her adored half-sister, Harriet Fisher. After Harriet's death her parents returned to The Braddons at Torquay.

Fanny had been writing *The Lottery of Marriage* during the Swiss visit, and dispatched the manuscript to Colburn in November of 1848. The story was set in Devon and Dover, and followed the fortunes of two match-making mothers. One, Mrs Codrington, kept her sixteen-year-old daughter in short pantaloons, hoping that she, herself, would appear younger than she was, and so win a suitor; and the other, Lady de Laurie, schemed and plotted to win a rich husband for her daughter so that the family fortunes might be restored. Two cousins, Julian and Augustus Oglevie, on holiday at Dover, were chosen as the targets. Cassandra de Laurie mistakenly picked the flirtatious and penniless Augustus with whom to elope, while Mrs Codrington's daughter, at last seen in adult clothes, won the gentle Julian from under the nose of her mother. As usual, it is the minor characters who provide the main interest. As the *New Monthly Magazine* said in the review of June 1849: 'Altogether, *The Lottery of Marriage* is shown to be one in which there may be many blanks, but in which there are also prizes; and while Mrs Trollope can exhibit the former in a most ominous and terrifying light, she can also depict the latter in such inviting and seductive colours, that the most lasting impression is to take a ticket.'[26]

Fanny's brother, Henry Milton, and his son John had been acting as her agents with Colburn, who was very slow in his payments. Fanny, forever in need of money, was annoyed. John Milton wrote to tell her that 'Colburn has paid the money, which I have lodged at Herries' Bank. C. appears well pleased with his bargain; and told me that he hoped my Aunt considered herself bound to furnish him with another novel at the same price, before the end of this year.' Her brother Henry said: 'Your much-wished-for return to England will, I trust, put an end to any similar annoyances in the future.'[27]

John Tilley's report of Cecilia's health was so alarming in the spring of 1849, that Fanny decided to go to England without any delay, and she set off at once to go directly to London. Tom and Theo went for a visit to the south of France and the furniture was left in storage.

The Tilleys were now living in London, at Allen Place, Kensington, where Fanny arrived on 10 March 1849. It was her seventieth birthday. She wrote to Tom:

> I had the unspeakable consolation of finding that my darling Cecilia had again rallied, and was able to converse with, and welcome me, as if in perfect health. Yet I am still told that there is *no* hope! This dreadful sentence is pronounced with a degree of certainty that precludes my daring to doubt it; but there are moments when it is difficult to believe. . . . The long and solitary journey was a dismal trial to my strength of all kinds. Thank God it is over, and that I am not too late![28]

Not only was Cecilia ill, but Henry Milton, Fanny's brother, was also seriously unwell, and had been sent to Brighton to recover. The house at Florence was closed; and Tom and Theo were away together. The carefully built up security of Fanny's world was beginning to crack. At once she set about nursing Cecilia, and finishing the promised book for Colburn. This latter was not easy, as she told Tom:

> What to do about my book I know not. The difficulty of finding a quiet half-hour here to write, is incredibly great. Sometimes I feel in absolute despair on the subject. John Tilley is *very* kind, but he has no power to help it. Cecilia sleeps in the back drawing room, and has the doors open day and night into the other, so I cannot work there. At night (the only quiet time), although I am sorely tired, I *would* try, had I a fire. But this I cannot have, because the fire in my room is laid for the morning, which is the only moment I can command. God bless you both my dear children.[29]

Colburn was getting impatient, and called on her in Kensington. 'He was prodigiously civil; told me I was a little behind my time; and twice muttered that, although he made nothing by it, he should be willing to make another engagement on the same terms. I said that when I had completed the present engagement, I would call upon him and talk about it. But when will this be? To write more than a page at a time, is pretty nearly impossible. And even so, I scarcely know what I am writing.'[30]

The book she was now working on was called *The Old World and the New*. Nursing Cecilia, the last of the children who had gone with her to America, her thoughts had returned to that time. This book is an idealized version of that disastrous journey; she wrote of how the expedition should have been. The tale is about Captain Stormont and his wife, who found themselves in financial difficulties, and decided the only remedy was to sell their possessions and go to America taking with them their two children. Their cousin Katherine, having quarrelled with her fiancé, elected to go with them, and to provide the financial backing to enable them to buy some land and become pioneer settlers. She also secretly bought up their furniture and employed their old trusted servants to accompany them.

Fanny thus gave her fictitious family the necessities she had so desperately lacked, and moreover, provided a strong husband for support. The party landed in New York, and found they had to decide between buying cleared and established land, or uncleared land. Captain Stormont, not wishing to squander Katherine's money, opted for the latter, and they travel in a Deerborn over corduroy roads to visit a property. Eventually they arrived. 'Where was the dear variety which the human heart so loved? It was all briars and brakes! Tall grass and tall trees! North, south, east and west – all, all, all the same.'[31] Fanny's sentiments on arriving at Nashoba.

The Stormont family, however, had a choice, and eventually found a house on some partly cleared land 10 miles out of Cincinnati in a place called Bloomfield Knoll. Here they settled with their own furniture and servants and began to prosper. Katherine decided to build a larger house designed by herself, to be three storeys high and each side 60 ft. 'Could Robert Stormont have looked into Katherine's writing desk . . . he would have been greatly startled, and greatly alarmed too, at finding it filled with rough pencil sketches of handsome mansions, with colonnades and without colonnades, with spreading lawns and graceful flower beds, and all sorts of gentlemanlike elegancies in all directions.'[32]

The house was built of wood according to local custom and only took twelve weeks to erect; it cost a quarter of what it would have done in stone or bricks. The surprisingly detailed description of the house sounds like a domestic version of the Cincinnati Bazaar. Katherine became part of the Cincinnati social scene, and all the local worthies vied with each other to entertain her (unlike Fanny's experience). Katherine quickly became tired of the endless parties and longed for the peace of Bloomfield Knoll. She returned to find that her erstwhile fiancé had turned up disguised as a Red Indian. (This was probably based on the Irish novelist, Charles Lever's, youthful exploits). Once she recognized him all was forgiven, and they returned to England, leaving America to the Stormonts. There is a sub-plot throughout the story in the form of a series of letters from a friend in Paris telling of the terrible uprising there; Madame de M.'s letters in a fictionalized form.

As Fanny struggled to complete the book while watching the dying Cecilia, there must have been many bitter memories and questions. To what extent had the terrible hardships endured in America been the cause of the premature deaths of Henry, Emily and now Cecilia? There is a poignant 'if only', quality to the story. The book was eventually to be finished in July after Cecilia's death.

The *New Monthly Magazine* found it interesting:

The progress of a new settlement in such a place opens a field for description as interesting as it is instructive. It is a step-by-step progress in which it is impossible not to feel the deepest interest – in every tree felled, in every paling put up, in every new lamb or every sucking pig born. . . . It would, indeed, be difficult for Mrs Trollope to write a novel that should not be replete with human interest.[33]

On 2 April Fanny wrote to Tom:

In general John Tilley has taken good care that I should not be disturbed at night. But last night he did not lie down at all; and I only for an hour or two. As to my hours by day, they are far from being at my own disposal. Cecilia's state requires constant, unremitting watchfulness both day and night. . . . Her patience, her trusting confidence in the fate that awaits her, and her tender thoughtfulness for everyone, are more beautiful and more touching than I can describe. [She adds in a note to Theo] It is the saddest scene that ever mother watched. Her poor dear devoted husband never leaves her side when not forced away by official duty. It is piteous to watch him hanging over her. Little Fanny is getting better, I hope. The other poor unconscious little things seem well. The boy is enchanting.[34]

Cecilia died on 10 April 1849, a month after Fanny had arrived. Anthony came from Ireland in time to see his sister, and Fanny wrote to Rose: 'She was like an angel falling asleep in happy certainty of awakening in heaven. I am very *very* glad my dear Anthony saw her on her deathbed. The impression left on his mind, however painful at the moment of receiving it, will remain with him for-ever, more as consolation, than sorrow.'[35]

After the funeral Anthony took the youngest child, Edith, back to Ireland to be looked after by Rose. Fanny broke the news to Tom:

Your dear sister breathed her last at midnight on Tuesday the 10th of April. It was as though she had fallen asleep. But for a day or two previous, she had suffered sadly. Sweet Soul! She longed – but never with impatience – for the moment of her release. I have, as you well know, my dear Tom, suffered ere now, and very severely; but I almost think the last month has been the most suffering period of my existence. . . . I cannot sleep as I used to do, and I am deplorably thin. But Tilley is everything that is kind and attentive; and, though I feel that I am almost too old for a *rally*, I will do the best I can to get over it.[36]

Fanny believed that 'every friend and every relation you ever heard of in your life has written to me', and of course she had to reply to them all. She was also very worried about her brother Henry, who was still unwell at Brighton. Fanny's depression was not helped by a severe attack of bronchitis which laid her low shortly after Cecilia's death. She had been seriously thinking of returning permanently to live in England, but the English winter affected her throat and chest so badly that she had to abandon the idea.

On 9 May Fanny was well enough to visit the Garnetts who were now living at Brighton. As she said, 'I feel that change of air and scene will be good for me; and I would willingly make my absence longer, were it not that I do not like to leave my dear good son-in-law alone. By degrees, I dare say, we shall emerge from the deep seclusion in which I have, of necessity, been living for the last nine or ten weeks. . . . Yes, dear Tom, I love to look forward *still*.' There was a scheme proposed that Fanny might later join Tom and Theo in western France, and make Pau their headquarters.

By 17 May she began to sound more like herself: 'I am greatly, *wonderfully* better, I think, and I attribute it entirely to my having passed a week with the Garnetts at Brighton; during which I took (under medical orders) three shampooing vapour baths.' Later she wrote: 'I have, much to my own surprise, begun to eat again. The next thing, I suppose, will be growing fat! At present I am greatly the reverse. My brother is, I trust, in a fair way towards recovery; but he has been very dangerously ill.'[37]

Grave fears were held for Cecilia's children. Fanny's namesake and granddaughter, young Fanny Trollope Tilley, was thin and pale and showing definite signs of consumption. Fanny thought the chances of saving her were not good. In early July Lady Sevestre came to stay at the Tilleys' house in Kensington, and Fanny went to dinner with some of her old Florentine acquaintances.

Fanny never finished one book without starting at least one to follow it.

The current book was *Petticoat Government*. It was set in the small town of Westhampton (based on her memories of Exeter), and in London. It is the story of four sisters: two unmarried and living in Westhampton, one married to a Colonel and living in India with a daughter, Judith, and one who had committed the unforgivable sin of eloping with her drawing master, and now widowed, lived with her son Charles in Rome.

Judith's parents died in India, and she was sent home as a Ward in Chancery to be cared for by her two aunts in Westhampton (inspired by cousins Mary and Fanny Bent). Aunt Barbara had ecclesiastical interests, especially in the clergyman Dr Wroughtley, and was cautious and mean. Aunt Elfreda was a bluestocking, interested in science and anthropology, who found Westhampton seriously dull, and moved to London. 'Drones in Westhampton, and Stars and Lights in London,' as Aunt Elfreda said. Once again the story followed the required romantic path, with both the spinster aunts vying to care for Judith (and her generous allowance).

Judith had sworn to find her disgraced third aunt, Mrs Worthington, in order to deliver some sapphires, left to her as a legacy by her sister, Judith's mother. This she did, and found her ill and in poverty, living in a garret with Charles her artist son. Most of the story takes place in London, in and around the prejudices of the upper classes, for Judith had become engaged to a lord. Judith finding that she could not conform to the expected role of a rich young society heiress, became sickened by the hypocrisy, especially the attitude to artists, broke off her engagement and left the country. Eventually she married her artist cousin, Charles Worthington, and lived happily with him in Austria at the Capo del Cadore.

Contemporary attitudes to both maiden aunts and artists were shown by Fanny with unflattering clarity. The two spinster Aunts were drawn with the loving detail of familiarity. Fanny had first-hand knowledge of the disapproval of artists as members of society, and she wrote with a purpose; this was a tribute to Auguste Hervieu, whom she had championed twenty years before. Following his satirical illustrations for Fanny's early books, and the portrait he painted of her in 1833, Hervieu had become a successful exhibitor at the Royal Academy in London and the British Institute, showing forty-seven paintings. He married a Swiss girl in 1842, and seems after that to have drifted away from the family. In 1866 Anthony mentioned to a correspondent that he thought Hervieu was still in London: 'But I never see him'.

On 23 July John Tilley and Fanny went to stay for three weeks in Ireland, with Rose, Anthony, and their sons, at their home in Mallow. Henry Merivale was three and Frederick James not quite two, the same age as little Edith, who was staying with them. Fanny enjoyed seeing her grandchildren. Anthony and Rose took her to Killarney, 'with which she was enchanted. . . . She walked through the gap of Dunlo as easily as if she had been twenty-nine instead of sixty-nine. And she was delighted with young Spellan, the bugler.' She was persuaded to take a ride on one of Bianconi's ramshackle-looking cars, which she much enjoyed. They took her to Glengariff which Rose reported was not a success. 'She was tired with her journey; the tea was rubbish; the food detestable; the bedrooms pokey; turf fires disagreeable, and so on. And now looking back on it all, I feel that she had grounds for complaint; and I should vote it – nasty.'[38]

Tom and Theo planned to return to England in the autumn, and they too wanted to visit Anthony in Ireland. However, they were summoned by the Garrows to Torquay in early August to look after Mrs Garrow who was seriously ill. Fanny, who was in Ireland, was very cross that she had missed them:

> That I should miss seeing you and my dear Theodosia when you pass through London, is *very* painful to me, I have been looking forward to your coming with so much pleasure! Of poor Mrs Garrow's state your mention is so vague that I know not whether she is drooping in consequence of her long journey, or from any malady. . . . You know she has been rather apt to fancy herself worse than she really is; and this may be the case now.

She told Tom that she planned to visit her sister Mary Clyde for a week at Charmouth, near Bristol, on the way back, and then, if Tom could get away to meet her, to go on to Exeter to stay with Fanny Bent. Could he let her know if he could be there on 21 or 22 August. She was worried, 'as you can as yet have formed no very assured plans for the future. But if you have any notions let me share them. I don't quite think it right that you and I should of necessity be parted for ever. Do you? . . . But *now* I feel as if everything were uncertain about you.'[39]

The suggested trip to Exeter had to be cancelled at the last minute as Fanny Bent became ill, and after staying with Mary Clyde, Fanny T. returned to John Tilley's house in Kensington, to help nurse his children. It was not a good time for the Trollopes or the Tilleys.

Fanny wrote to Theo after her return to London:

> . . . most cordially do I wish to see you! But truly the when seems lamentably uncertain. It is evident that your poor mother's state is very precarious, and that our poor Fanny is not less so. Under these circumstances it seems idle to speculate on what we can, or cannot do. . . . We pleased ourselves mightily while with Anthony and his wife, in plotting and planning a visit to them and their lakes in company with you and Tom. . . . Had I my will, wish, and way, you should never be very far from me.[40]

Fanny talked of going with John Tilley to Venice for a month in the spring, and hoped that Tom and Theo might go with them if she paid their expenses above £20, or failing that, maybe Paris. News from Torquay was not good. Mrs Garrow was a demanding patient, and Fanny disapproved. 'I cannot tell you how much I lament the close confinement to which dear Theo is subject. It is quite enough to destroy her health. And the medical man in attendance on her mother, ought to state this to the old lady, and order Theodosia, professionally, to take exercise in the open air at least twice a day. I am quite sure that she has not strength to endure such a life as she is now leading without permanent injury.'[41]

It was in September that Theo heard the welcome news that her half-sister, Harriet Fisher, had left her a considerable sum of money in her will. This was to make a difference to their plans.

Fanny was finding London deeply depressing. There was a cholera epidemic, and, 'The newspapers are filled with details of dirty drains, spasmodic convulsions, and horrid murders.' She told Tom: 'How I long to see you! And how vain does this longing threaten to be! After close upon forty years passed so very nearly together, the indefinite gulf that now divides us is very like being dead already, as relates to each other! But there seems no help for it.'[42]

In September she had another and more serious attack of bronchitis. She wrote to Tom on 17 September: 'Though not quite well yet, my dearest Tom, I think that I am sufficiently better to tell you that there does not at present appear to be any probability that I am going to be worse. And last evening I was well enough to get up for an hour or two.' Later, after Tom had visited her, she told him the doctor's opinion. 'He paid me (as he had done before) many compliments on my constitution; but accompanied them with the assurance that if I did not go south again in a year or two, I should – not die – but be a very suffering old woman for the rest of my life.'[43]

At the end of September Mrs Garrow died. Tom and Theo remained with Mr Garrow at Torquay, and he was very insistent that they should live there with him permanently; however, Theo's health was fragile, and had not been improved by the long days nursing her mother. Tom had very little money of his own, and where they were to live very much depended on which of the parents gave them a home. Theo felt responsible for her father, and Tom for his mother. Fanny, in Brighton, 'in the hope that sea air, and the vapour baths, might do me good,' was concerned about the future:

My health and spirits have been shaken by all the sorrow I have gone through. And I confess to you that I feel my separation from you to be almost too painful under my present circumstances. For very nearly forty years, my dear son, you and I have lived together in more perfect harmony than is often found, I believe, in any connection in life. And now, when I so very greatly need the comfort and support of your society, I am deprived of it. I should be very unwilling to put you and your dear wife to any serious inconvenience, but I feel that your coming to me for a few weeks now, might be very beneficial to me.[44]

Tom and Theo went to stay with her, and discussed how they could best untangle the conflicting demands. The most positive arguments in favour of their return to the south of Europe had come both from Dr Latham, who had been treating Theo, and Fanny's own doctor. Both had advised their patients that they must leave England and go south for their health. The stumbling block was Mr Garrow, who had no wish to move his residence or change his lifestyle. It was finally, and after much discussion, agreed that Mr Garrow would give up the house at Torquay, sell his furniture, and join his daughter and son-in-law abroad for that winter. Fanny was also to be one of the party and it seems that there was a certain amount of skilful negotiation. She advised Tom:

In speaking to him of the terms on which I should make one of your family, you ought to make him understand that my contribution includes *the entire household furniture.* I trust and fully believe that all will go smoothly now, and that no difficulties of any kind will arise to prevent Theodosia's making the prescribed transit to a milder climate as speedily as possible. If left too late it would probably be useless to do it at all. Make Garrow feel this truth as I feel it, and you will have, I trust, no opposition from him.[45]

Garrow prevaricated, and Fanny urged Tom to be more definite:

There are one or two points to which I desire to call your attention. The first is the *vital* importance of your adhering to your purpose of taking your wife southward *this* winter. Once make Mr Garrow (whose bark I am of the opinion is considerably worse than his bite) understand that this is your fixed purpose, and I am greatly mistaken if you do not find him disposed to avail himself of all your energy in getting through the needful business at a pace that will enable *him to go with you!* . . . Depend upon it the more the thing is pushed on, the easier it will appear to you all.

Fanny, to whom living with Tom was of such vital importance, and who had been used to making her own plans for so long now, must have found it irksome to have the health of herself, and Theo, jeopardized by the shilly-shallying of a selfish old man. 'In these first days everyone feels and knows

187

that things are out of joint; and the putting them into shape again is quite as easily done in one form or another, if a firm master-hand be set to the work.'[46]

Naturally enough, from Mr Garrow's point of view, to be induced to sell his family home and dispose of the furniture in the short space of two months, would have seemed unnecessarily rushed – it would have seemed rushed to almost anyone – except a Trollope. However, the 'firm master-hand' prevailed, and at the end of November the party set sail from Folkestone.

Anthony, told of their intentions, had written: 'Where do you mean to go? It is as well for you that some of the continental republican bubbles have burst. This time last year you would hardly have known where to pitch yourself. I suppose you can now go to Florence for the winter, if you so please.'

Florence was to be their eventual destination, but for the first few months they went to Pau, in the south-west of France to recuperate.

CHAPTER THIRTEEN

'A bluestocking who travels in seven-leagued boots'

Pau. December 1849–1852

Fanny and the young Trollopes spent the Christmas of 1849 at Pau; there is no mention of Mr Garrow, who may have delayed his departure from Torquay until he could move directly to Florence. Tom and Theo planned to take an apartment in Florence early in 1850, and then look for a suitable house large enough to accommodate both themselves and their respective parents.

After Christmas, Fanny was deeply saddened by news of her brother Henry's death. Anthony wrote to her on 29 January 1850: 'You will have been very much shocked to hear of your brother's death, for I am afraid that the previous accounts which you had received had not made you expect it – at least so suddenly. Till the last week I had no idea that he was in immediate danger. . . . His death will be a most severe blow to you and my Aunt Mary; for he was a most affectionate fond brother.'[1]

Other news from Anthony was that John Tilley was to marry Cecilia's cousin, Marianne Partington, according to Cecilia's deathbed wish, to provide care for John and the children. This meant that young Edith Diana was to be returned from Ireland; Anthony and Rose were, '*very sorry*. But we have no right to complain. Indeed incurring the chance of losing her at any moment after we had become fond of her, was the only drawback to the pleasure of taking her.'[2] Anthony had just finished *La Vendée*, his third book, and had sent it off to Colburn. His second book, *The Kellys and O'Kellys* had been published in 1848.

Once again Fanny had problems with money. Her brother Henry had been the trustee for her marriage settlement, and until a new trustee was appointed no one could collect the London rents for her. This was the vital £250 a year, salvaged when Thomas Anthony became bankrupt. The delay in obtaining the money created problems, for Fanny had been relying on it to pay her expenses. John Tilley suggested that her nephew John Milton be appointed in his father's place, and this was eventually done.

Tom and Theo departed for Florence in early February leaving Fanny in Pau working on the last chapters of *Petticoat Government*. The novelist, Sabine Baring-Gould, then a lad of sixteen, was staying in Pau and remembered:

The winter we were at Pau, Mrs Trollope, the authoress, was there as well, a good-humoured, clever, somewhat vulgar old lady. She took much notice of me. The English residents were not a little shy of her, fearing lest she should take stock of them and use them up in one of her novels; for she had the character of delineating members of her acquaintance, and that not to their advantage. Someone asked her whether this was not her practice. 'Of course,' answered Mrs Trollope, 'I draw from life – but I always pulp my acquaintance before serving them up. You would never recognize a pig in a sausage.'[3]

Fanny was feeling isolated now she had been left at Pau, and on 27 February wrote to Theo in Florence.

I will not say anything so very stupidly superfluous as that I shall long to hear again. I fear my letters when you do get them will appear very cross and grumbling. And it is abominable of me to make them so, because the people here are excessively kind to me. . . . But yet there is something indescribably desolate in the little solitary *home*.

I declare to you that it is very difficult for me to sit quietly and go on with my writing labours, for I am so much more inclined to meditate upon what you may be about at this very *now*. Is the house taken? Do you actually know where you are going to live? Well, if I live, I suppose I shall be there too ere very long; and if I die, it matters not where I am! Not that I am anticipating that particular event. I believe I am in good health, – only savagely melancholy.[4]

On 10 March she wrote again:

The mountains were fully, and most gloriously visible yesterday; and if you had been with me, I should have enjoyed it greatly. But I was ready to cry because I had no one to whom I could say how lovely I thought the view. I am ashamed of myself for complaining so bitterly of my own company. But it is my birthday, *voyez-vous*, and the *tristesse* is felt the more for that reason.'

Such self-pity was unusual, and she added a further note on 13 March: 'I am greatly ashamed of my preceding pages, but will send them *as a penance*. I am in much better condition now.'[5]

Fanny's seventieth year was indeed not a good year for her. She had lost both her brother and her daughter, and now it seemed, four of her grandchildren were too delicate to survive. Following Tom's marriage, and the plans for a shared house, she was no longer in charge. More and more she was handing over the control of her affairs to Tom, and with her fierce belief in a woman's need for independence, she must have found this difficult. It was a new role, and it was not easy to adjust. On 20 March she asked Tom to act for her:

> I must perforce talk to you a little, dearest Tom, about my own business, – which is yours too. I have a letter from John Milton, in which he tells me that he can receive no rents for me, because he can give no receipts. You have never told me whether you have received an answer from Robert Young to your question about a new trustee. . . . As it is, I have about £50. But when this is gone, what is to become of me?
>
> I am writing at my book as rapidly as stultified spirits will let me. And *if* I live to finish it, and *if* it gets safely to London, and *if* Colburn pays promptly, I shall have wherewithal to pay your money, and my board and other expenses for a year. But what is to become of my promised loan to you? If you still desire it dearest Tom, it is absolutely needful that this trustee business should be settled as soon as possible. . . . Think of my having this species of anxiety as the subject of meditation in my solitary den! But I shall enjoy what I hope is to follow, all the more for my present discomfort.

She enclosed a more cheerful letter to Theo: 'Though your houseless condition continues, my dear daughter, I nevertheless feel that your sweet letter breathes hope and cheerfulness, even in the midst of the tormenting anxiety which uncertainty must bring. . . . Remember me kindly to your father. *Have you got a cat?* If not, you and Mr Garrow will pine to death.'[6]

Tom and Theo, who were becoming concerned about Fanny's obvious depression, suggested that she join them at once in Florence, and not wait until they had found a house. But Fanny said that she would wait 'till you are a little more settled'. She had changed her hotel, and was nearer to her friend Mrs Monro, which made her feel less lonely. She wondered if Tom had any plans for the summer, because if so, 'I should like to join you.'

At the beginning of April a house was decided upon in Piazza Maria Antonia, later renamed Piazza dell' Independenza. Only part of the building was then completed, but Tom planned to finish and enlarge it to his own design. Fanny eagerly awaited letters:

> The only excuse for my impatience is that I *am alone*:– a condition so very uncongenial to my nature, as to render me not only miserable, but most savagely cross! And so full of moral angles that everything seems to hit against me, jar me, and shake me! . . . The letter you alluded to, never reached me. I am therefore, still as ignorant as ever as to the size of your mansion, number of rooms, arrangement, and the like: all of which would furnish food of a very agreeable kind to my solitary meditations. As

far as I understand the plan of *my* room, I like it vastly. Nothing could more nearly fulfil the idea of what I wished for.[7]

The news about the Tilley grandchildren was not good. They had caught measles, followed by whooping cough, and then she heard a few days later of young Cecilia's death on 13 April; there seemed no hope for Arthur. She felt for 'the fearful desolation of poor Tilley'.

In addition to all her other miseries at this time, there was an epidemic of mumps at Pau. Both Fanny and her friend Mrs Monro caught it. 'You may guess, both of you, dear children, the state of mind in which I have lived during the last ten days, during nearly the whole of which time I have been confined to my bed by an attack of that most painful malady, the *mumps*.' Her doctor 'has proved both a kind and skilful physician. I believe he has thought me *very* ill. He says that this place has *decidedly* disagreed with me, and reduced my strength so lamentably that – although his most earnest prescription is that I should leave it as soon as possible – he does not encourage me just yet to encounter a long journey.'[8]

By the end of April she was beginning to feel a little better, and wrote that she would 'hold myself in readiness to set off for Marseilles as soon as Dr T. shall tell me that he thinks I may do so with prudence. But I have no hope that this can be *quite yet*. I have not hitherto tried to do much more than stand upright for a few minutes at a time – and this is quite enough to make me very glad to sit down again. The weather is most melancholy. It is like a fretful child that smiles for a moment, and weeps for an hour.' She was delighted with the description of the house and told them to, 'value as highly as you can, there being no other inhabitants in it. The suite of reception rooms will, if skilfully managed, be very effective. And you both know me well enough to believe that it would be very difficult to call me to a consultation into which I should enter with so much zeal, and so much enjoyment, as the consultation about fitting them up.'[9]

On 6 May she was happy to tell Tom that her nephew, John Milton, who worked in the War Office, had obtained the money owing from Colburn. 'Your money was paid into Coutt's according to my directions. He sent me a third letter of credit which I thought would be amply sufficient to supply all my wants till I got to Florence. But my expenses have greatly exceeded my calculations.' The expenses were increased because she had had to have some teeth extracted. She had been suffering so much:

. . . that the replacing those I was obliged to lose was perforce delayed, because the whole face was too much swelled and inflamed to be touched. I am told I am in the hands of a very clever man, and I believe it: but would I were well out of his hands, his bill paid, and I *en route* for Florence! I think you will be rather shocked to hear that my physician, dentist, and druggist, will have cost me about £45 sterling before I have done with them! This has quite thrown me out.

I flatter myself, I hope not too fondly, that I shall be able to set out upon my journey to Florence about the 25th of this month. I am greatly better, but by no means strong as yet. I am taking bark wine, and sundry other restoratives, all of which seem to produce a good effect.[10]

She thought that if Tom's calculations were correct she should be able to make the journey without waiting for further money from London. Tom was so concerned about her health that he offered to go to Pau to fetch her but Fanny wrote again on 11 May to say that she was beginning to improve and had started to eat again. She felt that she would be in very fair condition for the planned journey on 25 May. 'God grant us a speedy and happy meeting, my dearest Tom!'

News came that John Tilley's marriage to Marianne Partington had taken place on 18 May 1850, 'His love was buried with poor Cecilia, and Marianne, tho' an amiable was not an attractive woman, and he married her from devotion to his wife's wishes.'

Fanny wrote to Tom and Theo again from Montpellier on 26 May:

Be not alarmed, my dear young ones, but I am coming down on you by a forced march, and shall probably reach Florence much before you expect me. . . . My journey (in a diligence coupé) has been very safe, and, thanks to George[s] Sand, as agreeable as a solitary journey could be. I left Pau on Thursday, and hope (DV) [*Deo volente*] to be on board a vessel to-morrow night going direct from Marseilles to Leghorn. As to the idea of your meeting me there – it is *bosh*! Keep your money to prettify your house, dear son! Wind and waves not being famed for the certainty of their action, I will not pretend to tell you when I arrive in Florence; but I am greatly in hopes that it will be at some hour on the 30th. Let me find some green tea, and I will ask for no other repast.[11]

Fanny was feeling better. She joined Tom and Theo in their apartment in the Borg Ognissanti, near the River Arno, and while Tom was busy supervising the building of the additional rooms at the new house, Fanny occupied herself with her next book. *Second Love, or Beauty and Intellect*, opened on the recently visited Glengariff–Killarney road, with the Selcroft family, who were on holiday in Ireland, admiring the scenery from a 'common Irish car, the construction of which obliged the family to divide themselves somewhat unsociably, two being on one side of it, and two on the other'. Fanny fictionalized her own visit to Ireland for the opening, including the bugler playing from the rocky heights of the Eagles Nest across Lake Killarney, and she gave detailed descriptions of the beautiful scenery.

The Reverend Selcroft, the vicar of Barton, who was of the Evangelical persuasion, had a lovely daughter who captured the heart of a fellow traveller, Henry Harley of Harley Court. After his betrothal, Henry Harley realized that his fiancée was beautiful but brainless, but, as a gentleman, he must keep his word and marry her. On a visit to Rome, and while he was still engaged, he met his true love Frederika, the intelligent and lovely daughter of Baron Rittesberg. He was unable to declare this love as he was betrothed to another, and, broken hearted, Frederika went to Venice where she met and married Lord Otway, aged sixty-five (she was only twenty-one). Henry's older sister, Fanny, in the meantime, had become the wife of the recently widowed Baron Rittesberg and went to live at his castle in Germany (memories of Baroness von Zandt). The story follows, through various countries, the twists and turns of these three unlikely marriages, and Fanny, again, showed how little control women, however independent and intelligent they were, had over their own destiny.

One of the sub-plots showed the contrast between Evangelical and High Church beliefs. Bishops of each persuasion were invited, separately, to the Reverend Selcroft's dinner table, where, in the hope of favours, he tried to ingratiate himself by adopting for each a very different code of behaviour. Once again Fanny wrote about her own familiar world.

All those who could afford to, left Florence in the summer to escape the heat, and early in July, Fanny and Mr Garrow left for the Baths of Lucca, originally a colony of Ancient Rome, where they stayed at Pagnini's Hotel. The Italians favoured Leghorn, leaving the Baths at Lucca an almost exclusively English resort, with many entertainments. There were assembly rooms, a reading room, the Baths, and a gaming table. Tom and Theo stayed in Florence, Theo was not worried by the heat as she was described as having 'an inertness of body, and disinclination to move', and Tom wanted to supervise the building alterations to their future home. Fanny urged them to join her at Lucca:

> It is no idle impatience for the enjoyment of your society which makes me thus anxious for your arrival, but a very deep conviction that the air in which you are living is not wholesome. The heat is trying; but it is not that I fear so much as the impure exhalations from the ten inches of filthy water which conceal from your eyes – though not from your lungs or your blood, – the abominations of the foul stream over which you daily hang to imbibe *fresh air*! Mr Garrow says that he was told when you took the lodgings, that you *must* not remain in them beyond the first of June. Why not go at once to your own house? My two rooms would suffice, and all the finishing might be left till you were gone. But better far than this, would be your coming here if it be possible. . . . We have very nice rooms here, and a north double-bedded apartment awaits your commands.[12]

Tom and Theo took her advice and moved into the two rooms at what was to be the Villa Trollope, but Theo was still enervated by the heat. She did not want to go to Lucca but Fanny urged her into action:

I think it very important that you should not be relaxed by remaining in the town. If you really and seriously 'hate' this lovely place so much as to make you strongly dislike coming here, I would strongly recommend your removing *somewhere* to the country. . . . People complain that this place is dull, but I do not find it so. The people I know are all very kind to me; and I have not spent a single evening alone. . . . Thus far I have fenced off Queen Zoe very well; – and I do not mean to give up this wholesome exercise![13]

Queen Zoe was the nickname give to Mrs Stisted, the unofficial Queen of the Baths. She and her husband Colonel Stisted lived in Lucca all the year round at The Cottage. Tom described her as:

. . . a stout old lady, with a large rubicund face and big blue eyes, surrounded by very abundant gray curls. She used to play, or profess to play, the harp, and adopted, as she explained, a costume for the purpose. This consisted of a loose, flowing garment, much like a muslin surplice, which fell back and allowed the arm to be seen when raised for performance on her favourite instrument. The arm probably was, or had once been, a handsome one. The large gray head and the large blue eyes and the drooping curls were also raised simultaneously, and the player looked singularly like the picture of King David similarly employed which I have seen as a frontispiece in an old fashioned prayer book. But the speciality of the performance was that, as all present always said, no sound whatever was heard to issue from the instrument! 'Attitude is everything', as we have heard in connection with other matters, but with dear old Mrs Stisted at her harp it was absolutely and literally so to the exclusion of all else.[14]

Mrs Stisted and her husband, the colonel, who was a keen violoncello player, used to drive out in the evening among 'her subjects'. One winter when they were visiting Rome her husband died. She was determined to take his body back to Lucca for burial; however, as Lucca and Rome were different states this was not permitted. The Queen of the Baths was not to be thwarted and hired a carriage with driver. She told him he was to convey a servant of hers, and a carriage of 'used second-hand goods' back to Lucca, for which she had obtained a border pass. In this guise the colonel and his beloved violoncello returned home, the only moment of panic occurring, 'by a sudden *pom-m-m* from the interior of the carriage, caused by the breaking of one of the strings of the violoncello'.[15] Fanny used this lady as a model for one of her house guests in *The Young Countess*.

At the beginning of August Theo agreed to join Fanny and her father at Lucca. Fanny was delighted: 'My heart dances at the idea of your prompt arrival.' Theo might arrive in time for the Levers' ball. Charles Lever, the Irish novelist, was staying with his family in the same hotel, and Fanny asked Theo that 'in addition to the four dozen whist papers which I ordered, to bring me four packs of whist cards, two blue, and two red. This contribution is the only way I have of sharing the nightly cost of Lever's pleasant whist table.'[16]

Charles Lever, born in Dublin in 1806, was reputed to have visited America as a young man and lived with the Indians, adopting their dress and mode of life. He returned to Ireland and took up the profession of medicine and wrote novels, mainly about experiences he had been through and people he had met. He was in Brussels when the Trollopes were in Bruges and was now living in Florence.[17] He was an inveterate, though rather unlucky, card player and was said to be wary of Fanny because he believed that she might use him in a novel. He probably had good reason, she may have already used him as her model for the Englishman disguised as a Red Indian in *The Old World and the New*.

It is not known exactly what was Fanny's contribution to Villa Trollope, apart from the furniture. There had been mention in one letter of a loan to Tom, and she sent a message to Tom via Theo 'whether it would be any convenience to him to have his 1st of August money paid before he leaves Florence. And if so tell me *how*.' Was this money for her share of the living costs, or was she still paying Tom an allowance? Whatever the arrangements were, her friends and family approved.

On 7 August 1850 Madame de M. wrote from Paris: 'I congratulate you dear friend, on Tom's house-buying. For although roaming about the world may be pleasant enough when one is in the wandering mood, it is no small comfort to feel that one has a nest of one's own wherein to roost.'[18]

Anthony said very much the same thing to Tom:

> To be sure there are certain very palpable delights in being *expeditus*: in living in other people's houses, being served by other people's servants, eating other men's roast and boiled, and having one's *gendarmerie* paid for by other men's taxes! But still there is a comfort, a solidarity, a *nescio quid decori*, in one's own armchair by one's own fireside, which after all I should not wish to want.[19]

In the autumn they all returned to the new house in Piazza dell'Independenza. Here Fanny was to live for the rest of her life. The house was referred to as Casa Trollope, Villino Trollope, and more commonly, Villa Trollope. It still stands in the north-west corner of the square. Now without its garden and hemmed in by new buildings, it has become the property of the Enteterrone dello Stato Compartmento di Firenze, and much of the inside is converted into small offices. The marble staircase remains, denuded of ornamentation, and disguised under a coat of institution grey paint. Over the outside of the door is a memorial tablet to Theo for her support in Italy's struggle for independence and unity. From the south-eastern corner the house looks over the trees of the Piazza. By the time Tom had finished his improvements it was an imposing building. As he later remembered:

> I had bought it when the speculator, who had become the owner of the ground at the corner of the space which was beginning to assume the semblance of a 'square' or 'piazza' had put in the foundations, but had not preceded much further with his work. I completed it, improving largely, as I thought, on his plan; adapted it for a single residence, instead of its division into sundry dwellings; obtained possession of additional ground between the house and the city wall, sufficient for a large garden; built around it, looking to the south, the largest and handsomest *stanzone* for orange and lemon plants in Florence, and gathered together a collection of very fine trees, the profits from which . . . abundantly sufficed to defray the expenses of the garden and gardeners. In a word I made the place a very complete and comfortable residence.[20]

Villa Trollope was described later as being in a situation which had the finest and purest air in Florence. There were spacious and lofty bedrooms; all having a pleasant outlook, also a large drawing room with a stage, which led onto open and covered terraces overlooking the garden. There was a picture gallery; a billiard and smoking room and also huge open fireplaces which would have been very cheering in the cold winter months. Kate Field, a young American friend of both Tom and Anthony, waxed lyrical in her description of the house:

> Ah, this Villino Trollope is quaintly fascinating with its marble pillars, its grim men in armour, starting like sentinels from the walls, and its curiosities greeting you at every step. The antiquary revels in its majolica, its old bridal chests and carved furniture, its beautiful terracotta of the Virgin and Child by Orgagna, its hundred *oggetti* of the Cinque Cento. The bibliophile grows silently ecstatic as he sinks quietly into a mediaeval chair and feasts his eye on a model library, bubbling over with five thousand rare books, many wonderfully illuminated and enriched by costly engravings. [There was also] . . . a cosy study where Puss and Bran, the honest dog, lie side by side on Christian terms.[21]

It was a palatial home. Elizabeth Barrett Browning told Miss Mitford:

> I hear that your friend Mrs Trollope has arrived in Florence from Pau, &
> that she, Mr Garrow, & the filial Trollopes have taken a house between
> them, containing all three establishments on different floors . . .
> according to Continental fashion . . . each floor as large as a house in
> England. I was told that they had taken it on a twenty-year lease, & are
> furnishing it. So Mrs Trollope has built her nest in Florence, 'for good',
> as people say.[22]

In her next book Fanny explored further the reasons, or lack of reasons,
for marriage. This time, however, in *Mrs Mathews*, the lady began to take
control. The heroine, Mary King, left motherless at an early age, had learnt
the value of independence. Her father was lazy and weak. 'If he was too
yielding, she was too tough. If he relied upon himself not at all, she,
generally speaking, relied too much upon herself.'

Mary King had inherited from her mother a large library which was
housed 'up thirty slight, narrow, crooked, twisting stairs, to the nest in
which his dear wife had lived, as he jocosely expressed it, with dead men's
brains'. Immersed in her beloved books, Mary King remained unmarried.
However, her father, fearing for her future, as she was now fifty and he
might not live much longer, urged her to marry Mr Mathews, a 62-year-old
neighbour. Mary, who found Mr Mathews a great bore, and could see no
need for his protection, refused, saying, 'I am very well as I am, thank you.'
Eventually, worn down by her father's weeping and worrying, she gave in,
but on her own conditions. She told Mr Mathews that she 'could not be
passively obedient to any one'. That she would 'make her own engagements,
and know how her property is to be disposed of'. The settlement was agreed
upon, Mary would remain in her own home, have £500 a year for her own
use, and was allowed to dispose of her own inheritance.

After their wedding, Mary began her married life as she intended to go
on. On the morning after her marriage day, 'Mrs Mathews mounted her
corkscrew staircase with the respectable deliberation acquired by fifty years
of existence; and then she seated herself in her queer-looking chair, at her
queer-looking table, tolerably well satisfied with herself, and with the
manner in which she had set about beginning her conjugal existence.'[23]

The household was disrupted, however, first by a young man claiming to
be the grandson of Mr Mathews, and shortly after, by a young girl, the
orphan daughter of Mrs Mathews' childhood sweetheart. Mrs Mathews
found her peaceful existence greatly altered, but on meeting Janet, 'was
happier at that moment than she had ever felt before in the whole course of
her life'. Janet, who she grew to love dearly, had to be outfitted and
introduced into society. Mrs Mathews who 'was very indifferent to, and

forgetful of, everything appertaining to dress', asked her maid-servant to deal with the problem of clothes.

There were dinner parties and picnics, walks and carriage rides, and much confusion as to who was going to be married to whom. Mr Mathews' grandson who turned out to be an impostor, was caught trying to steal some money, but managed to escape the law. Janet fell in love with Herbert, the son of Lord Otterborne who found, after his father had shot himself, that his whole inheritance had been gambled away and the family was destitute. 'All that it was possible to sell he had sold, and all that he could mortgage he had mortgaged.' With the help of Mrs Mathews, the Otterbornes rebuilt their lives, 'and no one guessed, no, not one, that for the first time since her marriage, Lady Otterborne was leading a very happy and a very cheerful life.'[24]

Fanny showed, in this novel, her strong, women characters leading their own fulfilled lives with no help from their men. There had been glimpses of this before in her novels with minor characters, and especially with the Widow Barnaby. Mrs Mathews, however, was a woman who made her own way happily and successfully and on her own terms. The book was published by Colburn in 1851, the year of the Great Exhibition, and sold well.

Tom, Fanny and Theo had planned to go to England in the summer of 1851 to see the Great Exhibition, but decided that because of the cost of setting up the Villa Trollope, the expense would be too great. Anthony was sadly disappointed. In March 1851 he wrote to Tom:

I grieve to find that you and Theodosia do not intend coming to London next summer. Your stay in Italy will, I presume, occasion my mother's. And there is our pleasant party broken up! I cannot tell you how I grieve at this. . . . As for the Exhibition itself, I would not give a straw for it, – except the building itself, and my wife's piece of work which is in it. I suppose you have nearly completed your decorations and improvements.[25]

Anthony wrote to Fanny on 7 May 1851:

It is May by the calendar, but February by one's feelings as affected by rain, winds, and cold air. . . . I regret more and more every day that Tom is not to see the Exhibition. I am sure it is a thing a man ought to see. John Tilley is enthusiastic, and knew all about it before it was opened. . . . I think he is right. It is a great thing to get a new pleasure. . . . Will there be no such thing as a cheap trip from Florence by which a man could come to London and go back within a fortnight or so? At present we are all agog about going to London. Rose is looking up her silk dresses, and I am meditating a new hat![26]

Anthony had a large collection of hats.

Fanny became seriously ill in early summer with what was thought to be English cholera, but managed to throw it off with unexpected rapidity. John Milton, Fanny's nephew, was transacting most of her business for her in London; collecting rents and dealing with Colburn. He wrote to Tom in July: 'Tell her . . . that I received in safety the MS. of her novel, vol. 2, pages 101 to 152. But I had the heavy tax of £1.0.3d to pay for it!' He went on to say that he would be in France from 5 August to 10 September, and if the entire MS. was ready for delivery to the publisher before that date she had better send it to John Tilley. (The manuscript was *Uncle Walter.*)

Fanny Bent was well, and Anthony had visited Aunt Clyde. 'Give our very kindest love to my dear aunt. Take good, very good, care of her. Don't let her have any more such attacks.'[27] John Milton became Accountant General of the Army in 1871 and was knighted in 1878. He died in 1880.

In September 1851, once his mother had recovered, Tom went alone to London, leaving Fanny and Theo at the Baths of Lucca. He probably took the rest of the book with him. He was away for only two weeks but was able to visit Anthony, Rose, and young Harry at Exeter where Anthony was then working. Frederick James had been left in Ireland. In December of 1851, John Tilley's second wife, Marianne, gave birth to a son, Arthur Augustus. She died a week later, but the baby survived. Cecilia's children were less fortunate. On 21 May young Arthur William died, followed by the death in June of Frances Trollope Tilley, aged eleven, and, on 3 August Anna Jane, the third daughter. In the space of two years John Tilley had suffered the death of two wives and four children.

This latest book of Fanny's, called *Uncle Walter*, is of particular interest because of its possible influence on Anthony's *The Warden*. The book took a humorous look at the various religious persuasions currently in contention, using Uncle Walter as the catalyst.

The story started with the elderly Reverend Harry Harrington preparing his Sunday sermon. He was Warden of All Saints College at the University of Oxford, Rector of St Martin's in London's West End, and Prebendary of the Cathedral Church of Glastonbury. The Sunday Observance Bills were not being kept, and he mused on the influence of the park versus the pulpit as he re-wrote one of his old sermons. 'The Doctor had a great objection to clergymen preaching sermons which were not their own composition. To do so, he argued, was to abandon all attempt at supplying the peculiar teaching which every different congregation required according to its circumstances and condition.'[28] The doctor was a pompous, self-satisfied man who spoke in meaningless platitudes. As Fanny said:

The words of very decent, well-behaved people, like the Doctor often require translating into plain English in order to be fully intelligible even to their own hearts. The key to this language is simply putting words indicative of the generous, the noble, and the great, in order to express thoughts shabby, dirty, and little. It is a figure of speech which furnishes enormous resources; and it may almost be said, that in the present state of society, *decency* could scarcely exist without it.[29]

The doctor was an Establishment man, married to Lady Augusta, the third daughter of the Earl of Bentley, and he went through the motions of religion. 'God knew he cared as little as most men for the pomps and vanities of life, but it was impossible not to feel that the Church must lose station and influence, if her aristocracy were not placed on a level with that of other professions.'[30] His wife, Lady Augusta, had an Evangelical sister, Lady Juliana, 'a thin and peevish lady much addicted to religion,' who believed that 'fêtes and finery can only be enjoyed at the risk of eternal burning hereafter', a risk which she prudently declined to take. Lady Augusta had, in her day, been a beauty. Not so Lady Juliana.

Hence in two narrow, ill-regulated minds, innumerable jealousies, heart-burnings, and mutual dislikes had sprung up from their earliest years. . . . To irreproachably elegant manners, a tolerable knowledge of the small world in which she moved (calling it, and believing it, the great world), and a fair share of common sense, Lady Augusta added that deep-seated vulgarity of mind which is the inevitable product of a life spent in looking up to that on which we ought to look down.[31]

Doctor Harrington and Lady Augusta had three children: Henry who was High Church, the Reverend James, a Puseyite with a country living, and Kate the youngest who was, as yet, unmarried.

Into this staid London home came Uncle Walter, the younger brother of the Doctor, who had been living on a sheep station in Australia for the last twenty years. A botanist and zoologist, he believed in the power of good and evil, and had a large and abiding charity towards 'the follies, faults and frailities of humanity'. He brought with him a large boa constrictor as a present for Regent's Park Zoological Gardens. Lady Juliana remarked disapprovingly: 'It was in her judgement a vain and sinful tempting of the Lord, to feed and cherish animals which He had selected as the fitting form of incarnation for the eternal enemy of man.'

Lady Augusta gave a ball for her daughter Kate, in the hope of finding her a rich and suitable husband. Lady Augusta had set her sights on the young, wealthy, and incredibly naive, Lord Goldsmith, whom Kate could not abide. Uncle Walter was horrified at the suggestion: 'No law, no sanction, no duty, authority, or any consideration whatever, can justify or excuse a woman for giving herself to any man whom she does not love. The doing so, my child, is an outrage against nature, and the God of nature.'[32]

Kate's elder brother, Henry, explained the system:

I must allow, that the young ladies intended for the market, are carefully and admirably trained to prepare them for it. I can assure you, uncle, that our practice in that respect puts the method of the Constantinople dealers to shame. There the fair ones, we are told, do shrink painfully from the exhibition made of them, and evidently dislike the *trotting out*. But with the superior methods of training for our market, the pretty creatures are fully as anxious for the sale, as the seller. . . . I have always been taught that marriage is a holy state instituted for the better securing of a handsome establishment and equipage, and that it is the bounden duty of a well-principled young lady to obey her parents, and keep these objects steadily in view in forming a matrimonial connection.[33]

Fanny, herself, speaks through Uncle Walter:

Is it not inconceivable . . . that the same society which thinks no language strong enough to upbraid the degraded creature who sells herself, when the price paid is to save her from starvation, should smile upon and approve the very same act, when not the necessaries, but the luxuries of life are the legalised payment? Not to mention that, in the latter case, the additional impiety is incurred of invoking the sanction of religion upon the sacrilegious atrocity?[34]

Fanny also introduced the scheming Mrs Fitzjames, who appeared in *Uncle Walter* as a beautiful and penniless widow. She was able to capture the rich, young, Lord Goldsmith with her seductive wiles, but was, no doubt in order to appease Victorian morality, eventually exposed as a bigamist and sent packing. Fanny explained in wonderful detail the calculated way in which Mrs Fitzjames made her conquests:

For example: supposing the sum total of one thousand to be the amount required for the achievement of any given conquest, she would systematically have set down the relative value of every separate manoeuvre somewhat in this wise:
First sight, under all advantages of dress, one hundred.
Under disadvantage of ditto, but not presumed to be actually disfiguring, fifty.
Morning occupation, with hands ungloved, and hair hanging in disorder (nicely arranged), fifty.
Caught reading a newly arrived review (if the chase be literary), twenty-five.
Transcribing music, if he be musical, one hundred and fifty.

A ball well lighted, with good reposing room, seventy.

Fancy dress ditto, one hundred and sixty.

Caught singing an Italian *bravura*, or a French ballad, if you have a voice, and he has ears, one hundred and seventy five.

To be seen at early church, if he be a Puseyite, seventy-seven.

At an Evening lecture, if he be an Evangelical, seventy-seven.

To be seen darning stockings, if he be a rich miser, one hundred.

To be seen embroidering in gold and seed pearls, if he be a poor elegant, one hundred.

A pic-nic, everything being *couleur de rose*, fifty.

Ditto with storm, seventy five.

Ditto with a moon, and a little dancing after, one hundred and fifty.

Ditto when matters are tolerably advanced beforehand, two hundred.

And so on, with an infinity of items, every one of which would have shown an admirable knowledge of the human heart.[35]

Kate, who unlike Mrs Fitzjames had no creditors knocking on her door, took Uncle Walter's advice and refused to marry the stupid Lord Goldsmith. She was locked in her mother's room and then bundled off to stay with her clergyman brother in his country parish, Lady Juliana was sent with her to keep watch. 'And thus it was authoritatively decided that Kate should be delivered over to the keeping of her Puseyite brother, and her Evangelical aunt, in order to be ground down to the necessary point of obedient submission by their joint efforts.' Kate tried to explain the Puseyite beliefs to her bewildered Uncle Walter:

I believe that a Puseyite thinks that the world was in its prime of life somewhere about the year 1500, or thereabouts; and that it has been going down hill ever since. I know that a proper Puseyite, thinks it far better to be a Roman Catholic than a dissenter; and that he wears a particular sort of waistcoat, generally made of black silk, pinned, without buttons, close under his chin. This, I know, is a very essential point. . . . He is greatly inclined to love and reverence all kinds of ecclesiastical ornaments; and if anything of, or belonging to the church, has an old name and a new one, he seems to think it a point of duty to call it by the old one.[36]

In this book, Lady Juliana's Evangelicism, the Reverend James' Puseyite practices, a Calvanistic widow, an educated Jesuit priest, and Doctor Harrington, the Warden of All Saints and a follower of the Established Church, are all examined in minute detail. 'Nothing can appear more puzzling in all the inscrutable ways of Providence than that the divinely appointed teaching of the Church shall prescribe to the faithful the doctrine of prevenient grace, perhaps, in Mary'bone, baptismal regeneration in Bloomsbury, election and reprobation in Pall Mall, and the operative efficacy of absolution in Piccadilly.'[37]

The two main themes of this provocative book were women's rights, especially in relation to their choice of a partner in marriage; and the contrasts in living and behaviour of clergy from the different religious factions. It was the last book Fanny wrote about the clergy, and she explored the latter in greater depth than she had ever done before, and with her usual satirical zest.

One elderly curate, promoted to Glastonbury, was asked:

'How shall you manage to be all things to all men? To all prebendal men, I mean, down at Glastonbury? Eh!'

'By minding my own business, which I take to be singing. . . . If I sing in tune, my doctrine will neither be found too high nor too low, I believe.'[38]

Anthony, in 1851, had written three books and one play, none of which had been very successful. Fanny's *Uncle Walter* was published in 1852, and it was in the summer of 1852 that Anthony, while visiting Salisbury, conceived the story of *The Warden*. As he said himself; 'I may as well declare at once that no one at their commencement could have had less reason than myself to presume himself able to write about clergymen. . . . I never lived in any cathedral city, – except London, never knew anything of any Close, and at that time had enjoyed no particular intimacy with any clergyman.'[39]

The kindly Uncle Walter had much in common with the gentle Mr Harding in *The Warden*, and Dr Harrington would have felt at home with Archdeacon Grantly. Anthony, who was frequently employed as a messenger between Fanny and her publisher, would have been familiar with the story. It is interesting to speculate that *Uncle Walter* may have been one of the foundation stones upon which Barchester was built.

In 1852 the *New Monthly Magazine* ran a series of articles on 'Female Novelists'. The first four to be featured were Jane Austen, Mrs Gore, Currer Bell (Charlotte Bronte) and the 'Author of Olive'. Mrs Trollope was number five. The anonymous author berated her for writing too fast and condemned 'the rash speed of her grey-goose quill'. He went on:

In vain have reviewers tried to keep up with her. A bluestocking who travels in seven-leagued boots may well run critics and criticasters out of breath – *she* triumphantly ascending the hill Difficulty, as fresh as a Daisy while *they* wallow, and struggle, and give up the race (and almost the ghost) in the Slough of Despond. Pant and puff as they will to run her home, she is in a trice miles out of sight, over the hills and far away, and wondering what those sluggard lameters are doing in the rear. What a

Lady Bountiful hath Mrs Trollope been to printers, Marlborough-Street puff-factors, Wellington Street advertising columns; provincial papermakers and eke, we fear, to universal trunk makers! . . . Nor does she ever betray symptoms of fatigue.[40]

However, Fanny, at the age of seventy-three, was starting to slow up. During the next four years she was to produce only four more books. The 'seven-leagued boots' were beginning to wear out.

CHAPTER FOURTEEN

'I am in truth grown most woefully idle'

Villa Trollope. March 1852–October 1863

The Trollopes and Mr Garrow spent a comfortable winter at the Villa Trollope, where Fanny continued to write, though now, thankfully, the financial need was less urgent. Anthony and Rose planned to visit Florence in the spring of 1852, but had to postpone the trip. Anthony wrote to Fanny and Tom in March 1852:

> I am delighted not to find myself scolded for having changed our proposed plans, I trust, when 1853 does come, I may find myself repaid for my patience by the *greenth* of your lawn. A twelvemonth does not seem so long to wait now as it did ten years ago. It ought to seem longer, for as one has fewer months to come one should make more of them. But somehow, the months and years so jostle one another, that I seem to be living away at a perpetual gallop. I wish I could make the pace a little slower.[1]

In April 1852 Fanny was delighted to receive a letter from Mary Russell Mitford. She replied: 'It was for a moment, very much as if I had been looking at you – and greatly did I rejoice at the sight, but alas! the precious bit of paper was soon exhausted, and then I only wished the more that I could get sight of yourself.'[2]

Miss Mitford wrote to another correspondent in the autumn of that year, 'My old friend Mrs Trollope, in spite of her terrible coarseness, has certainly done two or three marvellously clever things. She was brought up within three miles of this house . . . and is, in spite of her works, a most elegant and agreeable woman. I have known her these fifty years; she must be turned of seventy, and is wonderful for energy of mind and body. Her story is very curious; put me in mind to tell it you.'[3]

Once again, the summer of 1852 was spent at the Baths at Lucca. In July Fanny was overjoyed to hear that Theo was pregnant, although Theo herself found pregnancy very wearing and distasteful. She and Tom remained in Florence, and Fanny wrote encouraging letters. 'I should like a *daily* bulletin of poor dear Theo, although I know it would be silly to ask for it or to give it. But tell me how she is as often as you reasonably can. . . . Remember that the constant direction under such circumstances is "take care of the general health, in exactly the same way as usual."'[4]

Later she wrote to Theo: 'Did I think I could do you any good, I would offer to return to you at once. But this I know full well cannot be hoped for from anything but time.' She offered to pay for both Theo and Tom to visit Lucca for a few days if poor Theo improved a little, and on 3 August 1852 wrote: 'I think of you both *very* often. And did I not know to a very perfect certainty that my presence would do neither of you any sort of good, I should think myself a monster for enjoying myself here. . . . This is my fourth visit to this place; but it is this year in such perfection of foliage and atmosphere, that I am as much in raptures with it as if I were looking at its exquisite beauty for the first time.'[5] Fanny was content.

The book she was writing, *The Young Heiress*, is not one of her best; it is a run-of-the-mill romance, drawn out over three volumes.

By September Fanny was back in Florence, and on the 28th received a letter from Anthony:

We have heard a rumour (some one told John Tilley in Kensington Gardens!) that Theodosia is about to make Tom a father. If so, why has not Tom told us what we should have been so glad to learn from him? If it be true, I heartily wish Theodosia well through her trouble. . . . I have been expecting, dearest mother, to hear either from you or Tom these two months. I hope you have not both forgotten me!

He went on to tell her that he was now working in South Wales, and the family were all going to Gloucester for the winter. The Duke of Wellington had just died, and Anthony was getting dreadfully sick of him. 'The papers have no other subject, and people write, speak, and think, of nothing else. Oh that he was well buried, and there an end!'[6]

As Theo was barely three months pregnant and very delicate, it was not surprising that Tom was hesitant about broadcasting the news; however, he did then tell Anthony, and got a rumbustious letter in return:

5 October 1852.
I am glad you are to have a child. One wants some one to exercise unlimited authority over, as one gets old and cross. . . . One's wife may be too much for one, and is not always a safe recipient for one's wrath. But one's children can be blown up to any amount without damage, – at any rate for a considerable number of years. . . . Joking apart, I am heartily glad to hear the news, and assure you that, to my thinking, nothing that could happen to you would be so likely to add to your happiness as this.[7]

Beatrice Trollope, nicknamed Bice (pronounced Beechay), was born the following March, and was the delight of Villa Trollope. Once the baby was born, Theo adored her, as Tom said, 'Her intense worship of her "Baby Beatrice" was equalled only by – that of all the silliest and all the wisest women, who have true womanly hearts in their bosoms for their children. The worship was, of course, all the more absorbing that the object of it was unique. I take it that, after the birth of her child, I came second in her heart. But I was not jealous of little Bice.'[8]

In April 1853 Rose and Anthony finally visited Florence to meet young Bice, her parents and Fanny, whom they hadn't seen for four years. It was Rose's first visit to Florence and she wrote of her mother-in-law:

> She took me about everywhere, and explained everything to me. And she made me happy by a present of an Italian silk dress. She also gave me a Roman mosaic brooch, which had been a present to her from the Princess Metternich during her stay in Vienna. It is a perfect gem. At this time she used to have her weekly evening receptions, attended by some of the pleasantest of the English residents in Florence; and she always had her own special whist table. I thought her the most charming old lady who ever existed. There was nothing conventional about her, and yet she was perfectly free from the vice of affectation; and was worlds asunder from the 'New Woman' and the 'Emancipated Female' School. I do not think she had a mean thought in her composition. She was lavishly generous as regards money; full of impulse; not free from prejudice – but more often in favour of people than otherwise, – but once in her good books, she was certain to be true to you. She could say a sarcastic word, but never an ill-natured one.[9]

Elizabeth Barrett Browning saw the 'weekly evening receptions' slightly differently. She told Miss Mitford, 'Mrs Trollope seems to be quite strong again & as social as ever – with "an open day" once a week, filled up to the brim with the various nationalities & very various reputations for which this city is famous. Oh, we are by no means purists in Florence I can assure you, in any sense of that term.'[10]

Fanny's next book, *The Life and Adventures of a Clever Woman*, was about Charlotte Morris, who, in spite of Rose's perceptions of her mother-in-law, was quite definitely a member of the Emancipated Female School. The strong-minded daughter of a banker, Charlotte decided from a very early age to have her own way in all things. She was left in the care of her aunt, Mrs Buckhurst, who was aware 'of the utter hopelessness of her ever attempting in any way to control her high-spirited niece'. Charlotte decided to become 'a woman of fashionable consequence and intellectual influence in Society'.

She cultivated the well-connected, but impoverished, Knighton family, who agreed to introduce her to the 'right' people in return for a little material help. Charlotte, 'never forgot that, whatever we make up our minds to have, we must make up our minds to pay for'.

One of the fashionables she conquered was a painter, Mr Richards, who was much sought after as a dinner guest for his skill as a caricaturist and his ability to rhyme extemporaneously; an ability which 'is found wonderfully useful in helping on a dull evening'. However, in spite of his popularity as a guest, Mr Richards ran into financial trouble, and his pecuniary circumstances rendered it, 'desirable to go to Berlin for a few weeks'.[11]

Mr Richards was thought by Frances Eleanor to be drawn from a well-known London society figure; Fanny's reputation for caricaturing her friends made some of them very wary of her company.

Charlotte, the clever woman, found that being a society hostess cost rather more than her allowance would permit. She resolved to enter into a marriage of convenience with young Mr Knighton, knowing that the money which her father would advance her for the wedding, would pay her outstanding debts. 'I await my coming fate with great philosophy, or, in other words, with great indifference. Fortunately for my peace of mind, the only point on which I am not indifferent, is the only point concerning which I either do or can know anything with certainty, and that is concerning the security of my own fortune.'[12] However, when the intended groom was arrested for debt on the eve of the wedding, she was quite composed. The object had been achieved, the debts had been paid. 'It is so common to hear of the tyranny of fathers and husbands! And yet it seems to me as certain as the sun is in his Heaven, that fathers, and husbands too, may be managed with the greatest ease, if women would but set their wits a little more steadily to work upon the business.'[13]

When Charlotte again ran into financial difficulties she decided that this time she would marry Cornelius Folkestone, who 'disliked the idea of marrying exceedingly,' but who was 'greatly in want of money'. Although the settlement was to remain in Charlotte's name, Cornelius had great confidence in the law which stated, 'What belongs to my wife, is mine; what belongs to me, is my own.' Charlotte's father died, she inherited his money, and, for the sake of peace, agreed to pay some of her husband's debts. Cornelius told her that 'her settlement was a farce, for that there was no law, nor gospel either, which could prevent his locking her up, and keeping her upon bread and water till she obeyed his commands'. Charlotte was only too well aware of this: 'the law made and provided in this country, for regulating the extent of the husband's power over the wife, was somewhat uncertain'.[14] She resolved to flee to the Continent, but was not quick enough. Cornelius demanded payment of £1,000, and when she refused, imprisoned her, telling her friends that she was ill. With the aid of an old servant, Charlotte was freed, and, generously, paid Cornelius an allowance for life, as long as he stayed away from her. Fortunately he died within two years. She declared: 'for all this I care not a straw. I am thirty years old, and I well know that if I did not marry, my brilliant position in society would have been speedily converted, in the eyes of the world, into that of a disappointed old maid.'[15]

Charlotte Morris refused all further offers of marriage. She had achieved all that she set out to do, and stated firmly, 'I have assuredly great pleasure in thinking that this record of my remarkable life may be not only interesting, but useful to my fellow-creatures.'[16] Single-minded, strong-willed, and ambitious, Charlotte Morris was successful and triumphant, though not particularly likeable. She was a new kind of heroine. The *New Monthly Magazine* wrote about Fanny in 1852:

No one class appropriates her irony. No one pariah society is the recipient of her hard words. Wherever, high or low, she discerns what she honestly believes to be weak points or vicious abuses, she as honestly proclaims war, and incontinently fires a broadside. She is, in fact, one of the most Catholic of satirists – a very Ishmaelite in the impartiality of pugilism – one who looks out for squalls on every coast.[17]

In 1854, the year of the Crimean war, the Trollopes left Florence for the summer, going to the Villa Caprini in the hills. Fanny stayed there for a while, and then went on to visit friends in the Val d'Arno. When the full heat of summer set in she went again to her favourite Baths of Lucca. Tom, Theo and baby Bice returned to Florence, where Tom had a recurrence of his painful rheumatism. Fanny wrote to him:

Your account of yourself, my dearest Tom, makes me very uneasy. Dear Theodosia is so deeply incrusted with the notion that the heat of Florence in the month of August, is as genial to an active Englishman as the breezes of the mountain which surround it, that I will not bother her, or myself, by endeavouring to convince her of the contrary. . . . Give her my most truly affectionate love, and tell her that nothing but my long experience of what your constitution requires, could induce me to combat her intense aversion to move, or be moved. . . . Do you think it would be possible to persuade her to come here *bag and baggage?*[18]

While she was at Lucca Fanny was hard at work on her next book, *Gertrude, or Family Pride*. It was set in Austria, and the main theme of the story is Baron von Schwanberg's over-concern about the importance of his family pedigree. He had married a beautiful and intelligent wife who 'had long ceased to lament, with anything like bitterness, the fate which had given her one of the dullest men that ever lived as husband and companion.' A daughter was born, who was the darling of both parents. She was educated by her mother, whose passion was her library, and her father, whose passion was his exalted position, and who stated that no man should be allowed to marry his daughter whose name could not be found in the *Almanack de Gotha*, a book which, 'contains not only the pedigrees of all the reigning dynasties of the earth, but records also the names of all those noble persons who are in any way connected to them'. One day, when out riding, young Gertrude fell from her pony into a swiftly flowing stream and was rescued by Rupert, a village youth. As a reward, Rupert was installed in the castle as librarian and private secretary to the baron, who bestowed 'favours upon the low-born boy with no more caution than he would have thought necessary in petting a poodle'. Naturally, Rupert and Gertrude fell in love, but they realized that the prejudiced baron would never countenance the match, and it was only many years later, after the baron's death, the couple were at last married.

In *Gertrude* Fanny was considering the need for change to the, hitherto, rigid rules of class by which society had been divided. 'The system of enlarged *education* which is gaining ground among us, will do more towards lessening the inequalities of rank, than all the heralds will be able to withstand.' It is a long-winded story, and unfortunately, the theme 'Worth is better than family pride' is not enough to carry the reader through three volumes.

Elizabeth Barrett Browning, whose attitude to Fanny was a little waspish, reported to Miss Mitford:

Here is your friend Mrs Trollope who ebbs & flows like the sea – has attacks affecting vital organs, and recovers, and takes long walks again and writes half a dozen more romances. . . . From what I hear, she appears to be well, & has recommenced her 'public mornings' which we shrink away from. She 'receives' every saturday morning in the most heterogeneous way possible – It must be amusing to anybody not overwhelmed [by] it, & people say that she snatches up 'characters' for her "so many volumes a year" out of the diversities of masks presented to her on these occasions.[19]

It seems that Mrs Browning too, was indulging in the 'double gossip' she decried.

Fanny loved having a grandchild to spoil. She enthused in a doting grandmotherly way to Anthony in the Christmas of 1854 about Bice who was not quite two, and told him how she was already able to 'talk fluently of most earthly affairs'. Her musical talents were equally wonderful, and whatever tune she wanted played she could hum well enough for her mother to understand. She danced as well as an opera dancer, and 'as to pictures of all kinds her comprehension, and the delight she receives from them is quite unlike any thing I ever saw in one so young'.

Fanny and Tom met Anthony and Rose in Venice in May 1855, where they planned to take a holiday before returning to England together. Theo and Bice remained in Florence. Rose reported that: 'Mrs Trollope had not much scope for her pedestrian powers. But the stairs she climbed, and the walks she took on the sands of the Lido, were wonderful. She was then seventy-five years old.' One day when they were returning by boat from Murano, they were caught in a thunderstorm, and there was a nasty swell, causing the gondola to 'rock about more than was pleasant'. Fanny, who was not a good sailor, panicked. 'Her nerves gave way and she fairly broke down with terror.'[20] She recovered rapidly, however, once they reached land.

Fanny returned to England, ostensibly to see her grandchildren and her old friends, but there was another reason. In London at that time was a young Scotsman by name of Daniel Dunglas Home. He had just returned from living in America, and was staying in Ealing as the special guest of a solicitor, Mr Rymer, to conduct seances. There had been a craze for spiritualism in Florence, with friends gathering to hold seances and communicate with the other world, and Fanny wanted to see Mr Home. She became a constant attendant at the Ealing house, at the sittings of the medium, and was fascinated with the procedures. Tom, who was far more sceptical, went along as well and described how all the guests placed themselves around a large and heavy old-fashioned mahogany table and waited expectantly: 'Before long little crackings were heard, in the wood of the table apparently. Then it quivered, became more and more agitated, was next raised first at one end and then at the other, and finally was undeniably raised bodily from the ground.' Tom immediately flung himself under the table to observe that it was, without doubt, hovering some four or five inches from the floor, a phenomenon which he found 'wholly inexplicable'. 'That was the sum of what occurred. There was no pretence of the presence of any spiritual visitor.'[21]

However, Tom and his mother were both so impressed with Daniel Home that they invited him and Mr Rymer to stay with them in Florence in October 1855. Mr Home stayed at the Villa Trollope and sittings were held with the medium nearly every evening. Theo, who was very unimpressed, was not pleased. The results reported were again more physical than metaphysical. Tables were moved, heavy lamps twirled around in full view, a heavy American rocking chair violently rocked to and fro, and mysterious knots tied in handkerchiefs. Tom felt that Daniel Home was in the habit of adding to, or assisting, the manifestations. Fanny was reported to enjoy the sessions, but was not particularly agitated by the reports of family spirits said to be present at the meetings. One story went the rounds of the Browning circle that at one seance a table hurtled towards the door, and Fanny cried in great excitement 'Damn it, let it go!'[22]

It was during this time that Fanny wrote her last book, *Fashionable Life, or Paris and London,* in which she described just such a seance, and discussed the whole issue of spiritualism.

> I cannot believe . . . that Nature has any secrets which it would be a sin to penetrate . . . although there may be many which we may long to try and investigate in vain. . . . And we have, at least, the great satisfaction of knowing, that every onward step we take, renders the next more easy . . . and many an acute observer may be emboldened to hint at new discoveries *now,* from which he may have shrunk a hundred years ago.[23]
>
> I now again feel persuaded that it *may* be possible for a human agent to produce effects upon inert matter, such as you, and many others, have described; though the theory which refers the phenomena thus produced, to the *mesmerized* and *deluded* condition of the *spectator,* and not to any locomotive activity in the table and chairs, has, I am told, many advocates.[24]

For the third time, in this book, she explored the relationships between those with wealth, and those with breeding; and considered ways in which they could become less mutually exclusive.

In *Diary of a Clever Woman,* the protagonists had deliberately used each other for their own gain, and rejected the opponent when the goal was achieved. In *Gertrude,* the class prejudices of a parent, had blighted the lives of the young. Now, in *Fashionable Life,* Fanny put forward a scheme whereby the two classes could live together in harmony for their mutual benefit.

Clara, the rich heiress of a corn factor, travelled to Paris with her aunt, and there they met Lady Amelia Wharton and her daughter. Clara and Lady Amelia discussed the difficulties arising from poverty and a title (Lady Amelia), and riches and obscure birth (Clara), and decided to keep house together to solve the problem. A 'female co-partnership' was formed and:

> . . . in a marvellously short space of time, they found themselves leading precisely the sort of life they had imagined, intended, and desired. . . . It would have been difficult, perhaps, to find any other group of four females who, while each was so essentially different from the others, could, nevertheless, constitute a society in which each should so delightfully contribute to the enjoyment of the rest.[25]

They became part of the fashionable life of Paris, and went to many dinners and soirées, and even to one dissipated, 'tobacco Divan party', described in detail, where both the ladies and the gentlemen smoked and drank. Clara also became acquainted with an American 'medium', a Mr Wilson, and went to her first seance, which was described at length. Lady Amelia's daughter fell in love with Victor, a handsome but penniless young man, and Clara happily resolved to endow the daughter with £10,000 to give her financial independence. It was suggested the money be invested in a mining company, in Victor's name, 'which would suffice for his reception into the concern as a partner'. The money was paid to a Mr Roche, also residing in Paris, the chairman of the company, and a collector of pictures. Clara signed her name on the document as security, and the wedding took place.

Some time later, Victor told her that Mr Roche had suddenly left town, and the company was in a dangerous state. Clara tried desperately to remember what was on the paper that she had signed. 'How did I write it? Where did I write it? On what paper? At what table? Again and again her thoughts recurred to the scene when, with so gay a heart, and in so heedless a hand, she had written her name upon a sheet of folded paper, below a few written lines which he read to her rapidly.'[26]

She immediately went to Mr Roche's house and found it in disarray. All the pictures had been removed from the walls, 'some were already in packing cases, while others were lying on the floor . . . showing plainly enough, that the dispersion of the whole collection was in rapid progress. . . . The mining concern was a bubble! It had burst.'[27]

Victor, who felt responsible for the loss of Clara's money, killed himself; and Clara and Lady Amelia, deeply upset, resolved to return to England and live with Clara's old tutor in Crowton Rectory. But all ended happily, when Roche repented and returned all her money.

The particular interest in Mr Roche, who is described as a suave confidence trickster, lies in the possibility that Fanny intended him as a disguised portrait of Edward John Heseltine, Rose's father.

In Heseltine's obituary in the *Sheffield Times* of 1855, the writer observed: 'that it was probable that he was the oldest person alive who was a banker by training'. Fanny's Mr Roche had a father who 'was one of our first bankers'. Heseltine's obituary also declared that he was, 'a well-known connoisseur of painting, and often purchased valuable pictures for the price of their frames. One for which he paid a very few guineas, was purchased (after being cleaned) for the National Gallery for a large sum.'[28] Fanny's Mr Roche confessed to 'a passion for pictures. . . . But like all other expensive fancies, this could not be long indulged without making me feel that . . . I was not rich enough to indulge this new fancy without making or finding some means of increasing my revenue.'[29]

After his retirement in 1853, Heseltine was discovered to have embezzled a sum of £4,000 from the bank of which he was a manager. In 1853 or 1854 he fled to Le Havre, and he died in France on 15 September

1855. If Fanny intended Roche as a portrait of Heseltine, this would account for the otherwise inexplicable return of Roche at the end of the last volume, when he repented his evil ways and returned to Clara all the money he had embezzled. This section was written just after the death of Heseltine.

At the beginning of *Fashionable Life*, Fanny, in the character of Clara's father, mused on growing old and having to stop work:

Depend upon it . . . the mind is the most important part of that wonderful machine called man; and if this portion of it has worked too much, or too long, our general well being must suffer for it. . . . Before I decide upon taking so strong a measure [as giving up work], I wish you would give me a hint as to how you think I shall be able to employ my time. I have passed six or seven hours every morning of my life, for the last fifty years, and more, in my office . . . and I can't for the life of me, think how I am to get through that time.[30]

Fanny, now seventy-six, had already decided that this might be her last book. When she reached the end of the third volume of *Fashionable Life*, which was also the one hundred and fifteenth volume of her works, she laid aside her pen, and wrote no more.

In the summer of 1856 Fanny went to Leghorn instead of Lucca, and on 30 July she wrote to Tom to tell him that she had arrived safely. The view was wonderful. 'It is . . . like being on board ship without the horrors of being at sea!' She only stayed away for a very short time; she missed the comfort of the company at the Villa Trollope; she was also now without employment and the days must have seemed very long.

On 8 July 1856 she wrote to Anthony:

Age eighty (minus not quite three), Thermometer eighty (plus rather more than four) must be accepted as an excuse my very dear Anthony, both by you and my highly valued new correspondent [her Grandson] for not having acknowledged your very precious *packet* earlier. I am in truth grown most woefully idle, and worse still, most woefully *lazy*, and this symptom is both new and disagreeable to *me*. But the degree of activity of which I have been wont to boast, and on which I have so often been complimented might have been accounted in my very best days as positive *idleness* to what you manifest. Tom and I agree in thinking that you exceed in this respect any individual whom we have ever known or heard of – and I am proud of being your mother – as well for this reason as for sundry others. I rejoice to think that you have considerably more than the third of a century to gallop through yet before reaching the age at which I first felt inclined to cry *halte la*!

[Tom added a line on the end].

My mother is pretty well, though weak, and it is impossible not to see that the last year has made a greater change in her than ever any one year did before. She does not suffer in any way but from inability to exert herself.[31]

In 1857 Anthony and Rose again visited Italy and went to stay at the Villa Trollope. Anthony said of his mother, 'It was the first year in which she had not written, and she expressed to me her delight that her labours should be at an end, and that mine should be beginning in the same field.'[32] Rose felt that Fanny was much changed and broken, and showed little interest in either her afternoon drive, or her rubber of whist.

On 27 January 1859 Anthony wrote to Fanny from the ship which was to take him first to the West Indies; from there to Cuba, Panama, and then to America where he hoped to meet Rose.

In this way it will be 1860 before I can see you or Florence. But what could I do? . . . Tom will be in England, I presume, when this reaches you, looking after the family literature. John Tilley says he has done all he can. His house is now quite full, and he *cannot* stow away any more Trollope books. This is since the cheap editions have set in upon him! . . . I found your novels advertised with quite new names, – one by that horrid blackguard R. Should not this be stopped? And then there's *The Days of the Regency* by Mrs Trollope, brought out by Thomas Hodgson in his Parlour Library. Surely you never wrote a *Days of the Regency?* The worst is that it makes an appearance as tho' you were in league with the publishers in palming off old novels.[33]

Town and Country was re-issued under the new name of *Days of the Regency*, but it must have been difficult to keep an eye on unscrupulous publishers. A book was brought out by a French publisher purporting to have been written by a Sir Francis Trollope, the name was an assumed one. The publisher T.C. Newby, who had published Anthony's first novel, and who was known to be an opportunist, published a whole series of books between 1865 and 1880 under the name of Frank Trollope. The books, produced in the three-volume format, were poorly written in a florid, meandering style, and appeared with Trollope or F. Trollope on the spine. Nothing is known about the author, and one wonders if Newby 'borrowed' the name.

By 1859 Fanny was beginning to lose her memory. She still knew her family and could remember most past events, but her short-term memory was failing. She was now eighty. Anthony visited the Villa Trollope for six weeks in September, and on this visit met Kate Field, who was to become a close friend. One last letter to Anthony survives, undated and very short:

My darling Anthony,

You ask me to write – I and my pen have been so long divorced that I hardly know how to set about it – But you ask me to write and therefore write I will – though I have no news to tell you more fresh than that I love you dearly – I should like to see you again but can hardly hope it! God bless you my dear, dear Son!

Your loving mother,

Frances Trollope[34]

Fanny was no longer able to stride across the hills, but still walked every day around the loggia of the Villa Trollope, leaning on Tom's arm. At a certain time every afternoon the voice would call out 'I want Tom to trot me out',[35] and off they would go around the covered walk shaded from the sun, past ancient marbles and carvings, and smelling the scent of the wisteria and roses which grew around the stone pillars. The only photographs we have of Fanny were taken at about this time. She is sitting in a high-backed chair on the loggia, small, hunched, and wrapped in a shawl, and Tom is hovering protectively behind her. Theo gazes out into the garden, and her beloved Bice plays on the marble tiles at her feet.

Tom wrote in his memoirs that although his mother had almost entirely lost her memory for the last two or three years of her life, it was only in the last few months that 'she lost the use of her mental faculties'. Anthony took his eldest son, Henry, to Florence in September 1863, but Fanny no longer knew who they were.

When the end came for Fanny it was swift. She was confined to bed only for the last twenty-four hours and she died peacefully on 6 October 1863, at the age of eighty-four. Her last words were, 'Poor Cecilia'.

She had always had a horror of being buried alive and had made Tom promise to prevent this possibility by having a vein in her arm opened after her death. She was buried in the English Cemetery in the heart of Florence, near to Mr Garrow, and not far from Elizabeth Barrett Browning, who had died two years before.

The cemetery today is a forgotten place. A small island surrounded by major roads, with the endless roar and screech of fast cars thundering around it. Once inside the high fence, time dissolves. Wind blows the tops of the straggling pine trees which loom protectively over the crumbling broken marble, their scattered needles inches thick. Graves, nameless from erosion, huddle together. Eaten by pollution, broken by vandals, the headstones protecting the bones of a lost era are crumbling into dust.

However, something remains. Fanny wrote: 'Such people . . . do not quite leave this world when they die; a portion of their spirit is left behind them, and lives still in the memory of those who loved them.'[36]

Postscript

When Fanny Trollope died many papers carried her obituary. Even after her death she received mixed reviews.

The Spectator. 10 October 1863.
We regret to notice the death, at Florence, of Mrs Frances Trollope, the novelist, at the age of eighty-four. Though she began writing nearly forty years since, her works still sell, and, with some exceptions, deserve their popularity.

There is a vigour about them which, though it often degenerates into coarseness and caricature, still keeps the attention alive, and her sketches of Mrs Barnaby, of the Ward of Thorpe Combe, and the four Robertses, are valuable contributions to the anatomy of vulgarity. Her more refined personages are usually characterless.

The Gentleman's Magazine. December 1863.
In 1832 Mrs Trollope . . . made her first appearance as an authoress, and produced her caustic work termed *Domestic Manners of the Americans* which though manifestly written in a most unladylike spirit, and in a style of broad caricature, was favourably received in England – a fact that gave extreme offence in the United States. . . . It was soon followed by *The Refugee in America,* in which some fancied slights that she had received whilst there, and the comments that her former work had provoked, were repaid with interest. . . . Mrs Trollope's writings are characterised by great ability, but this is marred by a coarse unfeminine style.

The Illustrated London News. 17 October 1863
Frances Anne Trollope, one of the cleverest and most amusing novelists of her day, was the daughter of the Rev. William Milton. . . . Mrs Trollope's first appearance as a writer was in giving vent to a bitterness of feeling on account of the many désagréments she had experienced in a journey she took to America. . . . [This book] at once made her reputation, and she continued a long career of authorship, which has been as prolific as it has been prosperous.

The Athenaeum: 1863

It is scarcely thirty-five years since she commenced that literary career which made her one of the most remarkable women of her period. But at the time alluded to Frances Trollope was fifty years of age. She had fought a hard battle of life, and was grievously stricken in the contest. But she was a woman of stout heart, perseverance, and ability.

The wife of a barrister who had not been fortunate, Frances Trollope found herself, after an unsuccessful attempt to establish a home in America, here in England, with a world to begin again, a husband too ill to aid her, and children who needed aid and could as yet give none. Many men in like circumstances would have appealed to public charity, but the true woman's heart did not fail her. She wrote for bread, and reaped that honour. Her writings never bore the shadow of her circumstances. They were as bright at the first, as when, later, circumstances brightened. Her own sorrow, tears and anxieties were never intruded between her and the public. Frances Trollope had a heart above that; and such a heart with such an ability as hers, carried her triumphantly to fortune. . . . For some years this indefatigable worker, having fulfilled all duties as wife and mother, and accomplished the purposes for which she had toiled with unfainting heart, withdrew to Florence. She had been tested as few women have been.

When Tom's Theo died, in 1865, shortly after the death of Fanny, twelve-year-old Bice and her father were left alone in the vastness of the Villa Trollope. Tom wrote: 'My house was indeed left unto me desolate, and I thought that life and all its sweetness was over for me. I immediately took measures for disposing of the house in the Piazza dell'Independenza, and before long found a purchaser for it.' Almost at once he bought another house in Florence called Ricorboli, a huge neglected villa, and set to work to refurbish it. Bice was sent to England to stay with Anthony and Rose, and it was arranged that Frances Ternan would go every alternate weekend to Anthony's house, to give Bice singing lessons. Tom had met Frances in Florence through Charles Dickens; she was the oldest of the three Ternan sisters – of whom the youngest was Dickens' secretly beloved Nelly. Bice missed her life in Florence, and it wasn't long before she returned to live with Tom. In the summer of 1866 Frances Ternan joined them as her governess, and in the autumn of 1866 Tom and Frances, twenty-five years his junior, were married in Paris.

Frances Ternan Trollope never met her famous mother-in-law, but after Tom's death in Budleigh Salterton in 1892, she had access to all the family papers in Tom's possession. She therefore set to work to produce a two-volume biography of Frances Trollope which was printed by Bentley in 1895. This biography is now the only record we have of most of Tom's letters. In later life the three Ternan sisters all shared a house at Southsea. It is thought that the papers were destroyed by Nelly Ternan's son Geoffrey, who, when, years later, he learnt of his mother's relationship with Charles Dickens, destroyed many of her personal papers and among them probably those of Tom Trollope.

Fanny's beloved granddaughter Bice married Charles Stuart-Wortley, but died soon after the birth of her daughter Beatrice in 1881.

Fanny's grandsons, Harry and Fred, Anthony and Rose's sons, both married. Harry had two children, Thomas and Muriel, neither of whom married. Fred migrated to Australia at the age of eighteen and worked for two years as a jackeroo on Barratta Station in Victoria. He then bought a small sheep station, Mortray, located in the rough country near Grenfell in New South Wales, and married an Australian girl, Susie Farrand. Anthony and Rose stayed with them during their visit to Australia, and Anthony wrote *Harry Heathcote of Gangoil*, based on his son's life at Mortray. Unfortunately the property was too small to be viable, and Fred sold it at a loss. The remainder of his working life was spent as an Inspector for the Lands Department, which involved endless travelling on horseback around some of the most remote areas of New South Wales. He and Susie had eight children, and whenever possible his wife and family stayed with him at the country town where he was based, but when conditions were too harsh and rugged they remained in their cottage in Sydney. This was a pattern which Fred must have often experienced as a child when Anthony's work took him away from his family. Fred wrote to his mother Rose, from the remote inland town of Wilcannia in 1886; 'I cannot regret that I did not bring Susie and the children here. About a month ago some teams arrived from Bourke with flour, for three weeks prior to that we had been living on weevils which had been living on flour. Everything is bad and everything is dear.'

In 1883, at Anthony's urging, and much against Susie's wishes, Fred sent his eldest son Frank to England to be educated. Frank arrived there soon after his grandfather Anthony's death, and was sent to Mr Wharton Robinson's school at Margate, where he was most unhappy. He was used to the freedom of Australian life, and with the stigma of an Australian accent eleven-year-old Frank was made to feel an outsider who did not fit in. He managed to escape back to Australia in 1890 by joining the Navy, and then jumping ship in Melbourne.

Only two of Fred and Susie's eight children married: their daughter, Kathleen, had a son Joe, who died aged fourteen, and their youngest son Gordon had two sons and a daughter.

The baronetcy of the Trollopes of Casewick in Lincolnshire had, by death and default, now passed to the Australian branch of the family. In 1937 Fred's eldest surviving son became Sir Frederick Farrand Trollope (14th Bart). On his death in 1957 the youngest brother, Gordon, inherited the title. Gordon was the only Trollope who attempted to carry on the writing tradition. He wrote occasional articles for Sydney newspapers, and there remains with his family part of an incomplete novel written in about 1930. At his death in 1958 the title went to his son, Anthony Owen Clavering Trollope, and at his death in 1987, it went to the present holder, his eldest son, Sir Anthony Trollope, who lives near Sydney. Sir Anthony has two daughters while his younger brother, Hugh, has two daughters and one son, Andrew Ian, born in 1978, the presumptive heir to the baronetcy. Six generations later, these are the only direct descendants of the famous literary family.

Notes

CHAPTER ONE (pp. 1–12)

1 St Michael's Church, Bishop's Transcripts (BT) 37(a) 9. Cert. No. 10

2 Bristol Record Office, Will. Jn Milton. 24 Nov. 1777

3 James Woodforde, *The Diary of a Country Parson*, 1758–1802 (Oxford University Press, 1935), ed. John Baldwyn Beresford, 1935

4 Woodforde, *Diary*

5 Hampshire Record Office, Heckfield Parish Records

6 St Thomas's Church, Bristol, Parish Records

7 Hampshire Record Office, Heckfield Parish Register

8 St Thomas's Church, Baptism Register

9 St Michael's Church, BT, 9. Cert. No. 87

10 St Michael's Church, BT, 9. Cert. No. 27

11 St Michael's Church, BT, 10. Cert. No. 22

12 Sketchley's *Bristol Directory*

13 *Bristol Guide*, 1815

14 Burgess Book, 1781

15 Bristol Poll Book, 1781

16 FT, *Mrs Mathews*, vol. 1, p. 11

17 Bristol Record Office, Wills, Jn Milton 1788

18 TAT, p. 15

19 FT, *Tremordyn Cliff*, vol. 2, p. 35

20 Bristol Record Office, *Improvement of the Port of Bristol* [11168/5(c–d), 9(aa–bb)]

21 Nicholls & Taylor, *Bristol Past & Present*, vol. 3, p. 216

22 Ibid., vol. 3, p. 222

23 Ibid., vol. 3

24 FT, *Fashionable Life*, vol. 1, p. 74

25 MRMB, vol. 1, pp. 8, 9

26 W.J. James, *Heckfield and Mattingley: The History of a Hampshire Parish*, ed. Revd Patrick W.R. Kennedy & Colonel Colin Davy, 1963, p. 18

27 W.J. James, p. 21

28 FT, *Jessie Phillips*, Introduction
29 W.J. James, p. 42
30 Bristol Record Office [1168/5(c–d). 9(aa–bb)]
31 FT, *Town and Country*, vol. 1, p. 18
32 FT, *Tremordyn Cliff*, vol. 2, pp. 30, 33

CHAPTER TWO (pp. 13–24)

1   FET, vol. 2, p. 10
2   FT, *The Laurringtons*, vol. 1, p. 43
3   FET, vol. 2, p. 287
4   FT, *The Robertses on Their Travels*, vol. 2, p. 286
5   FT, *Fashionable Life*, vol. 1, p. 20
6   FET, vol. 1, p. 16
7   FET, vol. 1, pp. 16–19
8   FET, vol. 1, p. 20
9   FET, vol. 1, pp. 21, 22
10 FET, vol. 1, p. 23
11 FET, vol. 1, pp. 35, 36
12 FET, vol. 1, pp. 38, 39
13 Parish register, marriages, Heckfield
14 FT, *Uncle Walter*, vol. 1, p. 23
15 FET, vol. 1, pp. 39, 40
16 FET, vol. 1, p. 41
17 MRMA, vol. 3, p. 241
18 FT, *Fashionable Life*, vol. 1, p. 308
19 FT, *Gertrude*, vol. 2, p. 24
20 FT, *Hargrave*, vol. 1, p. 233
21 FT, *Love and Jealousy*, vol. 3, p. 156
22 TAT, p. 16
23 FT, *Love and Jealousy*, vol. 1, p. 78
24 FT, *Uncle Walter*, vol. 1, p. 53
25 TAT, p. 11
26 FT, *One Fault*, p. 168
27 TAT, pp. 5, 7, 8
28. FET, vol. 1, p. 46
29 TAT, p. 41
30 FT, *Town and Country*, vol. 2, p. 56, vol. 3, p. 115

CHAPTER THREE (pp. 25–39)

1   TAT, p. 45
2   TAT, p. 41
3   FT, *The Three Cousins*, vol. 2, p. 138
4   TAT, p. 41
5   FT, *Tremordyn Cliff*, vol. 1, p. 52
6   TAT, p. 53
7   TAT, p. 40
8   FET, vol. 1, p. 55
9   TAT, p. 65

10 TAT, p. 46
11 *Salamagundi*, ed. N. John Hall, Princeton, N.J., 1975
12 FT, *Uncle Walter*, vol. 1, p. 310
13 FET, vol. 1, pp. 167, 168
14 Helen Heineman, *Restless Angels, The Friendships of Six Victorian Woman* (Ohio University Press, 1983), p. 16
15 AT, p. 23
16 FET, vol. 1, p. 77
17 FET, vol. 1, p. 78
18 GPC, Trollope, Frances (Milton) 1780–1863, 25 letters to Julia (Garnett) Pertz; 1824–1852, bMS Eng 1304.2 (30), by permission of the Houghton Library, Harvard University
19 FET, vol. 1, p. 76
20 FT, *The Three Cousins*, vol. 2, p. 141
21 FT, *Tremordyn Cliff*, vol. 1, p. 5
22 FET, vol. 1, pp. 89, 90
23 MRMA, vol. 1, 4 November 1826
24 MRMB, vol. 1, pp. 159–65
25 MRMB, vol. 1, pp. 168, 169
26 FET, vol. 1, p. 95
27 AT, p. 29
28 GPC, FT to Julia Garnett. Harrow, 17 May 1827
29 TAT, p. 106
30 GPC, FT to Julia Garnett, Harrow, 7 October 1827
31 GPC, FT to Julia Garnett, 17 May 1827
32 FT, *The Old World and the New*, vol. 1, pp. 92–4
33 FT, *Town and Country*, vol. 2, pp. 184, 186
34 GPC, FT to Harriet Garnett, 7 December 1828
35 Francis Wright to Harriet Garnett, 20 March 1828, from the Frances Wright Collection
36 GPC, Harriet Garnett to Julia Pertz, 12 December 1827
37 FT, *The Old World and the New*, vol. 1, pp. 40–2

CHAPTER FOUR (pp. 40–53)

1   FT, *The Domestic Manners of the Americans*. All quotes in this chapter are from this book unless otherwise specified
2   GPC, FT to Harriet Garnett, 20 March 1828
3   GPC, FT & Frances Wright to Julia Pertz, 26 December 1827

4   FT, *The Old World and the New*, vol. 1, p. 234

5   FT, *The Refugee*, vol. 1, p. 212

6   FET, vol. 1, pp. 112, 113

7   *Cincinnati Gazette*, 28 March 1828

8   *The Domestic Manners of the Americans*, edited with a history of Mrs Trollope's adventures in America by Donald Smalley, New York, Alfred A. Knopf, 1949, note p. 63

9   GPC, FT to Julia Pertz, 12 March 1830

10   FET, vol. 1, p. 114

11   TAT, p. 124

12   Donald Smalley's introduction to *Domestic Manners*, p. xl

13   Monique Parent Frazee, *Mrs Trollope and America*, Publications de la Faculté des Lettres et Sciences Humaines de l'Université de Caen, 1969

14   FET, vol. 1, p. 118

15   FT, *Fashionable Life*, vol. 3, p. 60

CHAPTER FIVE (pp. 54–70)

1   TAT, pp. 118–21

2   MRMB, vol. 1, p. 191

3   FT, *The Refugee*, vol. 1, pp. 63, 65

4   GPC, FT to Julia Pertz, Harrow, 22 August 1831

5   FT, *The Refugee*, vol. 1, p. 214

6   Donald Smalley's introduction to *Domestic Manners*, and previous quote, pp. xlvi–xlix

7   FT, *Jonathan Jefferson Whitlaw*, vol. 1, p. 164

8   FT, *Mrs Mathews*, vol. 2, p. 31

9   FET, vol. 1, pp. 128, 129

10   Monique Parent Frazee, *Mrs Trollope and America* (Université de Caen, 1969)

11   GPC, FT to Julia Pertz, Baltimore, 12 March 1830

12   FET, vol. 1, p. 125

13   FET, vol. 1, p. 126

14   FET, vol. 1, pp. 129–31

15   MRMB, vol. 1, pp. 219–22

16   FT, *The Refugee*, vol. 3, p. 196

17   GPC, FT to Julia Pertz, Alexandria, 10 April 1831

18   MRMB, vol. 1, pp. 226, 227

19   HH, Letter from Walter Stirling to George Harrison, p. 73

20   GPC, FT to Julia Pertz, 22 August 1831

CHAPTER SIX (pp. 71–89)

1   AT, p. 27

2   AT, p. 29

3   AT, p. 30

4   AT, pp. 31, 32

5   TAT, p. 205

6   Greater London Record Office (GLRO), Acc 76/2278/23036

7   GPC, FT to Julia Pertz, Harrow, 22 August 1831

8   TAT, p. 158

9   GPC, FT to Julia Pertz, Harrow, 25 November 1831

10   FET, vol. 1, p. 136

11   FT, *Tremordyn Cliff*, vol. 1, p. 40

12   FT, *Mrs Mathews*, vol. 1, p. 311

13   FET, vol. 1, p. 42

14   MRMB, vol. 1, pp. 229, 230

15   FET, vol. 1, p. 143

16   FET, vol. 1, p. 150

17   FET, vol. 1, p. 152

18   FET, vol. 1, p. 152

19   Monique Parent Frazee, *Mrs Trollope and America* (Université de Caen, 1969)

20   Donald Smalley's introduction to *Domestic Manners*, p. ix

21   Ibid., p. x

22   TAT, p. 161

23   *Trollope: Interviews & Recollections*, ed. R.C. Terry, Basingstoke, Macmillan, 1987

24   FET, vol. 1, p. 161

25   MRMB, vol. 1, p. 234

26   FET, vol. 1, p. 166

27   FET, vol. 1, p. 167

28   FET, vol. 1, p. 169

29   FET, vol. 1, p. 180

30   *The Spectator*, 1833, No. 6, p. 526

31   FT, *Belgium and Western Germany*, vol. 1, p. 86

32   FT, Ibid., vol. 2, p. 267

33   FT, Ibid., vol. 2, p. 32

34   FT, Ibid., vol. 1, p. 147

35   FT, Ibid., vol. 2, p. 85

36   FT, Ibid., vol. 1, p. 1

37   GPC, FT to Julia Pertz, no date (spring 1834)

38   Ibid.

39   GLRO, Acc 76.2341/2362

40   GPC, FT to Julia Pertz, Bruges, 13 July 1834

41   GPC, FT to Julia Pertz, Harrow, Spring 1834

42   GLRO, Northwick papers, Acc 76/2374/2372

43 GPC, FT to Julia Pertz, Bruges, 18 July 1834
44 GLRO, Northwick papers, Acc 76/2374/2372
45 AT, *Autobiography*, p. 41
46 AT, Ibid.
47 FT *Charles Chesterfield*, vol. 2
48 AT, Autobiography, p. 42
49 FT, Letter to John Murray, 22 April 1834

34 TAT, p. 203
35 FT, *Belgium and Western Germany*, vol. 2, p. 143
36 TAT, p. 204
37 TAT, p. 205
38 FT, *Love and Jealousy*, vol. 1, p. 1
39 FT, *One Fault*, p. 223
40 AT, pp. 45, 46
41 FET, vol. 1, pp. 254, 255 (also previous quote)
42 FET, vol. 1, p. 255

CHAPTER SEVEN (pp. 90–105)

1   FET, vol. 1, p. 94
2   FET, vol. 1, p. 99
3   AT, p. 45
4   FT, *Fashionable Life*, vol. 1, p. 47
5   FT, *The Robertses on their Travels*, vol. 1, p. 108
6   HH, p. 117, FT Letter to Colonel Grant, 3 June 1834, from the Morris L. Parrish Collection, Princeton University Library
7   AT, p. 43
8   FET, vol. 1, p. 205
9   FET, vol. 1, p. 208
10 FET, vol. 1, pp. 208, 209
11 FET, vol. 1, p. 210
12 FT, *Tremordyn Cliff*, vol. 1, p. 57
13 TAT, pp. 211, 212
14 FET, vol. 1, p. 216
15 AT, p. 44
16 FET, vol. 1, pp. 223, 224
17 FT, *The Young Heiress*, vol. 1, p. 110
18 AT, p. 44
19 FET, vol. 1, p. 227
20 AT, p. 45
21 TAT, p. 174
22 FT, *Tremordyn Cliff*, vol. 1, p. 98
23 FET, vol. 1, pp. 227, 228
24 FT, *Tremordyn Cliff*, vol. 1, p. 243
25 FET, vol. 1, pp. 228, 229
26 TAT, p. 175
27 British Library, 46612. ff. 150, 156, 157, 201. Also HH, p. 130, FT Letter to Richard Bentley, 24 June 1835, from the Robert H. Taylor Collection, Princeton University Library
28 TAT, p. 175
29 TAT, p. 176
30 TAT, p. 182
31 FT, *Paris and the Parisians*, Intro. vi
32 FT, Ibid., vol. 1, p. 269
33 FT, Ibid., vol. 1, pp. 269, 270

CHAPTER EIGHT (pp. 106–125)

1   Frederick Cass, *Monken Hadley*, J.B. Nichols and Sons, Westminster, 1880, p. 186, note e
2   FET, vol. 1, p. 259
3   TAT, p. 207
4   FT, *Fashionable Life*, vol. 3, p. 104
5   FT, *Gertrude*, vol. 1, p. 1
6   FT, *Jessie Phillips*, p. 2
7   AT, p. 60
8   British Library, MSS, Correspondence and Agreements R. Bentley 1835–40. 46612, ff. 150, 156, 157, 201, 237–41. 46613, ff. 46, 309. 46649, ff. 189, 287. 46650, f. 71
9   TAT, p. 208
10 FT, *Love and Jealousy*, vol. 1, p. 68
11 FT, *Vienna and the Austrians*, vol. 1, pp. 181–5
12 FT, *Hargrave*, vol. 2, p. 128
13 FT, *Vienna and the Austrians*, vol. 2, pp. 240, 241
14 FT, Ibid., vol. 1, p. 243
15 FT, Ibid., vol. 1, p. 252
16 FT, Ibid., vol. 1, pp. 259, 260
17 FT, Ibid., vol. 1, p. 280
18 FT, Ibid., vol. 1, p. 305
19 TAT, p. 221
20 FT, *Vienna and the Austrians*, vol. 1, p. 314
21 FT, Ibid., vol. 1, p. 372
22 TAT, pp. 221, 222
23 FT, *Vienna and the Austrians*, vol. 2, p. 25
24 TAT, p. 231
25 FT, *Vienna and the Austrians*, vol. 2, p. 55
26 FT, Ibid., vol. 2, p. 69
27 FT, Ibid., vol. 2, p. 80
28 FT, Ibid., vol. 2, p. 176
29 FT, Ibid., vol. 2, p. 285
30 GPC, FT to Julia Pertz, Hadley, 26 January 1838

31 FT, *The Vicar of Wrexhill*, p. 88
32 EBB, vol. 1, p. 47
33 TAT, pp. 244, 245
34 FET, vol. 1, pp. 285, 286
35 GPC, FT to Julia Pertz, Hadley, 26 January 1838
36 FT, *The Widow Barnaby*, p. 153
37 FT, Ibid., p. 182
38 FT, Ibid., p. 282
39 FT, Ibid., p. 301
40 FT, *The Widow Married*, vol. 3, p. 116
41 FT, Ibid., vol. 3, p. 117
42 FT, Ibid., vol. 3, p. 223
43 FT, Ibid., vol. 3, p. 226
44 FT, *The Barnabys in America*, p. 66
45 FT, Ibid., vol. 2, pp. 44, 47
46 FET, vol. 1, pp. 289, 290
47 FET, vol. 1, p. 295
48 TAT, p. 246

24 Louisa Devey, *Life of Rosina, Lady Lytton* (London, 1887), p. 195
25 FT, *Charles Chesterfield*, vol. 1, p. 22
26 FT, Ibid., vol. 1, p. 36
27 FT, Ibid., vol. 1, p. 257
28 FT, Ibid., vol. 1, p. 175
29 FT, Ibid., vol. 1, p. 318
30 FT, Ibid., vol. 1, p. 204
31 FT, Ibid., vol. 2, p. 103
32 FT, Ibid., vol. 2, p. 102
33 FT, Ibid., vol. 2, pp. 276, 277
34 *Encyclopaedia Britannica* (1879), vol. 9, p. 419
35 EBB, 23–25 December 1841, vol. 1, p. 322
36 EBB, 11 January 1842, vol. 1, p. 327, n. 328
37 FT, *The Blue Belles of England*, vol. 1, p. 117
38 FT, Ibid., vol. 2, p. 42
39 FT, Ibid., vol. 1, p. 178

CHAPTER NINE (pp. 126–142)

1   FET, vol. 2, p. 260
2   TAT, p. 280
3   *New Monthly Magazine*, March 1839, p. 565
4   FT, *Michael Armstrong*, p. 35
5   FT, Ibid., p. 237
6   *New Monthly Magazine*, No. 57, p. 286
7   TAT, p. 285
8   TAT, pp. 255, 256
9   FET, vol. 1, p. 304
10 MRMA, vol. 3, p. 156
11 *New Monthly Magazine*, Memoir to Mrs Trollope, 1839
12 FT, *One Fault*, p. 382
13 FT, Ibid., pp. 41–3
14 GPC, FT to Julia Pertz, York Street, 26 September 1839
15 *New Monthly Magazine*, Female Novelist No. V, p. 19
16 FET, vol. 1, p. 306
17 GPC, FT to Julia Pertz, Paris, 24 May 1840
18 FET, vol. 1, p. 308
19 FET, vol. 1, p. 307
20 FET, vol. 1, p. 312
21 GPC, FT to Julia Pertz, 26 September 1839
22 T.H.S. Escott, *Anthony Trollope, His Work Associates and Literary Originals* (London. John Lane, Bodley Head, 1913), pp. 31, 32
23 AT, p. 62

CHAPTER TEN (pp. 143–155)

1   FT, *Town and Country*, vol. 1, p. 1
2   FET, vol. 1, p. 319
3   The British Library, MSS Dept. 40490, ff. 65–69
4   FET, vol. 1, p. 320
5   FET, vol. 1, p. 323
6   FET, vol. 1, p. 324
7   *New Monthly Magazine*, No. 67, pp. 555, 556
8   EBB, 29 March 1843, vol. 2, p. 194
9   FT, *Visit to Italy*, vol. 1, pp. 272, 273
10 FT, *Visit to Italy*, vol. 2, p. 393
11 AT, pp. 66, 67
12 FET, vol. 2, p. 15
13 TAT, p. 327
14 FET, vol. 2, p. 16
15 TAT
16 FT, *Jessie Phillips*, p. 81
17 FT, Ibid., p. 82
18 FT, Ibid., p. 189
19 FT, Ibid., p. 211
20 *New Monthly Magazine*, vol. LV, March 1839, p. 417
21 MRMB, vol. 1, p. 212
22 TAT, p. 331
23 FT, *The Laurringtons: or Superior People*, vol. 3, p. 339
24 FT, Ibid., vol. 1, p. 163
25 FT, *Young Love*, vol. 1, p. 29
26 *New Monthly Magazine*, No. 72, p. 437

CHAPTER ELEVEN (pp. 156–171)

1 TAT, p. 332
2 TAT, p. 333
3 EBB, 4 September 1843, vol. 2, p. 294
4 *The Letters of Charles Dickens*, ed. Madeline House, Graham Storey, Kathleen Tillotson (Clarendon Press, Oxford, 1974), 3 vols. Charles Dickens to FT 16 December 1842, vol. 3, p. 395, from the Berg Collection, New York Public Library
5 TAT, p. 489
6 TAT, p. 345
7 HH, p. 227, FT to Rose Heseltine 7 August 1844, from the Robert Taylor Collection, Princeton University
8 FET, vol. 2, p. 39
9 FET, vol. 2, p. 60
10 TAT, pp. 351–3
11 FT, *The Robertses on their Travels*, vol. 1, pp. 2, 6, 7
12 FT, Ibid., vol. 1, p. 108
13 FET, vol. 2, p. 44
14 FT, *The Attractive Man*, p. 293
15 FT, Ibid., pp. 295, 296
16 AT, p. 80
17 FET, vol. 2, p. 52
18 FET, vol. 2, p. 55
19 FET, vol. 2, p. 58
20 FET, vol. 2, p. 57
21 TAT, pp. 415, 416
22 FT, *Charles Chesterfield*, vol. 2, p. 247
23 FET, vol. 2, p. 60
24 FET, vol. 2, pp. 70, 71
25 FET, vol. 2, p. 62
26 FT, *Father Eustace*, vol. 2, p. 181
27 *The Spectator*, 15 October 1842, p. 995
28 FT, *The Three Cousins*, vol. 1, pp. 47, 48, 49
29 FT, Ibid., vol. 1, p. 173
30 FT, Ibid., vol. 2, p. 162
31 FT, Ibid., vol. 3, p. 112
32 FT, *The Old World and the New*, vol. 1, p. 116
33 TAT, p. 384
34 EBB, vol. 1, pp. 316
35 TAT, p. 386

CHAPTER TWELVE (pp. 172–188)

1 FET, vol. 2, p. 100
2 FET, vol. 2, p. 102
3 FET, vol. 2, p. 107
4 TAT, p. 379
5 FET, vol. 2, p. 109
6 FET, vol. 2, p. 101
7 FET, vol. 2
8 FT, *Love and Jealousy*, vol. 1, p. 69
9 FT, Ibid., vol. 1, p. 215
10 FET, vol. 2, p. 112
11 FET, vol. 2, p. 117
12 FT, *Town and Country*, vol. 2, p. 11
13 FT, Ibid., vol. 3, p. 48
14 FT, Ibid., vol. 2, p. 75
15 FT, Ibid., vol. 3, p. 123
16 FT, Ibid., vol. 3, p. 139
17 FET, vol. 2, p. 118
18 FET, vol. 2, p. 120
19 TAT, p. 389
20 GPC, Harriet Garnett to Julia Pertz, n.d. (1848)
21 EBB, vol. 3, p. 241
22 FET, vol. 2, p. 128
23 FET, vol. 2, p. 132
24 FET, vol. 2, p. 135
25 EBB, 30 January 1849, vol. 3, p. 265
26 *New Monthly Magazine*, June 1849
27 FET, vol. 2, p. 139
28 FET, vol. 2, p. 141
29 FET, vol. 2, p. 142
30 FET, vol. 2, p. 142
31 FT, *The Old World and the New*, vol. 1, p. 234
32 FT, Ibid., vol. 2, p. 120
33 *New Monthly Magazine*, No. 87, October 1849
34 FET, vol. 2, p. 143
35 HH, p. 236, FT Letter to Rose Trollope, 20 April 1849, from the Robert Taylor Collection, Princeton University
36 FET, vol. 2, p. 144
37 FET, vol. 2, pp. 145, 146
38 FET, vol. 2, pp. 161, 162
39 FET, vol. 2, p. 154
40 FET, vol. 2, p. 166
41 FET, vol. 2, p. 168
42 FET, vol. 2, p. 170
43 FET, vol. 2, p. 172
44 FET, vol. 2, p. 174
45 FET, vol. 2, p. 176
46 FET, vol. 2, pp. 176, 177

CHAPTER THIRTEEN (pp. 189–205)

1 FET, vol. 2, p. 178
2 FET, vol. 2, p. 179
3 Baring-Gould, *Early Reminiscences 1834–1864* (John Lane, Bodley Head, London, 1923), pp. 127, 128

4   FET, vol. 2, p. 190
5   FET, vol. 2, p. 191
6   FET, vol. 2, pp. 193, 194
7   FET, vol. 2, p. 198
8   FET, vol. 2, p. 199
9   FET, vol. 2, p. 200
10 FET, vol. 2, p. 201
11 FET, vol. 2, pp. 202, 203
12 FET, vol. 2, p. 207
13 FET, vol. 2, p. 209
14 TAT, pp. 368, 369
15 TAT, p. 370
16 FET, vol. 2, p. 211
17 *Encyclopaedia Britannica* (1879), vol. 14, p. 486
18 FET, vol. 2, p. 213
19 FET, vol. 2, p. 213
20 TAT, p. 519
21 *Trollope: Interviews and Recollections*, ed. R.C. Terry, 1987, p. 72
22 EBB, 15 June 1850, vol. 3, p. 300
23 FT, *Mrs Mathews*, vol. 1, p. 104
24 FT, Ibid., vol. 3, p. 137
25 FET, vol. 2, p. 217
26 FET, vol. 2, p. 218
27 FET, vol. 2, p. 220
28 FT, *Uncle Walter*, vol. 1, p. 24
29 FT, Ibid., vol. 1, p. 32
30 FT, Ibid., vol. 1, p. 29
31 FT, Ibid., vol. 1, pp. 169, 170
32 FT, Ibid., vol. 2, p. 307
33 FT, Ibid., vol. 2, p. 305
34 FT, Ibid., vol. 2, p. 309
35 FT, Ibid., vol. 3, pp. 128–30
36 FT, Ibid., vol. 2, p. 243
37 FT, Ibid., vol. 1, p. 51
38 FT, Ibid., vol. 1, p. 61
39 AT, p. 95
40 *New Monthly Magazine*, No. 96, pp. 19–27

CHAPTER FOURTEEN (pp. 206–217)

1   FET, vol. 2, p. 231

2   MRMB, vol. 2, p. 96
3   MRMA, vol. 3, p. 241
4   FET, vol. 2, pp. 235, 236
5   FET, vol. 2, pp. 236, 237
6   FET, vol. 2, p. 241
7   FET, vol. 2, pp. 242, 243
8   TAT, p. 514
9   FET, vol. 2, p. 244
10 EBB, 23 October 1853, vol. 3, p. 397
11 FT, *Life and Adventures of a Clever Woman*, vol. 2, p. 32
12 FT, Ibid., vol. 3, p. 135
13 FT, Ibid., vol. 2, p. 197
14 FT, Ibid., vol. 3, p. 244
15 FT, Ibid., vol. 3, p. 190
16 FT, Ibid., vol. 3, p. 305
17 *New Monthly Magazine*, No. 96, p. 27
18 FET, vol. 2, pp. 351, 352
19 EBB, 19 October 1854, vol. 3, pp. 411, 420
20 FET, vol. 2, p. 253
21 TAT, p. 261
22 Trollope: *Interviews and Recollections*, ed. R.C. Terry, 1987, p. 23
23 FT, *Fashionable Life, or Paris and London*, vol. 2, p. 113
24 FT, Ibid., vol. 2, pp. 140, 141
25 FT, Ibid., vol. 1, p. 242
26 FT, Ibid., vol. 3, p. 88
27 FT, Ibid., vol. 3, pp. 108, 109
28 *Sheffield Times*, 24 November 1855
29 FT, *Fashionable Life*, vol. 2, p. 216
30 FT, Ibid., vol. 1, pp. 4, 6
31 *The Letters of Anthony Trollope*, ed. N. John Hall (2 vols, Stanford University Press, 1983), vol. 1, pp. 44, 45, from the Robert Taylor Collection
32 FET, vol. 2, p. 297
33 FET, vol. 2, pp. 283, 284
34 *The Letters of Anthony Trollope*, ed. N. John Hall, vol. 1, p. 82, from the Robert Taylor Collection
35 FET, vol. 2, p. 299
36 FT, *Mrs Mathews*, vol. 1, p. 217

General Bibliography

Bristol Acts

Bristol Poll Book, 1781

Bristol, *The Guide,* 1815

Bristol Record Office, Wills, John Milton, 1777, 1786

Bristol Record Office, Improvement of the Port of Bristol [11168/5(c–d), 9(aa–bb)]

British Library, MSS, Correspondence and Agreements R. Bentley 1835–40

Browning, Elizabeth Barrett. *Letters,* ed. Frederick G. Kenyon, 3 vols, New York, Macmillan, 1897

Browning, E.B. *The Letters of E.B.B. to M.R.M. 1836–1854,* 3 vols, ed. M.B. Raymond and M.R. Sullivan, Armstrong Browning Library of Baylor University, The Browning Institute, Wedgestone Press & Wellesley College, 1983

Bryant, Arthur. *The Age of Elegance,* The Reprint Society, London, 1954

Escott, T.H.S. *Anthony Trollope, His Work, Associates and Literary Originals,* London, John Lane, The Bodley Head, 1913

Frazee, Monique Parent. *Mrs Trollope and America,* Publications de la Faculté des Lettres et Sciences Humaines de l'Université de Caen, 1969

Glendinning, Victoria. *Trollope,* Hutchinson, 1992

Hall, N. John. *Trollope,* Oxford University Press, 1991

—— ed. *Salamagundi,* Byron, Allegra, and the Trollope Family, Princeton, N.J., 1975

Heineman, Helen. *Mrs Trollope: The Triumphant Feminine in the Nineteenth Century,* Ohio University Press, 1979

—— *Restless Angels: The Friendship of Six Victorian Women,* Athens, Ohio University Press, 1983

James, W.J. *Heckfield and Mattingley,* The History of a Hampshire Parish, ed. by Revd Patrick W.R. Kennedy & Colonel Colin Davey, 1963.

Johnston, Johanna. *The Life, Manners and Travels of Fanny Trollope: A Biography,* N.Y., Hawthorne Books, 1978

Kissel, Susan. *In a Common Cause. The 'Conservative' Frances Trollope and the 'Radical' Frances Wright,* Bowling Green State University Popular Press, 1993

Latimer, John. *Annals of Bristol in the Eighteenth Century,* George's, Bristol, 1970, 2 vols.

L'Estrange, Revd Alfred Guy, ed. *The Life of Mary Russell Mitford, Related in a Selection from her Letters to her Friends,* 3 vols, London, Bentley, 1870

—— *The Friendships of Mary Russell Mitford as Recorded in Letters from her Literary Correspondents.* 2 vols, London, Hurst and Blackett, 1882

Lewes. *Mrs Fitzherbert and sons,* 1991

Mathews *Bristol Guide,* 1801

Milton, Henry. *Letters on the Fine Arts written from Paris in the year 1815,* Longman, Hurst, Rees, Orme and Brown, 1816

Nicholls, J.F. and Taylor, John. *Bristol Past & Present, Civil & Modern History,* Arrowsmith, 3 vols, Bristol, 1882

Pope-Hennessy, Una. *Three English Women in America*, London, Ernest Benn Ltd, 1929

Plumb, J.H. *The First Four Georges*, Fontana, 1966 (first pub. by B.T. Batsford Ltd, 1956)

Reid, Helen. *A Chronicle of Clifton and Hotwells*, Bristol, Redcliffe Press, 1992. Liz Marleyn ©

Sadlier, Michael. *Trollope: a Commentary*, London, Constable & Co., 1927

Stebbins, Lucy Poate and Richard Poate. *The Trollopes: The Chronicle of a Writing Family*, New York, Columbia University Press, 1945

Terry, R.C., ed. *Trollope: Interviews and Recollections*, Basingtoke, Macmillan, 1987

Tomalin, Claire. *The Invisible Woman. The story of Nelly Ternan and Charles Dickens*, Penguin Books, 1991

Trevelyan, G.M. *English Social History*, Longman Group Limited, London, 1979 (1st pub. 1944)

Trollope, Anthony. *An Autobiography*, London, Williams and Norgate, 1946 (1st pub. 1883)

Trollope, Frances. 25 Letters to Julia (Garnett) Pertz, 1824–52, by permission of the Houghton Library, Harvard University. bMS Eng 1304.2 (30)

Trollope, Frances. *Domestic Manners of the Americans*, with a history of Mrs Trollope's adventures in America, ed. Donald Smalley, New York, Alfred A. Knopf, 1949

Trollope, Frances Eleanor Ternan. *Frances Trollope her Life and Literary work from George III to Victoria*, 2 vols, Richard Bentley, 1895

Trollope, Thomas Adolphus. *What I Remember*, New York, Harper & Brothers, 1888

Woodforde, James. *The Diary of a Country Parson, 1758–1802*, ed. John Baldwyn Beresford, Oxford University Press, 1935

OTHER SOURCES

British Library
Cambridge University Library
Scottish National Library
Winchester Library, Local Studies Collection

Encyclopaedia Britannica, 1879
Gentleman's Magazine
Illustrated London News
National Dictionary of Biography
New Monthly Magazine
The Spectator
The Times
Victorian County Registers

Chronological Bibliography of the Works of Frances Trollope

Domestic Manners of the Americans, With illustrations by A. Hervieu, 2 vols, London, Whittaker and Treacher, 1832

The Refugee in America: A Novel, 3 vols, London, Whittaker and Treacher, 1832

The Mother's Manual: or Illustrations of Matrimonial Economy. An Essay in Verse, With illustrations by A. Hervieu, Treuttel and Wurtz and Richter, 1833

The Abbess: A Romance, 3 vols, London, Whittaker and Treacher, 1833

Belgium and Western Germany in 1833, 2 vols, London, John Murray, 1834

Tremordyn Cliff, 3 vols, London, Bentley, 1835

Paris and the Parisians in 1835, With illustrations by A. Hervieu, 2 vols, London, Bentley, 1836

The Life and Adventures of Jonathan Jefferson Whitlaw: or Scenes on the Mississippi, With illustrations by A. Hervieu, 3 vols, London, Bentley, 1836

The Vicar of Wrexhill, With illustrations by A. Hervieu, 3 vols, London, Bentley, 1837

Vienna and the Austrians, With illustrations by A. Hervieu, 2 vols, London, Bentley, 1838

A Romance of Vienna, 3 vols, London, Bentley, 1838

The Widow Barnaby, 3 vols, London, Bentley, 1839

The Widow Married: a Sequel to the Widow Barnaby, With illustrations by R.W. Buss, 3 vols, London, Colburn, 1840

The Life and Adventures of Michael Armstrong, the Factory Boy, With illustrations by A. Hervieu, R.W. Buss, and T. Onwhyn, London, Colburn, 1840

One Fault: A Novel, 3 vols, London, Bentley, 1840

Charles Chesterfield: or the Adventures of a Youth of Genius, With illustrations by 'Phiz', 3 vols, London, Colburn, 1841

The Ward of Thorpe Combe, 3 vols, London, Bentley, 1841

The Blue Belles of England, 3 vols, London, Saunders and Otley, 1842

A Visit to Italy, 2 vols, London, Bentley, 1842

The Barnabys in America: or Adventures of the Widow Wedded, With illustrations by John Leech, 3 vols, London, Colburn, 1843

Hargrave: or the Adventures of a Man of Fashion, 3 vols, London, Colburn, 1843

Jessie Phillips: A Tale of the Present Day, With illustrations by John Leech, 3 vols, London, Colburn 1843, 1 vol., 1844

The Laurringtons: or Superior People, 3 vols, London, Longman, Brown, Green and Longmans, 1844

Young Love: A Novel, 3 vols, London, Colburn, 1844

The Attractive Man, 3 vols, London, Colburn, 1846

The Robertses on their Travels, 3 vols, London, Colburn, 1846

Travels and Travellers: A Series of Sketches, 2 vols, London, Colburn, 1846

Father Eustace: A Tale of the Jesuits, 3 vols, London, Colburn, 1847

The Three Cousins, 3 vols, London, Colburn, 1847

Town and Country: A Novel, 3 vols, London, Colburn, 1848 (re-issued in 1857 under the title *Days of the Regency*).

The Young Countess: or Love and Jealousy, 3 vols, London, Colburn, 1848

The Lottery of Marriage: A Novel, 3 vols, London, Colburn, 1849

The Old World and the New: A Novel, 3 vols, London, Colburn, 1849

Petticoat Government: A Novel, 3 vols, London, Colburn, 1850

Mrs Mathews, or Family Mysteries, 3 vols, London, Colburn, 1851

Second Love: or Beauty and Intellect: A Novel, 3 vols, London, Colburn, 1851

Uncle Walter: A Novel, 3 vols, London, Colburn, 1852

The Young Heiress: A Novel, 3 vols, London, Hurst and Blackett, 1853

The Life and Adventures of a Clever Woman, Illustrated with Occasional Extracts from her Diary, 3 vols, London, Hurst and Blackett, 1854

Gertrude: or Family Pride, 3 vols, London, Hurst and Blackett, 1855

Fashionable Life: or Paris and London, 3 vols, London, Hurst and Blackett, 1856

Index

Index